The Sun of Knowledge

شمس المعارف الكبرى

شمس المعارف ولطائف العوارف

THE SUN OF KNOWLEDGE
SHAMS AL-MAʿARIF

An Arabic Grimoire

A SELECTED TRANSLATION

AHMAD IBN ʿALI AL-BUNI (D. 1225 AD)

TRANSLATED AND WITH COMMENTARY BY
Amina Inloes
ILLUSTRATED AND WITH EXTRA COMMENTARY
BY J. M. HAMADE

REVELORE PRESS
OLYMPIA, WA
MMXXI

شمس المعارف الكبرى

The Sun of Knowledge (Shams al-Maʿarif): An Arabic Grimoire
A SELECTED TRANSLATION

Book and cover design by Joseph Uccello.
Illustrations by J. M. Hamade.

Printed globally on demand through IngramSpark.

ISBN 978-1-947544-35-2

Revelore Press
620 73rd Ave NE
Olympia, WA 98506
United States

www.revelore.press

TABLE OF CONTENTS

CHAPTER 10

The first page of an illuminated manuscript of *The Sun of Knowledge*

HOUSED AT FEYZULLAH EFENDI MADRASAH, ISTANBUL, #1303

Foreword

THE READER HAS the distinct honor of holding one of the most infamous books ever penned in the Arabic language—indeed, one of the most infamous books in the history of Islam. Feared, banned, and burned, the *Sun of Knowledge*[1] has nonetheless survived the vagaries of time to rise to prominence as the most famous Arabic grimoire.

With that in mind, the reader might be surprised to discover that the *Sun of Knowledge* is actually quite pious. Identifying as a faithful Muslim, al-Buni takes a spiritual approach towards using his will to exert material change. Primarily, he employs the names of God (the Ninety-Nine Names of Allah in the Islamic tradition) and the Arabic letters, numbers, and verses of the Qur'an. While not every act he prescribes is benevolent, he does advise that acts of destruction be aimed at those who deserve it—and I am sure we can all think of a few miscreants who fit that category nicely.

Little is known about the author, Ahmad ibn ʿAli al-Buni (d. 1225 or 1232). His name suggests he was born in Buna (formerly

1 The Arabic title of the work is *Shams al-Maʿārif wa Laṭa'if al-ʿAwārif*, which can be rendered as "The Sun of Knowledge and the Subtleties of Comprehension," although it is usually simply referred to as *Shams al-Maʿārif*.

Although both *maʿārif* and *ʿawārif* are plural, they are rendered more smoothly into English in the singular. Both are challenging words to translate satisfactorily into English. They come from the word root *ʿa-r-f*, meaning to know, understand, recognize, or comprehend deeply. For instance, *ʿa-r-f* can be used to mean knowing a person, understanding something experientially, or having deep mystical knowledge. This is in contrast to the word root *ʿi-l-m*, which denotes knowledge acquired by study, such as the sciences.

Maʿrifah (the singular of *maʿārif*) and its cognates occur frequently in Islamic spiritual literature, as in a famous saying "whoever knows himself knows his Lord" (*man ʿarafa nafsahu ʿarafa rabbahu*), and the Shiʿi branch of Islamic mysticism is known as *ʿirfān* ("knowing" or "gnosis"). A related word is used for the Christian practice of confession. Thus, *maʿārif* are closer to mystical insights than mundane knowledge. The word root *ʿa-r-f* is also used for a sage or wise man of a village or tribe, as well as for divination. Perhaps all the shades of meaning are intended here.

Hippo Regius, the bishopric of Augustine, now the Algerian city of ʿAnnaba). His father was said to have been a Qur'an reciter, and al-Buni's strong familiarity with the Qur'an and Prophetic tradition—of which the reader will have a taste—suggests that he had a traditional religious education. Clearly a disciple on the mystical path, at some point, he began to study under a prominent Sufi shaykh in Tunis, ʿAbd al-ʿAziz al-Mahdawi (d. 1224), who also instructed the famous Muslim mystic, Ibn ʿArabi (1165–1240). However, while Ibn ʿArabi and al-Buni write on similar topics, such as lunar mansions, divine names, and jinn, Ibn ʿArabi takes a more visionary approach, whereas al-Buni takes a more practical approach.

Eventually, al-Buni migrated to Egypt, visiting Mecca at least once, as all Muslims are exhorted to do if they are able. In Cairo, he taught his students in the necropolis, a center of tomb-visitation practices linked to the cult of saints. He is said to have been buried in Cairo, and, for many centuries, his tomb was visited by people seeking his intercession and blessings. Despite the deep piety imbuing his works, he quickly moved from fame to infamy, and has alternated between being known as a scholar and a sorcerer, a saint and a heretic.[2] Perhaps the wisest approach is to eschew categories, and simply to take him as he is.

There is, of course, an elephant in the room: the question of whether al-Buni himself actually authored the *Sun of Knowledge*. This issue is compounded by the fact that, in the classical Arabic tradition, books were often produced by a teacher's students. Given the enormity of the *Sun of Knowledge* as printed today—about six times the size of this book—it seems reasonable that al-Buni may have authored a core work, to which other esoteric material was later appended, as a sort of running encyclopedia ascribed to al-Buni hon-

2 Primary sources discussing the life of al-Buni are listed in Noah Gardiner, "Stars and Saints: The Esotericist Astrology of the Sufi Occultist Ahmad al-Buni," *Journal of Magic, Ritual, and Witchcraft* 12.1 (Spring 2017): 39–65. See also A. Dietrich, "al-Būnī," in *Encyclopaedia of Islam, Second Edition*, ed. by P. Bearman, T. Bianquis, C.E. Bosworth, E. van Donzel, W.P. Heinrichs (Leiden: Brill, 2012). As for al-Buni's naysayers, Ibn Taymiyyah (d. 1328) and Ibn Khaldun (d. 1406) spoke of him as a "sorcerer" and a "heretic," although, admittedly, Ibn Taymiyyah considered a great many people to be heretics.

orifically.[3] In any case, what can be said is that the *Sun of Knowledge* is an authentic reflection of the Arabic esoteric tradition, which has been passed down throughout the ages under the spiritual aegis of a great master, and which today is the single most influential and comprehensive work in the Arabic occult tradition.

At this point, some readers may wonder about the use of the terms "Arabic" and "Islamic," since the two terms are related but not interchangeable: "Arabic" describes a language and culture, whereas "Islamic" describes a religion. Many Muslims do not speak Arabic as a native language. However, since Arabic is the language of the Qur'an, Arabic esoteric and occult traditions—or variants thereof—are practiced wherever Muslims live. Furthermore, not all Arabs are Muslim, and people of other faiths also engage in these occult and esoteric practices. Perhaps most importantly, some of what is discussed in this book predates Islam. Therefore, an attempt has been made to use the terms "Arabic" and "Islamic" sensitively and accurately. The term "Islamicate" refers to products of Islamic civilization, including things produced by people who were not Muslim but who were living in a majority-Muslim culture. In my view, it is the most apt term for this tradition. However, it has been largely avoided for the sake of ease of reading.

The prominence enjoyed by the *Sun of Knowledge* in the Arabic tradition may come as a surprise to some, given that the most popular work on Arabic magic and astrology available in English is the *Picatrix*. The *Sun of Knowledge* and the *Picatrix* share certain key paradigms, such as the Hellenic schemes of the planetary hours and days, and certain approaches to talisman-making and sympathetic magic. Yet the *Picatrix* is rather less pious, and the author of the *Picatrix* does not share al-Buni's concern with nurturing the spiritual growth and well-being of the practitioner. In practice, the *Picatrix* is rarely used in today's Arabic-Islamic esoteric traditions, whereas the *Sun of Knowledge* is commonplace.

3 Noah Gardiner, who has researched al-Buni extensively, is of the view that much of today's *Sun of Knowledge* was not directly written by al-Buni. See "Stars and Saints," *passim*.

Sometimes, given the secularizing pressures of modernity, it can be easy to forget that the Arabic literary heritage is replete with occult manuscripts—some original, some translated from ancient languages, and some pretending to be translations from ancient languages. This translation and composition process occurred during the flourishing of the sciences and literature during the 'Abbasid caliphate, in which occult and astrological sciences were treated like other forms of learning rather than being shunted to the local equivalent of New Age bookshops. Much of this literary heritage has not been printed and survives only in manuscript form; for instance, the Biblioteca Ambrosiana in Milan boasts an extensive collection of Arabic occult manuscripts, as do universities and libraries throughout the world. Therefore, the *Picatrix* had and continues to have extensive competition.

While the *Picatrix* was not the only Arabic occult work to enter Europe, there may be a couple reasons why it gained prominence, beyond mere accident. First, it does not employ the Qur'an. Second, as Liana Saif notes, it—along with a few other texts—"constituted to European natural and occult philosophers a body of works containing philosophical notions of astral generation and causation that validate astrology and astral magic in non-supernatural terms, or without 'Diabolicall Principles' as Lilly would say, thus contributing to the flourishing of European occult philosophy." Even then, Saif observes that, in Europe, the *Picatrix* only gained popularity in the early modern period.[4]

With that in mind, myself and J. M. Hamade decided to render at least part of the *Sun of Knowledge* into English—especially since up until now the *Sun of Knowledge* has eluded such a translation. While many worthy people have embarked upon this task, the *Sun* has still outstripped them. This is only natural, since the book is both long and abstruse. Therefore, we included here a translation of the first eight chapters of the book, along with excerpts from Chap-

4 Liana Saif, *The Arabic Influences on Early Modern Occult Philosophy* (Basingstoke: Palgrave Macmillan, 2015), 3, 73. For an overview of the spread of occult knowledge from the Arabic-speaking world to Europe, see also the introductory chapter of Idries Shah, *Oriental Magic* (London: Octagon, 1968).

ter 17 and Chapter 19, to introduce readers to the style and content of al-Buni's work, and to add to the growing body of literature on Arabic astrology, astronomy, and lettrism. Truly, there could have been no better time: currently, there is an unprecedented interest in Arabic astrology and magic. From university halls to occult bookshops, there is a growing demand for the Arabic and Islamicate occult. With that in mind, we are honored to present this excerpt. To those still laboring away at the *Sun of Knowledge*, keep working: it is an enormous book, and there is plenty of it to go around.Additionally, it is my hope that this work will contribute to promoting dialogue between faiths and civilizations in an era frequently characterized by intolerance. While there is today an increasing awareness of the mutual interchange between mediaeval Europe and the Islamic world, there is oftentimes still a sense of an invisible wall between "Islam" and "the West." However, as Michael Muhammad Knight observes in his book *Magic in Islam*, the occult has a particular capacity to tunnel beneath humanity's barriers.[5] Any reader familiar with Kabbalah will see immediate parallels with al-Buni's lettrism. This makes perfect sense: Jews and Arabs have lived side-by-side in the Middle East, and Hebrew and Arabic are sister languages. But what about similarities between the *Sun of Knowledge* and the European Solomonic tradition? Shared Abrahamic heritage between Christians and Muslims, and certainly the physical transfer of occult manuscripts between Muslims and Christians during the mediaeval era, facilitated common ground in Arab-Islamic and European-Christian employment of similar names of entities and angels; similar planetary correspondences and timings; and similar techniques including the use of protective circles, or browbeating entities into submission by uttering the name of the Abrahamic

5 Such barriers include orthodoxy and heterodoxy, modernity and tradition, as well as culture and geography. On the topic of religious orthodoxy, he writes: "No matter how many concrete walls, security fences, razor-wire coils, and surveillance towers a scripture's guardians set up to police its borders, there are always points of entry and exit—holes in the fence, tunnels underground—that expose the border as an illusion." Michael Muhammad Knight, *Magic in Islam* (New York: TargerPerigree, 2016), 108.

God. Of course, the latter also occurs in the Greek Magical Papyri which predate both.

Perhaps one of the main theoretical differences between a strict Christian and a strict Islamic framework is that, in mediaeval European Christianity, entities were typically identified as either angels or demons, and therefore, in theory, any non-angelic entity would be considered diabolical. Although this worldview does not reflect the diversity of popular belief in Europe—which admits to entities that are neither angels nor demons—this dichotomy likely underpins the continued popular association of occultism with Satanism in English-speaking cultures. However in Islam jinn occupy a more intermediate position and are held to have free will, even if some have a tendency towards the demonic.[6]

Although the *Sun of Knowledge* presents itself as a single Islamicate product, it contains many layers of cultural and religious influence, including various streams from ancient Greece, pre-Islamic Arabia, the post-Islamic Arab-Muslim Empire, and Judaism;[7] and the lunar mansions are held to have developed in India.[8] "Magic

6 For more on the similarities (and differences) between the Islamic and Western occult traditions, and the transmission of occult material between the two civilizations, see Saif, *The Arabic Influences on Early Modern Occult Philosophy*, *passim*; Mark Sedgwick, "Islamic and Western Esotericism," *Correspondences* 7.1 (2019): 277–99. See also the many works of Charles Burnett on this subject.

7 See "Stars and Saints," 45–51, in which Gardiner discusses Hellenistic and neoplatonic influences on al-Buni. Al-Buni himself alludes to the heritage of the Arabian peninsula in our present volume of the *Shams*, such as in Chapter 3 on "the rain-stars." Names and words of Hebrew origin pepper Arabic occult texts, including the *Shams* and others; for instance, see Chapter 9, under "Reconciling people, especially spouses." The famous and frequently-recited Birhatiyah adjuration also includes both Arabic and Hebrew (or, rather, Arabicized Hebrew) names of God, including names such as Ehyeh Asher Ehyeh, Adonai, El, Shaddai, and Tzeva'ot. Wahid Azal, "The Birhatīya Conjuration Oath and the meaning of its first 28 names" (2014), https://www.academia.edu/9799507/The_Birhat%C4%ABya_Conjuration_Oath_and_the_meaning_of_its_first_28_names, last accessed 20/6/2020.

8 The system of twenty-seven or twenty-eight lunar mansions is generally held to have developed in China or India, and found its way westwards towards the Arabic-speaking world after the advent of Islam, although some scholars root the ideas behind lunar mansions in the Hellenic or Babylonian traditions. See Philip Yampolsky, "The Origin of the Twenty-Eight Lunar Mansions,"

squares"—with which the *Sun of Knowledge* is replete—are held to have originated in China over two thousand years ago, and then to have migrated westwards.[9] Thus, the *Sun of Knowledge* can be read as part of the overall human heritage of occult and esoteric thought, and not only as something limited to the Arab or Islamic world. Beyond that, like any other grimoire, the *Sun of Knowledge* reminds us that human concerns remain basically the same: people everywhere crave love, health, wealth, fame, glory, and enlightenment...and a solid way to smite their enemies.

It should also be noted that the *Sun of Knowledge* is situated in a living tradition. Unlike in Europe where the chain linking master to apprentice was largely interrupted by modernity, in the Islamic world—as indeed in much of the rest of the world—occult and esoteric teachings have continued to be passed on from teacher to student, especially among Sufis.[10] As but one example, exorcism is in

---

Osiris 9 (1950): 44–61; Nicholas Campion, *A History of Western Astrology* (London and New York: Bloomsbury, 2008), 67. The *Picatrix* (I:4 and IV:9) attributes one list of lunar mansions to the "wise men of India" and another to Pliny, reflecting a conception of the heritage that is likely both historical and mythic. However this idea of the origin of lunar mansions may be oversimplified since star "stations" associated with the later concept of the mansions were used in the pre-Islamic Arabian Peninsula (see Chapter 3 of this present edition of the *Shams*). Furthermore, the Arabian Peninsula, India, and the Hellenic world had been connected through trade routes and other means long before the time of Islam, so it seems unlikely that the idea of a lunar mansion was a genuine novelty.

9 An interesting magic square found in both Chinese and Arabic cultures is the square known as the "*badūḥ* square," which has nine cells and adds up to fifteen in any direction. Not only is it considered to have magical and protective properties in the Arabic tradition, but it is also used in Feng Shui. See Ole Bruun, *An Introduction to Feng Shui* (Cambridge: Cambridge University Press, 2008), 151.

10 While traditional occult knowledge is still transmitted on a person-to-person basis across generations in the West, the majority of formal Western occultism today is also heavily focused on reconstructions of ancient or mediaeval traditions, as preserved in texts, or the efforts of relatively recent individuals or groups such as Aleister Crowley or the Hermetic Order of the Golden Dawn. In contrast, in the Arabic-Islamic world, as in some other places, occult traditions have primarily been passed on from teacher to student, with little reliance on books. Until recently, it was not uncommon to find young people apprenticed into the fields of spiritual healing or the spiritual arts, just as young people were apprenticed into other professions.

and of itself considered a normative practice in Islam, even if some approaches to it are not.[11] In virtually any Muslim-majority country, it is easy to hire professional exorcists, spiritual healers, and sorcerers. Therefore, like the Greek Magical Papyri, the *Sun of Knowledge* is not meant to be a self-study book; instead, it is more like a cookbook which lists the ingredients and assumes the chef knows what to do with them. Still, there are many things readers can adopt for themselves, should they have an interest in such matters.

To that end, J. M. Hamade, himself a student and teacher of the esoteric arts, as well as a visionary artist, has included a fascinating chapter outlining how some of this material may be put into practice, and offering deeper insights into the text. His chapter shows how the material in this text continues to form a backbone of esoteric exploration, even as, simultaneously, the esoteric tradition evolves in its own ways with each and every practitioner.

Lastly, we understand some of this material can be challenging. To that end, we leave the reader with al-Buni's advice:

> I have explained to you all things. Do not cede to frustration! For tedium and vexation are the bane of the student. Seek, and you shall find. Do not seek, and you shall not find. Know, and be guided![12]

We hope that the reader will find this work beneficial, and that it is only one of many works on the Arabic esoteric and occult tradition to come.

AMINA INLOES
February 2021

11 The religious legitimacy of exorcism and spiritual healing (*ruqyah*) is derived from narrations attributed to the Prophet Muhammad; for instance, in normative collections such as *Saḥīḥ al-Bukhārī* (the chapter on medicine). Views of classical and contemporary Islamic scholars on matters such as possession and exorcism can be found in Annabelle Böttcher and Birgit Krawietz (eds.), *Islam, Migration and Jinn: Spiritual Medicine in Muslim Health Management* (Cham: Palgrave Macmillan, 2021), especially chapters 3 and 4.

12 Al-Shaykh Aḥmad ibn ʿAlī al-Būnī, *Shams al-Maʿārif al-Kubrā* (Beirut: Dār al-Mīzān, n.d.), 304; some words omitted for ease of reading.

28 Stations: *Travelogue*

by J. M. Hamade

MUCH LIKE OUR familiar twelve-sign zodiac, the lunar mansions mark a divisional pathway through the open sky. The Western astrological iteration of this pathway—distinct from its *sidereal* (that is, bound to the fixed stars) origin in the Indian subcontinent—has metamorphosed into a curious and often perplexing mixture of solar and stellar/lunar time-keeping. The Egyptian decans (divisions of the 360° ecliptic into 10° segments, and their evolution therein) share much with the Western iteration of the lunar mansions. Similarly the decans originated using stellar time-keeping but have since attached themselves to the solar zodiacal calendar.

The initial stellar impulses of the lunar mansions have remained intact within the Vedic *nakshatra* system, wherein the mansions themselves are still attached to the sidereal location of the stars from which they derive their meaning. Though much of the lunar mansion lore originating in India has remained intact within the Arabic system, there has also been a strong admixture of various cultural additions—ranging from Hellenistic astrology to indigenous Arab star lore and much in between.

Observing the much-familiar *Picatrix* or *Ghayat al-Hakim*, the Arabic astrological text most often cited in the Western magical canon, we see a similarly aggregating process at work. It may be said that because we share the sky so universally it is only inevitable that practices, lore, and philosophies begin to coalesce. This begs a question in regards to our text at hand, the *Shams al-Maʿarif*: is there something unique about the prominence of lunar mansion magic within the Arabo-Islamic traditions? If so, how might it relate to the vast corpus of not-explicitly-astrological magic found both in the *Shams* and across a variety of Arabic grimoiric materials?

#26 Al-Fargh al-Muqqadam

An unorthodox point of initiation, yes. Deep-space in character and markedly in-between, this strange locale belies all standard measurements. This is a cold distance (or, perhaps a short-sighted illusion). Concordant with all tenuous threads.

The Square of Pegasus marks the ancient sky dwelling of Enki, deity of cunning, magic, and underground springs of freshwater. Adjacent to this we find the winged horse who bears the name of the constellation. Pegasus, born of the Gorgon-Serpent's blood, emerges as an embodied and resplendent manifestation of the fertility from below. The precious coral—another symbol of the Gorgon's brood—is both life and death, red and white, suffused to engender liminal bodies and radiant form. The water bearer Ganymede, of the constellation right nearby, also speaks to the fount of life-giving waters found in this region of the sky.

Fluids of immortality, yes, perhaps; yet at what cost?

We find time and time again this mansion used to bring about a "higher" state of love. The *Picatrix* uses the twenty sixth mansion for this very purpose. With the aid of sweet substances as well as white binding agents (white wax and mastic) we are told to engrave the image of a woman with hair flowing into a vessel. This same sentiment is echoed in the *Shams al Maʿarif*: the intended aim is to elicit genuine affection—potentially even true love—with whomsoever is involved.

True love? To what degree and with whom? Using the symbol previously mentioned, one might be better served to approach this less literally. The woman's hair becomes a symbol of the thread, *khayt* or *khatt* (line), wherein continuities of spirit are bound together in true Saturnine fashion. We would be greatly mistaken to confuse the love mentioned with something superficial or fleeting. The texts refer to this as nothing less than "love-divine." What may we surmise from this? These tenuous threads, the serpentine hair of the Gorgon, are nothing short of the cosmic connective tissue; here revealed through Saturnian binding as love of the most high. Akin to—seen through this window—the gravity of connection to one another that keeps the cosmos intact and alive.

Once more, there is a cost here; something to bind oneself too. Such is the nature of "true love" or "true freedom," never enough as a boundless and random pursuit unto itself. For lest we forget: Medusa's blood has been spilled. Lest we forget the abduction of Ganymede in true faery-like fashion. Another present danger is the manipulation of such-and-such binding through the magic of knots—well attested in Islam and Arabic traditions. Surah al-Falaq of the Qur'an warns us of this same manipulation of the threads which connect us: "[Protect us]...from the evil of those who blow on knots" (113:4).

The Andalusian mystic Ibn 'Arabi was well aware of this almost paradoxical nature when he dubbed this particular mansion that of the Jinn. Often deceptive and roundabout in their actions, the Jinn mirror Ibn 'Arabi's ascription of the name *al-Latif*, the Subtle—one of the 99 Names of Allah—to this mansion. For what is more subtle than the counting of hairs? The threads, tenuous, loosened, knotted, what-have-you, in which we are bound—and indeed the plenitude of strange spirit pacts strung throughout the ages—are what tie the cosmos together in unfathomable and frankly terrifying ways... Subtle indeed.

The Archaic Language of the Moon

It is not by accident that the 28 Letters of the Arabic alphabet have come to be associated with the 28 lunar mansions. First we must acknowledge the obvious. There are 28 lunar mansions and 28 Arabic letters. In regards to both of these systems there have been a series of historical variations that are worthy of note. For example, it is far more common to encounter 27 lunar mansions in the current Vedic nakshatra system as opposed to 28 (this would include the nakshatra Abhijat). Semitic variations of the Phoenician alphabet including Hebrew and Aramaic primarily use 22 letter systems: ideal for modern Tarot correspondences but not quite as clean when it comes to lunar mansions.

Perhaps a more appropriate correspondence may be found in the *Greek Magical Papyri*. Less reliant upon particular quantities and their alignment, the voices in the Papyri liken the phases of the moon to a series of sounds. From Hans Dieter Betz's *The Greek Magical Papyri in Translation*:

> I call upon you who have all forms and many names, double horned goddess, Mene, whose form no one knows except him who made the entire/world, IAO, the one who shaped [you] into the twenty-eight shapes of the world so that you might complete every figure and distribute breath to every animal and plant, that it might flourish, you who wax from obscurity into light and wane from light into darkness/(who begin to wane into a decrease).
>
> And the first companion of your name is silence, the second a popping sound, the third groaning, the fourth hissing,/the fifth a cry of joy, the sixth moaning, the seventh barking, the eighth bellowing, the ninth neighing,/the tenth a musical sound, the eleventh a sounding wind, the twelfth a wind-creating sound, the thirteenth a coercive sound, the fourteenth a coercive emanation from perfection.

This selection from PGM VII 756–94 goes on to list 28 forms presumably associated with the 28 mansions, many of them being explicit symbols of the goddess Hekate. Along with nods to Hekate, the goddess of the moon Selene, or Mene, is mentioned at the beginning of the passage. Mene is said to have been divided by IAO into 28 shapes so as to nourish and enliven the natural world.

Through the highly syncretic text that is the Papyri, we can see a variety of worldviews and cosmologies coalescing into something fairly coherent: that is, at least coherent enough to be used as a highly workable magical system. Once more, we find the prominence of aggregating practices dominating magico-religious spheres. We see remnants of ancient Egyptian priest-craft as well as Greek, Christian, Jewish, and a smattering of ancient Mediterranean forms existing simultaneously within the worldviews of the Papyri. And though Muslim thinkers would not be inclined towards an explicit polytheism as witnessed by the above, we would also be hard pressed to not find significant crossovers; most importantly in the domains of Sufism, esotericism (or *Batinism*), and of course magic.

Genesis attests it was God who breathed upon the firmament to elicit the creation of the world, as well as breathing upon the clay in the fashioning of humankind. The twenty-eight attributes of Mene listed in the papyri, being one multi-form of the twenty-eight lunar mansions, are associated with the varieties of animal and plant life of the biological sphere, and by our invisible animating breath which moves through them. We are reminded of our own forming of words and sounds, which similarly use the shape of the mouth and tongue to articulate the invisible breath and the form it takes to the surrounding air. Commingling in copresence, the two airs of concept and vibratory frequency become tangible through one another. This language is not limited to banalities and small talk, of course. Sacred chant, song, rhythm, and music of all sorts, as well as the spoken roots of poetry itself, may be found as emerging from these various shapes and their conjunction with invisible breath. Likened to a knowledge of bird song, the *Mantiq al-Tayr*, or Language of the Birds, forms a wonderful mystical analogue to the use and manipulation of said shapes for various metaphysical means. We must not forget that Thoth, Djehuty, 𓅝𓏏𓏭𓀭, bird-headed Egyptian deity of magic, mathematics, and language—was also strongly associated with both the Moon and Mercury: once more, the shape of the mouth as present phase as well as the articulation of the tongue in forming the invisible into intended purpose.

Quoted in Chapter 9 of the present text, Al-Buni uses passages from Surah an-Naml (27) in commanding the aerial jinn associated with Solomon's carpet; that is, flight. These passages, involving a letter to the Queen of Sheba as well as the instantaneous movement of a heavy throne from far away, recognize the power in sculpting the force of air to a desired end. Similarly an-Naml speaks to Solomon's relationship to the gathering jinn as well as the birds, once more highlighting the connection to bird language in the magic of forming the air to evoke effect.

#1 Al-Sharatayn & #2 Al-Batin

Recall the lesson of Iblis, that rebel angel (or jinn?) who refused to bow to Adam, perceived as an inferior creation. To this end, in the story told by Mansur al-Hallaj in his *Tawasin:*

> And Allah said to him: "Prostrate yourself!"
> He said: "Not before another than you."
> He said to him: "Even if my curse falls on you?"
> He said: "It will not punish me."
> "My denial is to affirm your purity. And my reason remains disordered in You.
> And what is Adam compared to You, and who am I, Iblis, to differentiate from You!"

According to Hallaj, Iblis is *majnun,* made crazy through his loving devotion to Allah. In this way we see his thunderous devotion penned into the Arabic letter ا, Alif, ever upright in its alignment to the Northern pole, *qutb.* Similarly, the lunar mansion typically seen as the point of initiation with 0° Aries, *al-Sharatayn,* roars with a lightning from heaven as if a falling star. As the *qalam,* this lightning inscribes the majesty and power of heaven onto the horizon below, *al-lawh al-mahfuz,* or the book of nature, the primordial *kitab.*

As a gift from this other world we have received the meteoric iron. An extension of the domain of the Pole, with its glimmering sheen and hardened edge, the iron—in its refusal to prostrate—may take us further ahead than we have ever gone just as easily as its opposite. The double-sided blade, the head of the axe: a technology from beyond with no allegiance but to the One True God.

With the power of the breath, *in hand,* the pen, *al-qalam,* we wield quite the mighty sword. To this, where may we tend this fire? Who among us can contain the lightning? *Al-Batin,* the interior, the house of the flame, is none other than the *telesma,* the *telos,* the completion—the manifestation of the action in concrete form. Additionally, *al-batin* is also esoteric; as in, the unmanifest. Here we find the concept of "Celestial Earth" popularized by the likes of Henry Corbin. This sacred geography is both theophanic as well as mundane; the potential exists for both. We might say it is "hidden in plain sight."

Between the Arabic letters ا and ب we possess a greater portion of the mystery at work, for what is the art of talismanic magic, language, art, and poetry, but writing in the book of nature; or, to the magician's end, the manipulation of such forces? These two lunar mansions speak to the magic of the talismanic art in general. This said, we should not underestimate the importance of these techniques within the greater purview of Islamic and Arabic forms of magic. To possess the fires of heaven within the container of the talisman is akin to wielding weaponry. Therefore these practices must not be taken lightly; as the example of Iblis' certainty attests. Passionate devotion, especially when concretized in material form into the cycles of generation, can easily become dogmatism if not outright tyrannical. *Al-Sharatayn* and its association with *al-Ahmar*—literally the color red as well as the burning jinn king of Tuesday and the planet Mars—reminds us of the dangers therein. The alchemical fires must be tempered to engender sustainable results. We would be want to neglect the earth, *al-batin*, the world of the interior, in our pursuits toward holistic practice. For the materials in which we work, intellectual or otherwise, will reap the rewards or disasters for which we have put in...

Books of Spelling

Along with the *Ghayat al-Hakim*, the present text of the *Shams al-Ma'arif* takes a strong liking toward the talismanic arts of inscribing a series of images and symbols onto a variety of materials. In these instances, astrological timing is of prime import. Thus far, we have illustrated how the talismanic art is inextricably linked to Muslim cosmology as well as older forms of religion and magic in the Mediterranean world. Similarly, the use of precise astrological timing has a deep precedent within this part of the world in a variety of forms. Commonly referred to as "Image Magic," or "Arabic Astral Magic," this combination of timing and talisman creation has born out one of the more distinct magical forms in the Islamic world.

Though the varieties of practice and techniques of Image Magic are still used in the Islamic world, it takes a far subservient position to the majority of magical forms represented in the present text. As noted in the Foreword of this present work, the *Shams* far exceeded the popularity and use of Picatrixian forms of magic in the Islamic world. To put an added emphasis on ultra-precise astrological timing and the mathematics therein—as is sometimes done in contemporary Anglophonic astrological discourse—would be a misrepresentation of the material at hand. The *barakah*, or power, of surahs from the *Quran* far outweighs the complex workings of astral magic in terms of accessibility, strength, and efficacy amongst a religious population. To add to this sentiment, the readiness and consistent efficacy found in what are called "folk magical" remedies—whether they be the use of plants, writing, places in nature, invocations of the prophets and saints, and the like—will also outweigh the complex and often grand pageantry of Picatrixian astral magic.

With all of that said, we return to our initial question regarding the distinguishing qualities of the present text: those which both characterize and contextualize it within similar but also distinct magico-religious traditions. First and foremost, one primary quality can be thought of as *necessity*, the lived and mundane reality of the vast majority of humankind, approaching 2 billion identifying as Muslim, which informs the material of magical practice. Once more, acknowledging biases of the present writer, to emphasize complex astrological calculation as fundamental in Islamic magical practice would be a misrepresentation. In fact, the moon and her archaic alphabet are very much a bridge between these worlds. The accessibility of the lunar phases should not be taken for granted among the magics *actually* practiced as opposed to those merely theoretical. Al-Buni includes the instructions for determining these phases and the placement of the moon in the various mansions for this reason. Though there is a learning curve to identifying these particular places as well as any given asterism, this curve is far easier to navigate than the complex world of mathematics necessary to calculate a fully detailed astrological chart; at least, before computer software. Along with a more sky-visible astrology we must return to the emphasis on written, drawn, and inscribed material being of great import. If one was able to procure a text such as the *Shams al'Ma'arif*, and possessed the ability to read it, surely one was capable of utilizing the letters of the alphabet in the construction of spells and charms. Similarly, one would most likely have a working knowledge of the Qur'an, and perhaps some ability to recognize the efficacy of certain surahs as protective, healing, combative, or magically operative in general. As most esoteric exegetes of Qur'anic text will at the very least allude to, the use of segments of the Qur'an for magic is something of an extension of the *ilm al-huruf wa al-asma*, or the science of letters and names. And though the use of letters and names towards magical ends is not uniquely Muslim within the widest history of magic, we can absolutely say that this particular iteration of it is both unique to the Muslim world as well as to the text at hand. That is, invisible breath in its animation of form to particular ends.

The *grimoire*, a book of grammar, has become the common parlance for "magical book" in the Anglophonic world. Seen another way, the book of grammar is more like a book of a particular language with imagery; that of spirit, magic, and things seen as occult or hidden. The grammar portion is akin to the means of putting said language and imagery together correctly to elicit the desired response: which is, by and large, a non-material causative to a desired end. With the frequent mention of letters in regards to the magic of the present text, it is no stretch to say that this is the dominant medium of magical change found in the *Shams al-Ma'arif*, whether that be through the Arabic letters, segments of the Qur'an, names or attributes of God, or similar kinds of "spelling."

Perhaps another uniquely Islamic iteration in the magic of letters and their inscription—truly emerging from the milieu of Islamic magic and esotericism—is that of *ilm al-raml*, or *khatt-al-raml*, the science of sand cutting, also known as geomancy. Here again we have the "tenuous threads" mentioned in the twenty-sixth mansion, that is, for use in connecting, binding, and weaving through the fabric of existence itself. Various esoteric disciplines of the Islamic world frequently attest to the significance of these lines of spirit—whether it be Arabic calligraphy, geomancy, or the music and rhythms of *zar* ceremonies—as a means of connecting invisible spirit back to the plane of manifestation. As Hallaj reminds us in his *Tawasin*, the primordial dot—of which we often identify the sixteen geomantic figures—is the fundamental form which extends into line as well as the varieties of shapes with which the moon comes to be associated. The patron of this science of the sand is no other than Idris himself, the Biblical patriarch Enoch, who is both a patron of sewing-threading as well as that of esoteric knowledge *par excellence*. In this way he is often likened to Hermes Trismegistus and the Hermetic arts in general; recalling again our bird-headed—and, naturally, bird-speaking—patron of the moon in Egyptian cosmology.

Idris, having ascended to heaven, partakes of the invisible dimension or *al-ghayb*, yet his signs have been left behind, those marks upon the sand, to be arranged in another primordial language. The sixteen figures of geomancy offer combinations of concrete symbols (as with "the red") and abstractions (regarding, for instance, "inner" and "outer thresholds") and thus present wide ranges of possibilities and engagements for spellwork, esoteric interpretation, and—most importantly—divination: marking the tracks of the train for a future time using what has come before.

A Brief Digression on the Bull's Eye: #4 Al-Dabaran

In observing the mansion list of the *Shams al Maʿarif*, we consistently find a series of diagrammatic dots associated with each one. These dots are the asterisms, or stars and sometimes constellations, associated with the particular mansion. More often than not there are multiple sets assigned to each mansion, as well as some that only amount to one or two dots at different angles. In comparison with similar sets of asterisms seen, for example, in the astronomical works of al-Qazwini, most of the images map—perhaps somewhat crudely due to naked eye (lack-of-)visibility—to their related set of stars.

Hallaj's dot and the extension therein leave an opening for the imagination worth exploring. Image magic need not be limited to that which is strictly representational, but more importantly, an enlivening of picture into multiple levels of reality; the animation through invisible breath.

And it has been through imagistic correspondence in authors like Al-Buni and Qazwini that particular asterisms have come to be associated with particular geomantic figures. One of the earliest correspondence systems to be incorporated into Arabic geomancy was that of the seven classical planets and their related signs and temperaments. In fact, some have even argued that geomancy as we understand it is simply another extension of astrology rather than a self-existing system unto itself; at least, in the beginning. Such discussion is beyond the purview of the work at hand, but suffice it to say that the connections between the geomantic figures and the stars runs incredibly deep.

Some iterations of the *Shams* have the geomantic figure *al-Lahyan*, or *Laetitia* as it is known in the Latin West, as the asterism for Mansion #4 *al-Dabaran*—or perhaps it is the other way around. Nevertheless, the relationship has been reified and established. Scholar of Islamic science Emilie Savage-Smith has shown, in analysis of engraved geomantic-divinatory devices, this very same relationship between *al-Dabaran* and *al-Lahyan*.

Al-Lahyan is often translated as "the bearded," "the laughing one," and sometimes "the repetitive." *Al-Dabaran* is simply the name of the large reddish star found in the eye of the Taurus bull, Alpha Tauri, respectively. Per the elemental schema used by both Eastern as well as Western geomancers, the figure of *al-Lahyan* is depicted with one catalyzing point of Fire placed upon three lower segments of the less active elements, in descending order, from Fire to Air to Water to Earth. Seen through the context of the Vedic nakshatras, the red star of Aldebaran was representative of a powerfully passionate and erotic force known as Rohini; so powerful in fact that this force was able to initiate the verdantly lush growth of Spring through its very pull. How might this relate to the strange figure of *Laetitia*? One could say that both translations of the figure's name, whether in Arabic or Latin, connote something of a rarefied quality which therein requires repetitive upkeep for the maintenance of said state. Laughter, joy, and pleasure are all states of being which require immense amounts of energy to consistently experience. This is why these states are often seen more as "peak" points of experience as opposed to something constant or common. In this way the active flame atop the figure of *al-Lahyan* must have fuel to feed its light. If this is not so, more dangerous means are often turned towards to "keep the high."

Similarly the nature of the Spring season is to burst forth with energy, to push the plants through the frozen skin of Winter. As this energy progresses through the season it inevitably reaches its apex in the Summer Solstice, the longest day of the year, which is also the inevitable tempering of that initial impulse of the sun. Left unchecked the Bull of Aldebaran would trample the land to dust just as the Springtime sun must fall to keep from scorching the earth. Quite appropriately this lunar mansion has a strong tectonic quality. Al-Buni reminds us of this in Chapter 3 as he refers to *al-Dabaran* by its other name, *al-Atiq*, the mountain, evoking strong volcanic imagery. These emergent fires from the peak are the visible manifestation of something quite vast at work; albeit out of sight for the uninquisitive eye. The joys which we experience on the surface of the earth—bounties of food, drink, and lovely weather—are only possible through deep underlying mechanisms of sacrifice in other times, places, and below the surface: huge movements of earth, sea, and sky (the other three elements less active in *Laeticia*) at work for our fleeting and precious moments of joy.

#10 Al-Jabhah

A burning ember...slow, smoldering, the fire that never ceases, as if fed by the stolen breath of those who have passed away. This air is stale yet consistently present. Situated in the constellation of the Arabic Lion, *Al-Asad*, we may sense the pang of hunger. Yet the kill is swift only when it must be. Relaxation—as a form of waiting—endows us with stature as we sit comfortably within our form at the apex of creation.

But is this so? Or, rather, is our throne built upon the generations who have sacrificed and tread the paths before us? Is our palace, like that of Solomon's, not built by other beings endowed with agency unto themselves? The star Regulus and the Vedic nakshatra Magha, both associated with this mansion, speak of the heights of rulership in *this* world as a throne built upon the ancestral world. Our power is borrowed. We have been deputized. To overstep this notion is to embrace the inception of tyranny.

Prominent Al-Buni scholar Noah Gardiner has suggested that Al-Buni's material was explicitly intended for an exclusively Sufi-oriented crowd of esotericists. In Al-Buni's lifetime, such groups often met within the greater Egyptian necropolis known as the Qarafah cemetery. This point is critically important yet often grossly underemphasized in Islamic magical discourse. While Sufic chains of transmission from teacher to student, a *silsila*, are well considered in contemporary discourse, Islamic esotericists and magicians alike have not sufficiently addressed the role of the Dead within these various practices.

The discussion around Al-Buni's original intentions runs parallel to the discussion around authorship of the *Shams al Ma'arif* in general; some claiming that Al-Buni was not the sole author of the entirety of the work. If it is indeed the case that he did not author the text in its entirety—and in comparison with similar magical texts it truly does seem to be so—then regardless of Al-Buni's original intentions towards exclusivity, these practices have disseminated to a large range of interested parties composed of various classes and creeds. As is often the case with the grimoiric milieu, the name of Al-Buni has taken on certain legendary dimensions akin to Saint Cyprian, Solomon, Moses, and other significant religious figures who have had books attributed to them through the function of the *imagination*, that is, in opposition to that of literalist and linear forms of attribution history. In this way, these sorts of aggregated books of magic continue to elude both the fundamentalist religious and scientific strains; and rightfully so!

One might argue that through these literary masks and the dissemination of such works—including the present translation of the *Shams* and the commentary therein—we see the emergence of the Dead in forms both palpable and *acceptable* to the audience at hand. If we are to take this entire cosmology seriously then we must reckon with the fact that these letters are very much alive. Furthermore, implied within this notion of animate language, is also that of death and potential resurrection.

In other words, the language and commentaries of those who have attached themselves to the aggregating work that is the *Shams al-Maʿarif* are the voices of those both living and dead. In this way we see the never-ending hermeneutics of esoteric interpretation unfolding in living time. The pedagogy of Al-Buni within the necropolis is testament to this, as the words, thoughts, prayers, poetry and time transcending love of long dead Sufi masters are both reckoned with and interpreted by the living descendants, standing upon the structures built by those same ancestors. To this, it is not enough in our current age to draw boundaries around material in the hopes that it will never meet the eyes of those uninitiated masses. Rather, we must continue to reconcile the fact that these works possess a life of their own, distinct from any particular name which might attach itself to them. The trees used for paper, the blackening inks, the breath and saliva spilled in conjuration, as well as the necessities of everyday people who approach this magic seeking whatever they may—all congregate within the living and dying entity we see before us. This liminally encountered force is pure *barzakh*, both the tomb itself and the meeting of two waters of a different kind: the revivification of tradition in the form of lived experience and the imagination.

#13 Al-Awwa, م

Israfil, that great angel of music, how sweet is your song. How terrifying your call. My heart rings as if a bell, the resonance of which… an ocean which dissolves the temple.

The skeleton, the salt, what has been built. Sediment, as if scales upon the fish. Dissolving the temple once more. The immortal waters of Khidr upon this shore… The full moon of my being, illumined, darkened, the mirror he calls.

And I step out, knowing not where my feet will land…

#21 Al-Baldah

What is the nature of the lunar station? *Manzil*? *Maqam*? Much effort has been spent in describing the various grades of the cosmos, all the way from celestial planetary hierarchies to the stations of saints, prophets, and deities alike. The *Shams* is not altogether different in this regard as planets and letters are situated in spherical schemas of rulership from the mundane terrestrial world to the throne of God itself, *al-'Arsh*. We might say that these pursuits come from a fairly well-established human desire to organize the world around us into comprehensible parts. Similarly, one might liken Christ to the sun in exhibiting warmth, radiance, and renewal. This analogical tendency is fundamentally poetic, yet functions as a theological device in the sense that it both reifies and potentially invigorates one's presence with the divine. In this way it comes as no surprise that Al-Buni devotes much of the text to explicating cosmological schemas. For what is the efficacy of such magic if not an underlying divine-order?

Offering up another distinction, it would seem that many attributes of the celestial and divine signs and powers have historically been less amenable to alteration. This does not seem to be the same in regards to the lunar stations. In the section on the lunar mansions in the present text we see their likeness to "weigh stations" or rest stops on the journeys of Bedouin peoples crossing the ancient

Arabian desert. Unlike celestial phenomena of more complex visibility—the movement of the planets and their interactions with stars in particular—there is a stark imminence to the interplay of moon, sun and land in the everyday existence of a traveling desert dweller. These stops on the greater journey of the Bedouin take on a more ambiguous quality amongst the seemingly infinite desert horizon. This is not an entirely blank canvas any more than it is something obvious or outright.

Given the lunar mansions, decans, and various stellar systems are no longer bound to the stars, we must acknowledge there is something entirely different at work when speaking of a station in this respect in comparison to that of a planet or other celestial body. Even the Hindu nakshatra system, still very much situated within sidereal movements, must delineate space through *ayanamsa* (points in space used as starting places for the zodiac) as well as standardizing stellar mansions with degrees of varying sizes; some matching physical space more than others. The important factor here falls upon the delineation of open space as opposed to the tracking of discrete bodies.

Lacking the context of nomadic desert travel, the analogy of a theatrical stage may be used as a similar if not more familiar image. Regardless of the astrological system in which one abides, there still must be a generally agreed upon determination of where our performance is going to occur. This seemingly simple act of demarcating one from the other is not to be taken for granted, for many of the creation stories the world over describe something similar at "the beginning." Even the scientific explanation referred to as the Big Bang posits such an origin. There was nothing followed by the beginning of something. With this, it must be asked again. What do we choose to focus on? How do we shape the invisible? Where is the performance—or the sacred even—and where is the mundane?

This same imagery is readily visible in the twenty-first Arcanum of the Tarot, also known as *The World*. The four corners are established through the Lion, Human, Eagle, and Bull, as well as any iteration of cardinal directions we have come to know as marking the framework of existence. Even more importantly we have the human figure and the planet earth below, or, the upward and the downward directions respectively. Through the act of situating ourselves within the cosmos we have established the world as we know it. Through the act of renegotiating what that situation is, and could be, we re-establish the world in new and hopefully harmonious ways.

Out, Amongst the Darkness

In a time of so much perceived agency it often feels as though we have none. Whether it be guidance by spiritual elders, assistance in navigating the complex world of the occult arts, or even daily life in a media saturated flurry of superficial buffet options, more often than not we don't know how to use the things we already have. If guidance through magical books with the help of those more experienced is an option, this is always the preferred route. For those who do not have such options, as it will be for many, how does one situate themselves in these twenty-eight places? In the open and ambiguous imaginal realms in general?

We return to our initial question in regards to distinguishing qualities of the work at hand. The twenty-eight stations of the lunar mansions, as well as the twenty-eight letters of the Arabic alphabet, are culture specific forms of situating oneself; of demarcating space, which, as we have seen, is not something to be taken lightly. It is these forms, and importantly the way that we combine and create with them, that give form to the invisible and animating breath behind all things. As we can see from Chapter 10 of the present text on the Ring of Solomon, even the lowliest of elemental jinn may be swayed and moved by the uses of *the word*. Al-Buni's extensive treatment of one of the most important Islamic affirmations of God, the *bismillah*, is testament to the power with which our words—*and the letters therein*—can bring both levity and destruction to the world around us. As the text often reminds us, we are the ones who will be responsible on the Day of Judgment for the ways in which we choose to use these abilities. Do we choose to grow our light upon light, *Nur an-Nur,* or perhaps contain and obscure our light as if the darkness of the new moon.

In the grand scheme, the voices of the *Shams al-Maʿarif* are those who possess a cadence of the faithful. If the letters employed have the power to reveal the word of God, whether spoken or written, then being of steady faith is of the utmost importance in utilizing the majority of what lays before you. Though these words no doubt contain an efficacy unto themselves, the dabbler who has not *situated* themselves to the word will not reap the same rewards. It must be said that the same applies to heresy, as the opposite cannot be said for those fundamentally bland in their temperament to the material at hand. To embrace and relinquish the structures of orthodoxy is to become passionate, and it might be said, involved in the dramatic struggle that is the quintessential marker of the living, *al-Hayy.* This performance that is our existence, acts upon the twenty-eight stages, and is spoken through the twenty-eight letters. If this is the language that we choose, and these are the places in which we act, then perhaps the sun that is the *Shams* may be our guide.

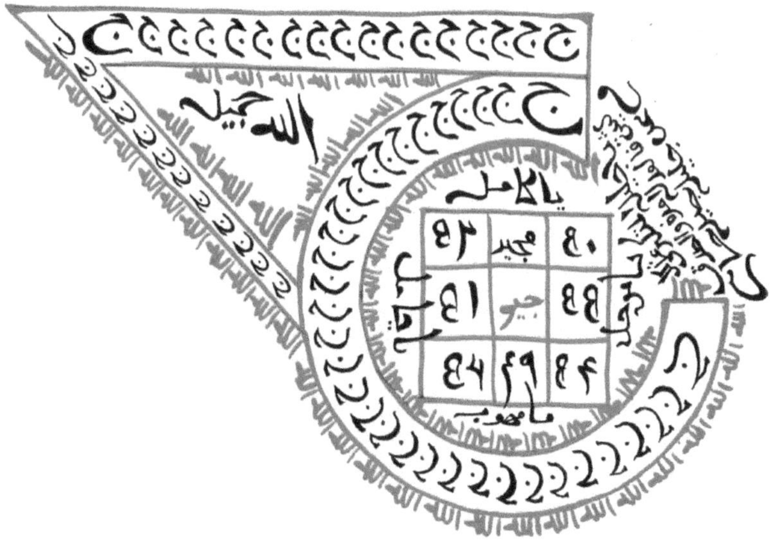

SELECTED BIBLIOGRAPHY

Al-Hallaj, Mansur, The *Tawasin*, translated by Aisha Abd ar-Rahman at-Tarjumana, Diwan Press, 1974.

Betz, Hans Dieter, The *Greek Magical Papyri in Translation*, The University of Chicago Press, 1992.

Burckhardt, Titus, *Mystical Astrology According to Ibn 'Arabi*, Fons Vitae, 2001.

Corbin, Henry, *Spiritual Body and Celestial Earth*, translated by Nancy Pearson, Princeton University Press (Bollingen Series) XCI:2, 1977.

Cordero, Jaime Coullaut, *El Kitab Shams al-Ma'arif al-Kubra de Ahmad b. Ali al-Buni*, Tesis Doctoral, Universidad de Salamanca, 2009.

Gardiner, Noah, "Stars and Saints: The Esotericist Astrology of the Sufi Occultist Ahmad al-Buni," *Magic, Ritual and Witchcraft* 12, 1 (Spring 2017).

Johnson, Kenneth, *Mansions of the Moon: The Lost Zodiac of the Goddess*, Archive Press, 2002.

Savage-Smith, Emilie & Smith, Marion B., "Islamic Geomancy and a Thirteenth Century Device: Another Look," *Magic and Divination in Early Islam*, Ashgate, 2004.

Skinner, Stephen, *Terrestrial Astrology: Divination by Geomancy*, Routledge & Kegan Paul, 1980.

Warnock, Christopher & Greer, John Michael, *The Illustrated Picatrix*, Renaissance Astrology, 2010.

ACKNOWLEDGMENTS

We would like to extend our utmost gratitude to everyone who provided moral or material support to this project, especially the anonymous donors who provided manuscripts and background literature, and those who took the time to offer their thoughts on obscure phrases. A special thanks goes to one friend who repeatedly asked, "Is it done yet?" Motivation is priceless; and it is our pleasure to confirm that it is now, indeed, done. While their names have been omitted out of respect for their personal or professional privacy, this work would not have happened without you!

TRANSLITERATION

The following conventions have been used to render Arabic letters and words into English. To avoid overwhelming the reader with a slew of diacritic marks, diacritic marks have omitted from proper nouns except in cases where the spelling or pronunciation of the names might be unclear, such as the non-Arabic names used in evocations.

a	ا	ṭ	ط
b	ب	ẓ	ظ
t	ت	ʿ	ع
th	ث	gh	غ
j	ج	f	ف
ḥ	ح	q	ق
kh	خ	k	ك
d	د	l	ل
dh	ذ	m	م

r	ر	n	ن
z	ز	h	ه
s	س	w	و
sh	ش	y	ي
ṣ	ص	ah	ة
ḍ	ض	ʾ	ء
a	َ	ā	ا
i	ِ	ī	ي
u	ُ	ū	و

NOTES ON THE TRANSLATION

The indented text is commentary on the translation. It is hoped that the commentary will assist the readers in navigating this challenging work. Additional annotations have been included in the footnotes; none of the footnotes are present in the original work. While many of the section headers have been translated directly from the text, some have been added for ease of reading. Furthermore, since some of the chapter and section headers in the original text come across as rather florid in translation, they have been pruned for ease of reading. For instance, "On the Secrets of *Bismillāh* and what Lies in it of Special Characteristics and Blessings and Mysteries" has been gently redacted to "The Secrets of *Bismillāh*." We are sure al-Buni will understand.

Several sources were consulted in the preparation of this edition, which primarily relied upon a beautiful handwritten manuscript with gold leaf from the Feyzullah Efendi Madrasa in Istanbul and which is dated 1645–1646 CE (year 1055 in the Islamic Calendar), as well as a copy from 1875 housed at Princeton. The Egyptian lithograph and subsequent printed edition published in Beirut by Dar al-Mizan Press were also consulted, although they contain typographic errors. Where appropriate, material from varying sources was integrated. Most of the drawings and diagrams have been modelled upon the diagrams in the Feyzullah Efendi manuscript, apart from the diagrams in the last two chapters, which are reproduced from the lithograph.

One challenge throughout the work was how to handle the question of gender inclusivity. Invariably, classical Arabic uses the pronoun "he" to refer to people generically, and is written for an implied male heterosexual audience. For instance, the reader is sometimes addressed as "brother" and presumed to wear a turban. However, while, in the mediaeval Islamic world, scholars, astrologers, mystics, belletrists, and the like tended to be male, women also occasionally participated in these endeavors—a point that is sometimes lost today. Furthermore, even before al-Buni's time, classical Islamic literature acknowledged that some people did not fit into a gender binary or were not heterosexual. Thus, these conventions can be taken to some degree as stylistic idealizations. Therefore, in some places in the translation, the gender-neutral, although not wholly grammatical, pronoun "they" was used; in other places, "he" was retained, especially when men were being specified. Additionally, in some places, awkward and wordy third-person constructions were converted to the second-person, not the least because, sometimes, the text shifts from third-person to second-person partway through a paragraph.

The other question was what pronoun to use for God. In the Islamic tradition, God is neither male nor female, since masculinity and femininity are traits of created beings, not the Creator—something that would not have been lost on a mystic like al-Buni. However, in practice, "He" is also used in Arabic for God. In deference to that, and also to common English-language usage, "He" was used for God, although some translators today have moved towards an avoidance of using a gendered pronoun for God when translating classical Islamic texts.

Translations of Qur'anic verses were prepared by the translator but inspired by the rich corpus of Qur'anic translations of the past century.

An apocryphal "original" *Sun of Knowledge* with the true secrets of the heavens and the earth is rumored to exist in the hands of elect; purported copies of it are occasionally offered for sale at prices rivalling those of manors in Beverly Hills. While we do not claim to hold this philosopher's stone, it is hoped that the more conventional manuscripts translated here will be a suitable stand-in.

Author's Introduction

In the name of God, the Compassionate, the Merciful is the first line of the Qur'an and traditionally prefaces classical Islamic works. Classical Islamic works also traditionally begin with a pious sermon or homily praising God and confessing to the core Islamic beliefs, while, at the same time, foreshadowing the themes of the book. Therefore, in his introduction, al-Buni situates himself a theurgist, and as one of the faithful, while hinting to the reader that his book will unveil the secrets of the cosmos. He also expresses the belief that occult workings are akin to prayer; and, just as the readers should be confident that God will answer one's personal prayers, they should be confident that their occult workings will bear fruit.

Al-Buni penned this section in florid rhymed prose, a traditional style of Arabic writing. He peppered it with phraseology from the Qur'an, Islamic philosophy, and Sufism, which the educated reader would have recognized, and hence required no further elucidation, but which can seem muddled or perplexing in translation. Therefore, some efforts were made here to simplify this section. However, regardless of what language his introduction is read in, his sincerity, his humility, and the value he ascribes to seeking mystical knowledge and the secrets of the universe shine through.

In the name of God, the Compassionate, the Merciful.
O God, make this task easy for me!

Know that the elect draw knowledge from the light of this testament, just like people scoop up water from a river. An eternal, sacred hierarchy in the confession of faith[1] links the angels to the enlightened. This confession of faith is a snapshot of eternity. If you understand it, you shall witness the celestial realms.[2] The celestial secrets shall be unveiled to you, and you shall gain access to the forms of all things, and all of the divine wisdom.

I ask God—the ever-living, the ever-subsisting!—to help me offer this work as a sincere, selfless gift. I am bequeathing my secrets. And I ask God to grace me with His satisfaction, to illuminate the way for you and me, and to bestow on you and me the light of the desire to attain truth.

This here is but a glimmer of the dazzling suns—the gnostics' and aspirants' paths, the treasures of the righteous as they ascend towards the divine presence. God—the lord of the worlds, the lord of lords! God clears the way, raises the veils, creates things afresh and anew, and lives outside the confines of time and space. Eloquently and perpetually praised, eternal from beginning to end—He it is who elevates people in spiritual status and wisdom, and who unfurled the material realm.

There is no god but God—the magnificent, the lofty, veiled with veils of light, the secret of secrets. He is hidden from people's eyes but knows what they see.[3] His essence is hidden in eternity, but his attributes are manifest for all time. He manifests his names through His acts. The first and the last, the eternal and perpetual—manifest in his timelessness, unhindered by dimensions or substances. He neither wearies nor wears out. He neither struggles to attain His aims, nor is He ground down by the vagaries of time. Night and day hinder Him not. Thusly I praise Him. Exalted and glorified be He! He has measured out everything in creation. God—the knower of the unseen, the witness, the magnificent, the high.

1 *Al-shahādatayn*: The two testimonies of faith Muslims profess; namely, that there is but one God and that Muhammad is a prophet of God.

2 *Al-malakūtayn*: The invisible, higher metaphysical realms which angels and other spiritual beings inhabit, which are above the material realms but beneath the divine environs. Also sometimes identified with the imaginal realm or Plato's World of Forms.

3 An allusion to Qur'an 6:103.

I bear witness that God is God alone, with no partner; this confession of faith accompanies souls as they step through the otherworldly realms.[4] And I bear witness that God has enumerated all of his creatures, the living and the dead, and has provided them sustenance and strength.[5] He knows the past and future, and will enliven the dead after they have turned to dust.

And I bear witness that Muhammad is God's servant and messenger, the sun of the faith, who rescued God's servants[6] from idolatry and misguidance, and who, through his call to faith, set into motion the machinery of monotheism. The suns of his wisdom shone, casting the mischievous stars into shadow. Monotheism dawned happily and fortuitously. So may God's peace and blessings be upon him, and may God be pleased with his truthful, aspiring companions. May God be pleased with all of them, and may these prayers reach them in their lofty spiritual heights.

I shall now proceed to our subject here.[7] There are guide-posts on the way to truth, there is an order to reality, and souls long for mystical knowledge. While they grapple for it, it ultimately must be gifted to them. Thus, they aspire towards eternal light, happiness, and perfection through honoring the religious law.[8] The people with

4 *Al-barzakhiyāt*: In Islamic eschatology, it is held that, after death, a soul goes to an intermediate realm called the *barzakh* before arriving at its final destination in heaven or hell; the only things that a soul carries from the worldly realm are its faith and deeds. Therefore, souls would carry this testimony with them. The *barzakh* is also identified as a layer of the subtle or astral realm where one might communicate with non-corporeal beings.

5 Insofar as one of the themes of the book is the secrets of the numbers, one can presume that the author did not select this phrase accidentally, just as, in the next paragraph, he refers to the Prophet Muhammad as the "sun." Regarding sustenance, in Islamic eschatology, it is held that the deceased will still consume some sort of otherworldly food to perpetuate their existence.

6 In classical Islamic thought, the word "servants of God" (*ʿibād*) is used to mean "all human beings" as a reflection of the belief that God created people to serve Him, even if they individually choose otherwise. Furthermore, all people are bound by certain matters of fate, such as matters of life and death.

7 This section begins with the transitional phrase *ammā baʿd*, used after the opening sermon to indicate that the author or orator will now discuss the subject at hand.

8 *Sharīʿah*: Islamic law. The implication here is that obeying the letter of the law with respect to religion might make a person more qualified before God to re-

the highest spiritual status are those who do works and guide aspirants. God's religion has no place for a person devoid of knowledge, just as a corpse cannot survive without a soul. Those who make light of the religious law or who dispense with the strictures of seeking truth will find themselves furthest away from happiness and success.

I looked to what our sages have said, and found vast horizons of perfection and wisdom; their blessings permeate all of creation. They compiled works on the employment of the divine names, the secrets of the letters, invocations, and adjurations. I was asked by people near me to clarify the treasures stored in them. Thus, I responded, although I fully acknowledge that I can never comprehend everything that our forebears and spiritual guides understood. Thus, I besought God to assist me and infuse my soul with His grace, so that my words might benefit those who aspire to truth, and that I might present it truly and well.[9]

Help comes from God, and in God we trust.

My goal in the chapters of this book is to present the revered knowledge of the names of God: the oceans of jewels and secrets and refined wisdom. I also hope to explain how to employ the divine names through invocations and adjurations, and similar matters pertaining to the letters of the chapters and verses of the Qur'an.

I have organized this book in distinct chapters so that the readers may locate various forms of knowledge pertaining to the divine presence without enduring needless tedium, and so that the readers may also accomplish their earthly aims. Although this is an insufficient, humble work, I have given it a title expressing grand knowledge: The *Sun of Knowledge and the Subtleties of the Lofty Heights*,[10] since it contains sophisticated knowledge of how to employ these things, and the results.

Should this book fall into your hands: you are not allowed to di-

---

ceive divine knowledge. The author is not speaking of being born with occult talents or "gifts," as is sometimes popular to say today.

9 The translator shares this sentiment.

10 The title in Arabic is *Shams al-Maʿarif wa Lataʾif al-ʿAwarif*.

vulge it to the unworthy or reveal it in the wrong places.[11] If you do that, God will impede you from benefitting from this book or enjoying its blessings. Only touch this book when you are pure[12] and while remembering God, that thereby you may succeed in attaining from it what you desire. Only use it in a way that pleases God.

For this is a book intimately tied to God's near ones: the righteous, the obedient, the seekers, the workers, and aspirants. Be miserly with it. Be greedy! Do not neglect anything in it, great or small. Have firm faith in it. Have faith in the truths in it, for God judges acts according to people's intentions and recompenses people according to their intent.[13]

Once you have resolved to perform a working, have faith in it, for the Prophet said, "Do not pray for something without being certain that there will be a response." Be certain that your working shall succeed, for the Prophet said, "When you pray for something, be confident in the response; avoid niggling doubts." Have faith in the outcome, and know that your works shall go aright. As the Prophet said, "Your prayers are answered when you do not rush to conclude, 'I prayed for this, but it didn't happen.'" Do not be impatient! Even if the response seems slow, live in confident expectation that it shall be done.

Thusly I have compiled these rules and secrets throughout the chapters of this book, that the intellect might ponder them.[14]

11 Thus, we will presume that the reader is worthy!

12 This is an allusion to Qur'an 56:79—"none may touch it except the purified"—which is either taken to mean that one must be ritually pure before touching the Qur'an, or else that a person will not understand it unless their heart is pure. By using this expression here, al-Buni is conveying a sense of sanctity about his book and putting it in the same overall category as sacred scripture.

13 This is a commonly cited saying from the Prophet Muhammad, speaking of how, in the afterlife, God judges people's deeds based on their underlying intentions. However, it is not usually mentioned in this context.

14 The introduction concludes with a full list of chapters of the book, which has been omitted here.

Chapter 1
THE MYSTERIES OF THE LETTERS

The Islamic worldview is divided between matters of the worldly life and matters of the afterlife; both are often discussed with reference to each other. The classical Islamic tradition exhibits an overarching concern with bringing about happiness both in this life and the afterlife, not only in the material world. Thus, al-Buni commits himself to this goal here.

I SHALL NOW SPEAK, and upon God I rely. People seek two types of goals: worldly and otherworldly. Each of these categories can be further subdivided according to what a person is seeking. My predecessors have already discussed how to construct magic squares,[1] astrological timings, ascetic practices, and making talismans; these things were mentioned before I set pen to paper for this book. People covet this knowledge; when they have a little, they want more, especially if they see that it produces practical results. However, overfocusing on the material world harms a person in the hereafter; this is something the ancient sages and even common wisdom concur on. Therefore, I would like to swim against the current and tell you of things that will benefit you both in this world and in the hereafter.

THE FOUNDATIONS OF THE LETTERS

This section reflects a classical mediaeval cosmology, common to both the Islamic world and Europe, in which each of the plan-

1 Singular, *wifq*; plural, *awqāf*.

ets inhabits its own celestial sphere. It then provides numerical and alphabetical correspondences for these planetary spheres. For this section—and, indeed, the remainder of the book—it is helpful to keep in mind that each letter of the Arabic alphabet corresponds to a number; in pre-modern times, letters were often used in lieu of numbers, sometimes as a secret code. A table of letter-number correspondences has been included in the appendix.

KNOW THAT THE numbers have secrets, just as the letters have effects. Know also that the celestial realm extends to the lower realm. Similarly, the realm of the divine throne extends to the realm of the divine seat;[2] the realm of the divine seat extends to the sphere of Saturn; the sphere of Saturn extends to the sphere of Jupiter; the sphere of Jupiter extends to the sphere of Mars; the sphere of Mars extends to the sphere of the Sun; the sphere of the Sun extends to the sphere of Venus; the sphere of Venus extends to the sphere of Mercury; the sphere of Mercury extends to the sphere of the Moon; the sphere of the Moon extends to the sphere of heat; the sphere of heat extends to the sphere of moisture; the sphere of moisture extends to the sphere of cold; the sphere of cold extends to the sphere of dryness; the sphere of dryness extends to the sphere of the element of air; the sphere of air extends to the sphere of the element of water; and the sphere of water extends to the sphere of the element of earth.

Therefore, the sphere of Saturn corresponds to the letter *j* (ج, pronounced *jīm*) and, in short, the number three. However, its extended value is fifty-three. This is because *jīm* is comprised of three distinct letters—note that they are also three! The letter *m* (م) corresponds to the forty, the letter *y* (ي) corresponds to ten, and the letter *j* (ج) corresponds to three. In the lower realms, it corresponds to the

2 The "throne" (*ʿarsh*) and "seat" (*kursī*) are spoken of in the Qur'an and are part of the higher metaphysical realms where God wields authority.

letter ṣ (ص) which has the value of ninety.

The sphere of Jupiter corresponds to the number four and the letter *d* (د). It is employed through a four-by-four square.

The celestial sphere of Mars, in short, corresponds to the number five and the letter *h* (ه). It is employed through a five-by-five square.

The sphere of the Sun corresponds to the number six and the letter *w* (و). It is employed through a six-by-six square.

The sphere of Venus corresponds to the letter *z* (ز).[3] It is employed through a seven-by-seven square.

The sphere of Mercury corresponds to the number eight and the letter *ḥ* (ح). It is employed through an eight-by-eight square.

The sphere of the Moon corresponds to the number nine and the letter *ṭ* (ط). It is employed through a nine-by-nine square.

Scholars and sages concur that Saturn is employed through a three-by-three square. Understand, and be guided!

HOW THESE RELATE TO THE HUMAN BEING

Navigating this section requires knowing that the definite article in Arabic is *al-*. Half of the letters of the Arabic alphabet are elided into the prefix *al-* and are called the "Sun letters" (*al-ḥurūf al-shamsiyyah*). The other half of the letters which are not assimilated into *al-* are called the "Moon letters" (*al-ḥurūf al-qamariyyah*). For instance, *al-salām* is pronounced as *as-salām* because *s* is a "Sun letter"; however, *al-kitāb* is pronounced as *al-kitāb* because *k* is a "Moon letter." Here, the author links this to the lunar mansions. Additionally, each lunar mansion corresponds to an Arabic letter, as will be discussed in Chapter 2. While the expressions "Sun letters" and "Moon letters" are used in common parlance, they are not usually discussed alongside the mansions of the Moon.

3 The numerical value of ز is seven, but the author does not specify that here.

THEREFORE, THE DIVINE throne corresponds to the letter *alif* (ا), the divine seat corresponds to the letter *b* (ب), and Saturn corresponds to the letter *j* (ج). Continue similarly until you reach the Moon, as mentioned above.

Alphabets are of different types. Some are written from right to left, such as Arabic; and some are written from left to right, such as the Roman and Coptic alphabets. Scripts that are written from right to left are connected in cursive when written, whereas scripts that are written from left to right are written in separate, disconnected letters. The Arabic alphabet consists of twenty-eight letters. The definite article *al-* is not a separate letter; if it were, the alphabet would consist of twenty-nine letters.

There are also twenty-eight mansions of the Moon. Fourteen mansions appear above the horizon. Those correspond to the letters which are elided into the definite article, and they are the letters *n* (ن), *t* (ت), *th* (ث), *d* (د), *dh* (ذ), *r* (ر), *z* (ز), *ṭ* (ط), *ẓ* (ظ), *l* (ل), *ṣ* (ص), *ḍ* (ض), *s* (س), and *sh* (ش). The other letters, which are not elided, are *alif* (ا), *b* (ب), *j* (ج), *ḥ* (ح), *kh* (خ), *k* (ك), *m* (م), *ʿayn* (ع), *gh* (غ), *f* (ف), *q* (ق), *h* (ح), *w* (و), and *y* (ي).

The first of the letters is *alif*. Then come the letters that are the same shape as *ẓ*, like *ṭ*, *l*, and *r*; all these physically resemble the *alif*. Upon examining the letters, you will find that they have an internal orderliness which pre-existed before their forms came into being; understand that.

The letter *alif* (ا) corresponds to the number one, and hence is the "one" of the letters. Numbers have subtle spiritual powers. The secrets of speech are founded on the numbers, just as the secrets of acts are founded upon the letters. In the human world, numbers have secrets and benefits which God has assigned to them, just as God has assigned the letters secrets and benefits. For instance, letters may be used to recite prayers, incantations, exorcisms, and other things which produce measurable effects—each enacted through different types of words.

Know that the letters are not bound by time. They may be used for ascetic practices and specific acts, whenever a person wishes.

The numbers may be used for constructing talismans, but are subject to the celestial spheres.[4]

THE LETTER *D* (*DĀL*)

THE LETTER *D* corresponds to the number four. Therefore, one may draw out a four-by-four square on a pure piece of parchment and write in it the appropriate numbers. This should be done on Tuesday, the day on which the Prophet Muhammad was born, the day that he was appointed as a prophet, and the day when he died. Additionally, this should be done when the Moon is at its degree of exaltation in the sign of Taurus—that is to say, at three degrees of Taurus—and when the Moon is not in any ill astrological aspects.[5] It should also be done during the planetary hour of the Moon. At this time, while in a state of ritual purity,[6] perform two units of prayer,[7] in which you recite the Throne Verse and the Qur'anic chapter on God's unity one hundred times.[8]

God will protect whoever carries this square. He will make it easy for them to learn and understand things, and elevate their status in the heavens and on earth. A prisoner who keeps this square close to themself will go free, by the will of God. A person who hangs it aloft a standard of war shall be protected from enemies, the godless, and the depraved. Anyone who gets into a fight or quar-

4 That is to say, one does not have to observe astrological timing to do workings solely based on the letters. However, when making numerical talismans, one should observe astrological timings.

5 Such as squares, oppositions, or conjunctions with planets traditionally considered malefic, such as Mars or Saturn.

6 Islamic law provides methods of ritual washing before prayer; for someone who is not Muslim, one might presume that bathing would suffice.

7 A "unit" of prayer is comprised of a specific set of ritual recitations and actions in the Islamic prayer which is recited five times a day.

8 The Throne Verse (*āyat al-kursī*) is Qur'an 2:255, which is often recited for protection. The Qur'anic chapter on God's unity is Chapter 112 (Sūrah al-Ikhlāṣ); it is not overlong. Since Muslims believe that the Arabic text itself has special properties, the Qur'an is always recited in Arabic, whether or not it happens to be a person's native language. Thus, the expectation here would be that these Qur'anic excerpts would be recited in Arabic.

rel while carrying it shall prevail. For its numbers are placed in a four-by-four square, and four is the number of Jupiter, which is a fortunate planet. While the letter *d* is inherently cold, altogether, the elements number four: fire, air, earth, and water. Furthermore, the humors number four: yellow bile, phlegm, blood, and black bile. Thus, a four-by-four square has a natural, intrinsic power and balance.Similarly, the letter *d* (د) appears in the names and attributes of God, such as *dāʾim* ("the eternal") and *wadūd* ("the loving"). Nothing precedes the letter *d* in the word *dāʾim* or succeeds it in the word *wadūd*. Similarly, the letter *d* is at the end of the names Ahmad and Muhammad.[9] This indicates that the Prophet shall exist perpetually beyond the end of time, but that he did not exist perpetually before time. However, since the letter *d* begins the word *dāʾim*, this shows God has existed perpetually, before time and after time.

This letter is associated with the divine throne since the throne is unchanging, for it was the first created thing and thus is the first everlasting thing. Towards it, spirits ascend; in it, the hierarchy of intellects resides; and, in it are the lights of mercy. This is what some of the mystics have discovered, similar to Harithah, may God be pleased with him:[10]

> The Messenger of God[11] asked Harithah, "How are you today, Harithah?"
> Harithah said, "O Messenger of God, I awoke as a true believer."
> The Messenger of God asked, "What is the reality of your faith?"
> Harithah said, "I woke up unenchanted by this world. To me, stone seemed the same as gold. Life struck me the same as death, and wealth the same as poverty. It was as if I could see the throne of the Merciful[12] clearly, and people being driven forward to their final reckoning, to heaven or hell."
> "You have understood," the Prophet replied. "Hold firm to that."

9 Ahmad is another name for the Prophet Muhammad.
10 Harithah was one of the companions of the Prophet Muhammad.
11 That is, the Prophet Muhammad.
12 Another name for God.

And the Prophet said regarding people's souls:

> If you fall asleep in a state of ritual purity, your souls will ascend to the realm beneath the divine throne and bow in worship.

And the letter *d* holds the secrets of eternity and perpetuity.

Here, the author digresses to an excursus on the spiritual topography of the heart; the discussion on the letter *d* will be resumed afterwards. In the classical Islamic world, the heart was envisioned as the seat of the emotions as well as the intellect, and as the primary organ of spiritual vision. In contrast, today, the intellect has been relegated to the brain, although still a person might know "in their heart." The Arabic language also boasts a great many words for "love," four of which feature here. In spiritual writing, love can refer to love between human beings, or the love of God.

The divine name al-wadūd ("the loving"). The divine name *wadūd* comes from the word-root *w-d-d*,[13] meaning "affection," and affection is the outer manifestation of love (*ḥubb*). Love is the inner feeling; genuine displays of affection arise from an inner feeling of love. Therefore, affection resides in the heart and reveals the worlds of the heart. Passion (*ʿishq*) is a refined strain of love, between regular love and affection, and resides in the enamored (*shaghaf*). Therefore, love is an inner aspect of passion and resides in the impassioned depths of the heart.

For the heart has three chambers. The first, which is the highest and thickest, is a shining light and is the place where one might submit to God; here, the meanings of the letters take form. It is also

13 As in Hebrew, most Arabic words are derived from three-letter roots. So, for instance, from the root *w-d-d* come *wadd* and *widd*, meaning "affection" and *widād*, meaning "friendship."

the seat of the power of speech. Thus, from here, what is inside a person emanates as words. Next comes the middle chamber. This is where a person thinks and remembers. It is a shining light where one finds inner peace, and is the seat of the imaginal faculty which inspires the soul. The third is the last chamber, which is the subtlest and most delicate. Through here pass faith, the intellect, light, power over nature, secrets, and wisdom. Here, the intellect and the subtleties of wisdom find balance. These are the depths of the heart which experience love; this chamber is the seat of the natural life and is characterized by the element of heat.

This deep zone of the heart has an illuminated eye which perceives the astral realities and the celestial secrets, both in their entirety and in the individual things that populate them. This is the inner vision or insight (*baṣīrah*) which a person uses to truly see. The Qur'an says: "It is not the physical eyes that are blinded; rather, it is the eye of the heart that goes blind" (22:46).

The middle chamber of the heart is where passion (*ʿishq*) resides. It has an illuminated eye which pinpoints what it desires; from it emanate determination and the desire to acquire what is sought. Its subtle essence attaches to people quicker. This sense is what perceives the physical plane (*ʿālam al-mulk*) and God's creations on it. It also decides what is good, agreeable, or beautiful.

The first chamber of the heart has an illuminated eye which perceives sensible realities, things with compound natures, and the mysteries and realities of the letters; it comprehends well the secrets which God has placed in them. And the greatest secrets which God has placed in the letters pertain to the divine names. God wanted His servants to understand them, and, upon understanding them, to glorify Him. Thus, God blessed the heart with the capacity to unveil the secrets of the sensory world. This is the heart's inner vision in its entirety, except that these capacities can vary in different situations.

I have discussed elsewhere how the spirits responsible for revealing the divine book are three: the "trustworthy spirit," the "holy spirit," and "the spirit of divine command."[14] The revelation delivered by the "trustworthy spirit" interacts with the first chamber of the heart, since it interacts with immaterial realities which lie between speech and the tongue. Therefore, it is the first level of revelation. Whenever God swears by it, He is referring to revelation and divine inspiration received by the heart. After it comes the "holy spirit," and it is composed of lights radiating what is inscribed in the Eternal Tablet.[15] It visits the second level of the heart, thereby establishing faith, insight, and thought. From these lights, wisdom manifests, and these lights are a divinelike substance and the subtleties of faith.

Then there is the third level, which is the seat of the sacred light, hearing, and the intellect. God said to His Prophet: "You cannot make the dead hear, nor can you make the deaf hear the call" (Qur'an 27:80). He was not referring to physical deafness; rather, he was referring to the death of the thinking capacity and, hence, transgression. They may indeed be able to physically hear, but their hearts' ears hear not. Therefore, this is where the "spirit of command" settles; when this happens, this indicates a stable union with God. This spiritual position was reserved for the Prophet Muhammad, may God's peace and blessings be upon him. We discussed these matters pertaining to the heart, insight, and such in our book entitled *The Ultimate Stations and Ascetic Secrets* (*Mawaqif al-Ghayat fi Asrar al-Riyadat*); contemplate it, and matters will become clear.

God says: "The Merciful shall ordain love for those who believe and work righteous deeds" (19:96). This means that God shall place divine love in their hearts; they will love God, and God will love them. In their hearts, they will enjoy remembering and approaching God; when their heart tells them to do something for the love of

14 *Rūḥ al-amīn, rūḥ al-qudus*, and *rūḥ al-amr*: These phrases are used in the Qur'an to describe the mechanisms through which the Qur'an was revealed from God to the Prophet Muhammad. By "it has already been said," the author is referring to his previous work.

15 The Eternal Tablet (*al-lawḥ al-maḥfūẓ*) is said to refer to the eternal tablet of the Qur'an in heavens, from which the worldly Qur'an descended. It is also said to contain matters which are fated.

God, they will always do it. They will not love themselves until they have severed their worldly affections and attachments, and then a wash of love from God infuses them. Then, they are moved to speak about matters of wisdom to perform acts which raise their spiritual status. Their souls long for the realities of faith and true submission to God. They yearn for the light of the secrets of the religious law and religion; they wish for the imprints of these to be manifest in their souls.[16] Thus, they gaze towards the hereafter to unveil what God has set in store there: delight for His near ones, and misery for His enemies. Thus, in their very nature, they become more and more inclined towards the return to God and desire what is with Him. Their intellect craves further reflection on the creations that God has hidden the secrets of His signs in. They leave behind the things and people they are attached to. They wish to carry out the divine command—which is founded on purity, since God only commands things which are good and beneficial. When theirs hearts experience love, they return to gazing towards the wondrous secrets of the astral realms, inspired discourses with the divine, and the celestial truths.

We have spoken long here.

RETURNING TO THE UNIQUE APPLICATIONS OF THE LETTER *D* (*DĀL*)

SO, AFTER THIS excursus, let us return to the letter *d* and how it may be used.

Prosperity. Write the letter *d* (د; pronounced *dāl*) thirty-five times—which is the numerological sum of the letters *d-ā-l*. Write it in the form of a four-by-four square upon a white piece of silk while the Moon is in its house secure from any unfortunate aspects with

16 Insofar as Islam has strict prescriptions for forms of ritual worship, throughout Islamic history, a number of treatises have been written on the inner dimensions of outer acts of worship, to stave off excess ritualism. Thus, these people would be concerned with the inner dimensions of the ritual prayer, rather than merely the external form.

Jupiter, and then write the letter *d* around it thirty-five times. Then place it in the recess of a ring at that time. Wear it while in a full state of ritual purity, while fasting, and with a pure inner self. God shall bless whoever does that with continual prosperity.

Reciting the divine name *dā'im* ("the eternal") copiously garners the same effect. We have already mentioned the bulk of the secrets pertaining to the divine name *dā'im* and the letter *d* in *ḥamd* ("divine praise") in our book The *Banner of Guidance, Secrets, and Wayfinding* (*'Alam al-Huda wa Asrar wa al-Ihtida'*). Therefore, there is no need to repeat it here; if you wish to know more, you may refer to that.

Audience with kings. If you write it and carry it with you, you shall attain whatever you seek from kings. Everyone who sees you will love you.

Love, fortune, and influence. You may also write it on a piece of yellow silk. Do this while the Moon is in Cancer, its domicile; or else in the house of Jupiter, and secure from any unfortunate aspects with Jupiter. Any pleasant-smelling incense may be burned. If you do that and carry it with you, you shall accomplish all of your goals and attain you want from kings, judges, and officials; women will also love you. You will enjoy great fortune, and any woman who sets eyes on you will love you. You shall achieve greatness, status and position which shall never fail. Here is a drawing of it. Know, and be guided:

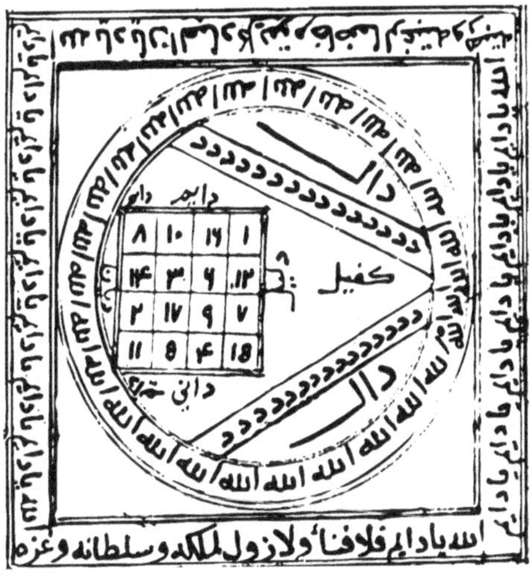

Prosperity, happiness, and pious works. A sage once said that if you write "Muhammad is the messenger of God; Ahmad is the messenger of God"[17] thirty-five times on a slip of paper after the Friday prayers[18] and carry it with you, you shall be gifted with prosperity, strengthened in your obedience towards God, and blessed abundantly. You shall be protected from the temptations of malicious spirits (*shayāṭīn*).[19] If you gaze long at that slip of paper and envision the Prophet's names "Muhammad" and "Ahmad," and consider how these two blessed, glorious names are perfected through this noble letter—that is, the letter *d*—and, in particular, if you gaze at that slip of paper at sunrise while praying for blessings upon the Prophet, God shall make it easy for you to obey Him and bring you great happiness. For sincere intent and inner purity elicit divine acceptance; that is a subtle secret indeed.

Protection. If you write the square with the numbers and carry it, God will protect you from your enemies, human or otherwise.

Fever. If you write it, then wash off the ink with water and give the water to an ill person to drink, that person will be protected from fever.

Snake or scorpion bites. Similarly, if you give that water to someone has been bit by a scorpion or snake, God will ease that person's pain; it can also be used in similar situations.

A sharp memory; chest pains. You may write the square containing letters, wash off the ink with rainwater and honey, and drink it. This dispels forgetfulness and sharpens the understanding and intellect. It also helps someone suffering from chest pains.

Scorpions. Write them upon a piece of copper, then heat the cop-

17 *Muḥammadan rasūl Allah; Aḥmad rasūl Allāh.* "Muhammad is the messenger of God" is the second testament of faith in Islam. "Ahmad" is another name for the Prophet Muhammad.

18 The noontime weekly congregational prayers in Islam. Here, presumably, the person writing is benefitting not only from the spiritual mindset that accompanies worship and prayer, but also the spiritual energy of the mosque and congregation.

19 *Shayāṭīn* are "mini-satans"; that is, malevolent or evil spirts that might cause harm or strive to derail someone. Although the phrase is generally used for spirits, it can be applied to malevolent humans as well.

per in a fire. This protects against the scorpion's sting. This must be written while the Moon is in Scorpio and in an unfortunate astrological aspect with Mars. Then, after the seal has been constructed, dip it in water and drink the water.

4	14	15	1
9	7	6	12
5	11	10	8
16	2	3	13

LETTERS AND NUMBERS

The author will now celebrate some of the special properties of the numbers one through sixteen in light of Islamic cosmology and mediaeval philosophy. The numbers are split between even and odd.

Throughout this book, the numbers in the squares have been converted from traditional Arabic-style digits to the digits used in the English language. Should any readers unfamiliar with Arabic wish to reproduce the squares using Arabic-style digits instead, a chart of Arabic-style digits has been included in the Appendix.

This four-by-four square is comprised of four of the letter *alif*—which is the secret of the intellect, the secret of the soul (*rūḥ*), the secret of the inner self (*nafs*), and the secret of the heart[20]—for the

20 *Rūḥ* and *nafs* can be used for the human soul interchangeably. However, *nafs* also sometimes carries the connotation of the individual self as well as the

letter *alif* has the inherent number of one. When four is multiplied by itself, the result is sixteen, and sixteen is largest of the numbers in it.

For the divine Throne, the divine Seat, the seven heavens, and the seven "earths" all add up to sixteen.[21] Sixteen is also the final sequential number to appear in this four-by-four square, which has sixteen cells.

The even numbers. It includes the number fourteen, which is the sum of the seven heavens and the seven "earths." It also includes twelve, which is the number of signs of the zodiac. It includes eight, and there are eight bearers of the divine throne. It includes six, which is the number of physical directions: up, down, right, left, forward, and backward. It includes four, which is the sum total of the groups celebrated in the Qur'an known as the prophets, the truthful, the martyrs (or witnesses), and the righteous.[22] And it includes two, and there are two testaments of faith: there is no god but God, and Muhammad is the messenger of God.

The odd numbers. Those are seven even numbers. Then, there are the odd numbers. It includes fifteen, which is the sum of the divine seat, the seven heavens, and the seven earths. It includes thirteen, which is the sum of the Divine Pen, the Eternal Tablet, the Form, the Holy Spirit, the divine Seat, the divine Throne, and the seven heavens.[23] It includes the eleven, which is the sum of the five senses—hearing, seeing, smelling, tasting, and touching—plus the six directions (above, below, right, left, forwards, and backwards). It includes nine, which consists of the human being plus his eight constituent substances. That is, it contains the four basic qualities

---

more animalistic or self-centered inclinations.

21 As mentioned previously, the Qur'an speaks of seven "heavens" and seven "earths," although it does not specify what precisely is meant by these terms. Here, the adding consists of 1 throne + 1 seat + 7 heavens + 7 earths = 16.

22 A reference to Qur'an 4:69: "...Those whom God has graced: the prophets (*nabiyyīn*), the truthful (*ṣiddiqīn*), the martyrs (or witnesses, *shuhadā'*), and the righteous (*ṣāliḥīn*)—what an excellent fellowship!"

23 *Al-qalam, al-lawḥ, al-ṣūrah, rūḥ al-qudus, al-kursī*, and the seven heavens. The "Holy Spirits" (*rūḥ al-qudus*) should not be confused with the Holy Spirit in the Trinity.

of heat, dryness, cold, and moisture. It also contains the four humors: yellow bile, which is hot and dry; and air, which is hot and moist and of the nature of blood; phlegm, which is cold and moist; and black bile, which is cold and dry. These latter two sets include eight items.

It includes seven, which is the number of the celestial spheres; that is to say, the spheres of Saturn, Jupiter, Mercury, the Sun, Venus, Mercury, and the Moon. The days of the week also number seven, as do the seven heavens, and the seven "earths"; all of these are sevenfold. It includes five, which is the number of the five daily prayers.[24] It includes three, which is the number of realms: the realm of the worldly life, the intermediate realm (*barzakh*), and the realm of eternal life (heaven and hell).[25] And it includes one, which represents the intellect; the intellect is alone.[26]

All of these combine in the number sixteen. There are eight odd numbers and eight even numbers. The even and odd numbers all include each other. For instance, when you add one plus one, you arrive at two; when you add three plus three, you arrive at six. Thus the sequence continues, generating even numbers. The digits used here are the Indian numerals, for they are better and truer; it is more appropriate that they contain wondrous secrets vis-à-vis the letters.[27]

Worldly and otherworldly blessings. You can also inscribe this, with letters in place of the numbers. Do this after fasting for two weeks,

24 The five daily prayers which Muslims are exhorted to perform at dawn, noon, afternoon, sunset, and evening.

25 In Islamic eschatology, it is held that, after a person dies, their soul goes to an intermediate place called the *barzakh*. Then, after all the world has ended, they will pass away again in the *barzakh*, then be resurrected and proceed to judgment for their deeds and an eternal life in heaven and hell.

26 *ʿAql*.

27 What are spoken of as the "Arabic numerals" in English are called "Indian numerals" in Arabic. This is because they are believed to have originated in India, then to have been adopted in the Arab world, and from there transferred to Europe, whereupon swarms of grateful mathematicians adopted them in lieu of the bulkier Roman numerals. That being said, the forms of the numerals used alongside the Arabic script differ slightly from the numerals used alongside English script. A table of Arabic-style numbers has been included in the appendix.

not eating anything except some dry bread at night, while carrying out ascetic practices, remaining in a state of ritual purity, and continually remembering God. Then, after praying two units of prayer, in which you recite the first chapter of the Qur'an and the Throne Verse one hundred times, and the Qur'anic chapter on sincerity one hundred times, inscribe these letters on a pure, blank piece of tin, while you are facing Mecca.[28] This should be done at sunrise on a Thursday, the day of Jupiter, at a time when the Moon secure from being in an unfortunate astrological aspect with Jupiter or the Sun, and when Gemini is rising. Every Thursday, incense it with mastic and white sandalwood. Then keep it on your person. God shall ease for you both worldly and spiritual matters. It facilitates righteous deeds and acts of obedience to God. It makes a person prosperous; God blesses whoever has it.

Better sales. Write it and hang it in your shop or put it your cashbox or storage-box; your wealth will multiply. There is more to say about earning one's daily bread, increasing prosperity, and attracting divine blessings; these things shall be discussed later, God willing.

Protection from thieves and accidents. Write it on a Thursday at sunrise on a piece of parchment made from gazelle skin, then sew it into your clothes. God willing, you will be protected from thieves, mishaps, and whatever you fear[29]—of course, after you write the appropriate things. But beware of carrying it with you while ritually impure.

This is my first discussion on the numbers. I shall speak more about the numerical secrets which God has disclosed, and how to use the numbers for benefic and malefic purposes. I shall also speak of the secrets of the letters in the Qur'an—that is, the curious, disjointed letters at the beginning of various chapters of the Qur'an; twenty-eight chapters of the Qur'an begin with them, but only the elite of this creation know what they mean.[30] I shall also speak of

28 Surah al-Fatihah (Qur'an 1), *āyat al-kursī* (Qur'an 2:255), and Surah al-Ikhlas (Qur'an 112).

29 Talismanic shirts, armor, and battle-wear were quite common in the premodern era, especially in Ottoman Empire.

30 Some of the chapters of the Qur'an begin with disconnected letters of uncer-

the names and attributes of God, which are a treasure-house of mysteries, and the secrets of the greatest name of God, not found in any book. Anyone who reads this shall benefit from it and understand what is meant, God willing.

Here is the diagram:

د	يد	يه	ا
ط	ز	و	يب
ه	يا	ي	ح
يو	ب	ج	بج

An invocation accompanies it, composed from its letters; namely: *a* (ا), *b* (ب), *j* (ج), *d* (د), *h* (ه), *w* (و), *z* (ز), *ḥ* (ح), *t* (ت), and y (ي). The letter *y* is added to them—and it is the tenth letter, with the numerological value of ten—to construct this invocation:

> O God! I beseech You by all of Your beautiful names, those which I know and those which I do not know. O He! O One! O Single! O Guide! O Good! O Creator! O Seeing! O Inventor! O Expander! O Eternal! O Glorious! O Everlasting! O Inheritor! O Loving! O Living! O Forbearing! O Truth! O Wise! O Pure! O Purifier! Reply to my call, and do what I need! Answer, O Isrāfīl[31]—you and your celestial and sublunary helpers and servants, may God bless you![32]

tain meaning, such as *a—l—m*. While there are many guesses, mystical and practical, about the meanings intended by the letters, Muslim scholars generally agree that the true meaning of the disconnected letters is a mystery. In fact, twenty-nine chapters of the Qur'an begin with them, but the manuscript says twenty-eight.

31 Isrāfīl is of the four archangels in the Islamic tradition, said to be tasked with blowing the trumpet heralding the end of the world.

32 These names of God each involve the associated letters of the alphabet, in order. In Arabic, it reads: *Allahummā innī as'aluka bi-asmā'ika al-ḥusnā kullihā*

It has already been mentioned that just as there are twenty-eight letters of the alphabet, there are twenty-eight lunar mansions, fourteen of which appear above the horizon while fourteen have set beneath the horizon. When one mansion sets, its sister-mansion fifteen slots forward has risen; thus it continues, perpetually. Similarly, fifteen of the Arabic letters have dots, and the remaining fourteen do not have dots. The letters with dots are: *b* (ب), *t* (ت), *th* (ث), *j* (ج), *kh* (خ), *dh* (ذ), *z* (ز), *sh* (ش), *ḍ* (ض), *ẓ* (ظ), *gh* (غ), *f* (ف), *q* (ق), *n* (ن), *y* (ي). Similarly, the letters without dots are: *alif* (ا), *ḥ* (ح), *d* (د), *r* (ر), *s* (س), *ṣ* (ص), *ṭ* (ط), *ʿayn* (ع), *k* (ك), *l* (ل), *m* (م), *h* (ه), and *w* (و).

Know—may God grant you and me success!—that the undotted letters correspond to the auspicious mansions, and the dotted letters correspond to the inauspicious mansions or the mansions of mixed fortune. The letters with a single dot correspond to the mansions which are not too unfortunate and which are closer to the fortunate mansions. The letters with two dots correspond to the mansions that are moderately unfortunate, and the letters with three dots correspond to the mansions that are deeply unfortunate. For instance, the mansions corresponding to the letters *th* (ث) and *sh* (ش), each of which have three dots, are direly inauspicious. Ponder on that.

God created the constellations of the lunar mansions in different forms; not a single one is identical with another. God created the Moon to be cyclical, and also the Sun. There is a hidden secret in this which cannot be explained, for revealing the divine secrets hither and thither is itself an act of faithlessness. There are many things to be said, however, about what happens when the first lunar mansion rises; but alas, the walls have ears. Thus, in the next chapter, we shall speak of some of this. But do keep this secret! Understand my implications; reflect, and you shall be guided.

---

mā ʿalimtu minhā wa mā lam aʿlam. Yā hū, yā wāḥid, yā aḥad, yā hādī, hā barr, yā bāriʾ, yā baṣīr, yā badīʿ, yā bāsiṭ, yā bāqī, yā jalīl, yā dāʾim, yā wārith, yā wadūd, yā ḥayy, yā ḥalīm, yā ḥaqq, yā ḥakīm, yā ṭāhir, yā muṭahhir—ajib daʿwatī wa aqḍi ḥājātī, yā rabb al-ʿālamīn. In some sources, *ẓāhir* and *muẓhir* ("O Manifest" and "O Manifestor") is written n place of "O Pure" and "O Purifier."

Chapter 2
ASTROLOGICAL TIMINGS

KNOW—MAY GOD MAKE you and me obedient towards Him and help us understand the secrets of His names—that God mentioned the Sun and Moon in His book, when he said: "Each gliding in its orbit" (Qur'an 21:33).[1]

When the Moon enters the first lunar mansion, called "the Butting" (*al-naṭḥ*),[2] it links to the letter *alif* and shares in the secrets of the letter *alif*. Therefore, when the Moon enters this mansion, the spirit of the letter *alif* descends from that mansion and manifests anger throughout the world, mostly among the rich and famous. People find themselves constricted, powerful, and enraged, to the degree that these faculties have been developed inside themselves; a person who generally lacks those things will find them.

Therefore, at that time, it is best not to do anything. Instead, busy your limbs with worship, copious prayers, and ascetic practices. Remember God, and remain in a state of ritual purity. This should be done while the Moon is in that mansion, and a bit beforehand. For, during this time, a person feels a strange disquiet in the self without knowing why, and turns inward. This is because the letter *alif* is the first of the letters and numbers;[3] there is nothing like it. Therefore, uneasiness befalls the sublunary realms. Understand that!

Vexing tyrants. If you want, when the Moon is in this mansion,

1 The full verse reads: He is the One Who created the night and the day, the Sun and the Moon, each gliding in its orbit.

2 The first lunar mansion is also known as *al-sharaṭayn*; both names are used in the book.

3 Arabic letters also have numerical values and can be used for numbering, with *alif* corresponding to 1. The Arabic number 1 also looks like an *alif*.

you can vex the ruling classes—especially people who are tyrannical or pompous—with unease. Truly, it is most befitting to torment and entrap them with the letter *alif* since the letter *alif* is hot and dry. It is the phase of Aḥmar, the Red; and red is hot and dry, sharing the nature as a blazing fire.[4] So if you invoke it with hot, dry names of a similar nature when the Moon is rising from the eastern horizon in the first mansion, the Butting (*al-naṭḥ*), it will turn out as I have said.

AN IMPRECATION FOR VENGEANCE

WRITE THE LETTER *alif* (ا) 111 times on a piece of red copper, iron, or a shard of red pottery along with the name of the person you want to vex and dispirit, and bury it in your home after incensing it with appropriate incense which has a heat similar to that of the letter, and invoke the names 111 times—which is the numerical sum of the word *alif*.[5]

To do that, separate the letters of the name of the person you wish to vex. See which letters correspond to which element, and see which element is preponderant—heat, dryness, cold, or moisture. Then, take the hot and dry letters from the name, inscribe them on a tablet, and hold it. Add the letters of Mars (*marīkh*), the first mansion (*al-naṭḥ*), and the Moon (*al-qamar*), and, from them, make names of God.[6] Invoke these names the aforementioned number of times while concentrating on overpowering and suppressing that person. It shall be so.

Here is an example using the name ʿAmr (عمرو). Write the letters as such, unconnected and separated:[7]

4 Al-Aḥmar, "the Red," alludes to the jinn king al-Aḥmar, who rules Tuesday as well as the planet Mars. Both the planet and the jinn king would be considered hot and dry.

5 *Alif* (1)+*l* (30)+*f* (80)=111.

6 The divine attributes, such as those known as the "99 names of Allah," e.g. *al-nūr*, *al-hādī*.

7 The author has written the letters from the name ʿAmr followed by the letters of the word "Mars" (*marīkh*), the first mansion (*naṭḥ*), and the word "Moon"

ر م ق ح ط ن خ ي ر م و ر م ع

r m r ḥ ṭ n kh y r m w r m ʿ

There are 14 letters here, which are of the nature of fire, air, earth, and water; namely:

Cold: *w*, *y*, and *n* (ن ي و)
Moist: only *q* (ق)
Hot: *m*, *m*, *m*, and *ṭ* (ط م م م)
Dry: *ḥ*, *ʿayn*, *r*, *r*, *r*, and *kh* (خ ر ر ر ع ح)

There are three hot letters and one moist letter. So, the original fourteen letters are divided as such. Most of these letters are hot, and heat is dry. Therefore, we deduce from this the names of God for this conjuration and say:

> O Samsamāʾīl![8] I adjure you, by the one who created you, fashioned you, and made you a light in the heavens, be my necessary equipment (*ʿuddah*),[9] for I have proclaimed authority over you.
>
> Aid me in taking vengeance against X. Strip him of his senses! Infuse his hot-headed nature with the heat of Mars! Light fires in him through repressing his limbs! Clench his belly and heart! Destroy his intellect; set upon him the angels of punishment and the fire of Mars. Beset him with fever, headaches, and multitudinous pains! By the right of Mars, and its calamities and fire—by the right of your lofty station—by the way you mete out vengeful dry heat towards nefarious oppressors and criminals—inflict the body of this transgressing, haughty, vile tyrant with the

---

(*qamar*), as specified in the text. The author mentions but does not actually use the name Zayd, although "Zayd" is a typical name used to refer to a sample person, similar to "John Doe"; therefore, it was omitted here. The letters are separated insofar as, in Arabic, most letters are generally connected to each other when written and not written out separately.

8 The angel in the Islamic tradition who rules over Mars.

9 *ʿUddah:* necessary preparations or equipment, such as a sail, a harness, or whatever one needs to do something.

spirits of disease! Make his stomach gnaw with might, anger, and vengeance!

For I have adjured you by the Strong (*al-qawī*), the Encompassing (*al-muḥīṭ*), the Apparent (*al-ẓāhir*), the Living (*al-ḥayy*), the Eternal (*al-qayyūm*), the Light (*al-nūr*), the Bestower of Security (*al-mu'min*), the Expediter (*al-muqaddim*), the Delayer (*al-mu'akhkhir*), the Emanator of Lights and Bestower of Secrets. I have adjured you by the right of the fire, sparks, and the Red Planet. And I have adjured you by the right of God, the One, the Overpowering.

Answer obediently, hastening to obey the names of the Lord of the Worlds.

With it, draw out a five-by-five square.

THE TWENTY-EIGHT LUNAR MANSIONS: AN OVERVIEW

This is the first and shortest of several sections on the lunar mansions, or *manāzil*. *Manāzil*, which is the plural of *manzil*, means "house" as well as a waystation that one might stop at on a journey, or a place where one makes camp. Since the Arab Bedouins were nomadic, their homes would have been at the places that they stopped before moving along. Thus, like a nomad, the Moon moves across the night sky, abiding in each waystation for a day or so before moving along.

The section after this addresses the types of works to be done during the mansions in more detail, followed by discussions of the constellations in the mansions. Since some of the lunar mansions were known by multiple names, al-Buni uses different names for the same mansion; this has been noted in the text or footnotes.

The astute reader will notice that the letters associated with the mansions do not follow today's Arabic alphabetical order. This is because they are associated with a pre-modern ordering of the letters from which the numerical values of the letters are derived. (For a table, see the Appendix.) Just as there are twenty-eight lunar mansions, there are twenty-eight letters of the Arabic alphabet, so it is a perfect fit.

THE FIRST MANSION (0° Aries–12° 51' Aries): It is called the Two Signs (*al-sharaṭayn*).[10] It rules the letter *alif*, which has a great magical square (*wifq*) pertaining to the element of air. Its planet is Mars, and its servant is al-Ahmar. It is a powerful, effective letter and is the limit of the units. If you use it as in the example above, you will experience obedience.

Know, my brother, that this noble letter is more powerful than all the other letters, since it is like the father of the letters. Understand that!

Using the letter alif (ا) *for love.* One of its uses is for love. In an auspicious hour (*sāʿah saʿīdah*),[11] write the name in the way we have explained. Your working will be better and stronger if you mix the name of the person you seek with the letters of the square (*wifq*). Then say this invocation:

> I adjure you, O Samsamāʾīl! I adjure you, your servants, your celestial and sublunary helpers, and the servants of the letter *alif* altogether. Hear and obey! Inflame the passions of X! Infuse X with love towards Y!

10 Also known as "the Butting" (*al-naṭḥ*); al-Būnī uses both names. The translations of the names of lunar mansions used in the work have been adapted in part from Danielle Adams, *Rain Stars Set, Lunar Stations Rise: Multivalent Textures of Pre-Islamic Arabian Astronomy and the Hegemonic Discourse of Order* [PhD thesis] (University of Arizona, 2018).

11 See the following section on fortunate and unfortunate hours.

> By the right of this adjuration—by the right of the letter *alif*—by the divine secrets which only the sages know—and by the right of the letters of the alphabet and their virtues—reply obediently, for I have called you! Do what I have tasked you do to.

This is a diagram of it. Know and be guided!

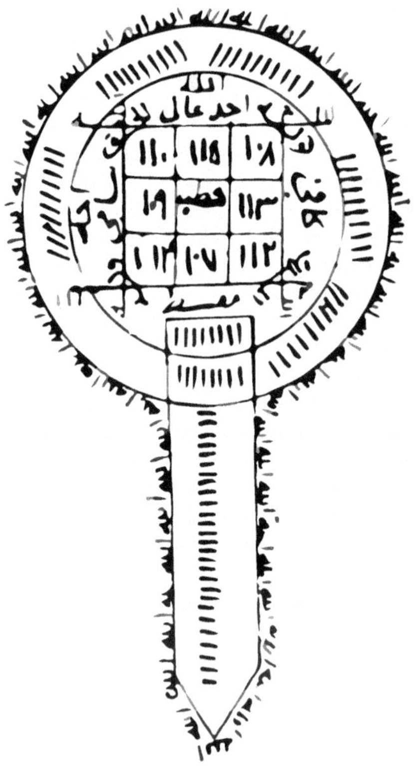

A general invocation with alif (ا). This is an invocation using the letter *alif* which can be recited the aforementioned number of times:

> Glory be to You! There is no god but You, O Lord and inheritor of all things. O God of Gods, of elevated glory. O living, O eternal, O originator of the heavens and the earth!

Pursue whatever workings you wish with this that are appropriate to this; by God, your efforts shall succeed and be blessed.

Destructive workings. If you wish to carry out a destructive work—such as perplexing, upsetting, or destroying someone—do as we said before, then do what you will; you shall accomplish your aim. God speaks the truth and guides to the right path.

THE SECOND MANSION (12° 51' Aries–25° 43' Aries): The second mansion is called the Belly (*al-baṭīn*). It rules the letter *b* (ب). By the command of God, when the Moon alights in this mansion, a spiritual power emanates from it that spurs on works of anger and things like what we just spoke of. In it, take medicine and mingle with nobles, worldly scions, and kings, for it begins in the second face of Aries which is the face of the Sun.[12] Its degree of exaltation (*sharaf*) is at nineteen degrees on the fourth of April.[13] The Sun is fortunate (*saʿīdah*) in it, and it is hot and dry, so it is fortunate and exalted (*sharaf* and *saʿīdah*) in this face.

While the Moon is in this mansion, do workings to take audience with kings and to urge them to grant your requests. During this time, needs are fulfilled. Also do works aimed at instilling love and acceptance, and endearing yourself to people's hearts. You may also pursue divine wisdom and prepare golden elixirs.

THE THIRD MANSION (25° 43' Aries–8° 34' Taurus): The third mansion is called the Mansion of the Pleiades (*al-thurayā*). It rules the letter *j* (ج). When the Moon alights in this mansion, a spirit combining heat, moisture, and cold emanates from it. It is moderately fortunate. Travel, mix with nobles, and socialize with the famous, worldly lords, and belletrists. The Pleiades consists of many stars; therefore, these meetings shall be fruitful.

This mansion has a great magic square (*wifq*). Draw it when it is in its dignity, and carry it on your person. Abu Jaʿfar al-Barmaki[14] had one. Because of it, the caliph Harun al-Rashid took him into his court and gave him whatever he wanted. If you carry it and stand

12 Each zodiacal sign is divided into three "faces" or decans (*wajh*).

13 This date is presuming that the Roman months are aligned with the beginning of spring, and hence the zodiacal signs, which is no longer the case.

14 Abu Jaʿfar al-Barmaki (767–803), a Persian vizier of the ʿAbbasid caliph Harun al-Rashid. The Barmaki family had a long-standing association with the caliphate.

before kings and notables, you will also get whatever you want from them; none shall oppose your will. This is what it looks like. Understand—may God guide you—and know!

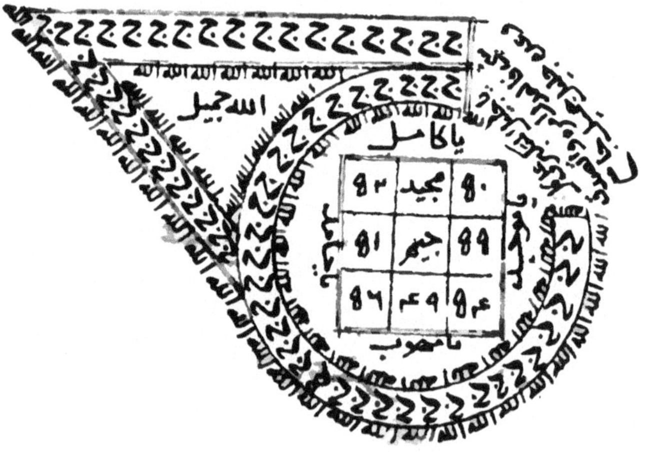

THE FOURTH MANSION (8° 34′ Taurus–21° 26′ Taurus): The fourth mansion is called the Follower (*al-dabarān*, also referring to Aldebaran). It rules the letter *d* (د). When the Moon alights in this mansion, a wicked, malicious spirit emanates from it. Do suitably appropriate harmful and destructive works.

THE FIFTH MANSION (21° 26′ Taurus–4° 17′ Gemini): The fifth mansion is called the Hair Whorl (*al-haqʿah*). It rules the letter *h* (ه). When the Moon alights in this mansion, a moderately hot, indeterminate spirit emanates from it. Do good works, and also not-so-good works.

THE SIXTH MANSION (4° 17′ Gemini–17° 9′ Gemini): The sixth mansion is called the Leaning Stars (*al-hanʿah*). It rules the letter *w* (و) and is a fortunate mansion. Work to instill friendship and affection, and to reconcile enemies, for a virtuous spirit emanates from it. Diagnose diseases so they may be treated. Do works which are for the sake of kindly and godly aims, for health and restoration, and for success.

THE SEVENTH MANSION (17° 9′ Gemini–0° Cancer): The seventh mansion is called the Forearm (*al-dhirāʿ*). It rules the letter *z*

(ز). When the Moon alights in it, a virtuous spirit emanates from it which aids in diagnosing diseases for the sake of curing them. Possibly, if you persevere in ascetic practices during this time, you will experience a vision of the celestial realms. It is good for spiritual retreats and seeking the truth, and it is suitable for all works.[15]

THE EIGHTH MANSION (0° Cancer–12° 51' Cancer): The eighth mansion is called the Nose-tip (*al-nathrah*). It rules the letter *ḥ* (ح). When the Moon alights in it, a spirit which is not overly good emanates from it. Perform acts of destruction.

THE NINTH MANSION (12° 51' Cancer–25° 43' Cancer): The ninth mansion is called the Twinkling Eyes (*al-ṭarfah*). It rules the letter *ṭ* (ط). When the Moon alights in it, a wicked, malicious spirit emanates from it, as before.

THE TENTH MANSION (25° 43' Cancer–8° 34' Leo): The tenth mansion is called the Forehead (*al-jabhah*). It rules the letter *y* (ي). When the Moon alights in it, a spirit which is both good and evil descends from it. Act accordingly in the works that you do.

THE ELEVENTH MANSION (8° 34' Leo–21° 26' Leo): The eleventh mansion is called the Mane (*al-zubrah*). It rules the letter *k* (ك). When the Moon alights in it, a goodly spirit descends from it which makes it easier to increase wealth and prosperity, and to acquire what you need. Act accordingly in the works that you do.

THE TWELFTH MANSION (21° 26' Leo–4° 17' Virgo): The twelfth mansion is called the Weather-Change (*al-ṣarfah*). It rules the letter *l*. When the Moon alights in it, a spirit which is both good and evil emanates from it. Act accordingly in the works that you do.

THE THIRTEENTH MANSION (4° 17' Virgo–17° 9' Virgo): The thirteenth mansion is called the Howling Dogs (*al-ʿawwāʾ*). It rules the letter *m* (م). When the Moon alights in it, a mixed spirit descends from it. Do nothing apart from setting off to sea—nothing else.

THE FOURTEENTH MANSION (17° 9' Virgo–0° Libra): The fourteenth mansion is called the Sky-Raiser (*al-simmāk*). It rules the let-

15 Ascetic practices—*dhikr*, often used for the repeated recitation of the names of God. Celestial realms—*malakūt*, discussed in the notes to previous chapter. Spiritual retreats—*iʿtikāfāt*, often used for spiritual retreat in the mosque, as opposed to full isolation, which is often prescribed for spiritual workings.

ter *n* (ن). When the Moon alights in it, a spirit which is not bent on good descends from it. Do not do anything at all.

THE FIFTEENTH MANSION (0° Libra–12° 51′ Libra): The fifteenth mansion is called the Shrouded (*al-ghafr*). It rules the letter *s* (س). When the Moon alights in it, a virtuous spirit descends. It is good for all material and spiritual endeavors. Do whatever will; your works shall succeed.

THE SIXTEENTH MANSION (12° 51′ Libra–25° 43′ Libra): The sixteenth mansion is called the Claw (*al-zubānā*). It rules the letter *ʿayn* (ع). When the Moon alights in it, an indeterminate spirit descends from it. Only strive for good.

THE SEVENTEENTH MANSION (25° 43′ Libra–8° 34′ Scorpio): The seventeenth mansion is called the Crown (*al-iklīl*). It rules the letter *f*. When the Moon alights in it, a spirit descends from it that is not associated with good works. Carry out works pertaining to wholesome worldly matters, and you shall succeed.

THE EIGHTEENTH MANSION (8° 34′ Scorpio–21° 26′ Scorpio): The eighteenth mansion is called the Heart (*al-qalb*). It rules the letter *ṣ* (ص). When the Moon alights in it, a spirit descends from it that is associated with good works. Do good works.

THE NINETEENTH MANSION (21° 26′ Scorpio–4° 17′ Sagittarius): The nineteenth mansion is called the Stinging Tail (*al-shawlah*). It rules the letter *q* (ق). When the Moon alights in it, an indeterminate spirit descends from it. Do not engage in any worldly matters in it.

THE TWENTIETH MANSION (4° 17′ Sagittarius–17° 9′ Sagittarius): The twentieth mansion is called the Ostriches (*al-naʿāʾim*). It rules the letter *r* (ر). When the Moon alights in it, a mixed, pure spirit descends from it that purifies hearts and gladdens souls. It is excellent for all worldly and otherworldly endeavors.

THE TWENTY-FIRST MANSION (17° 9′ Sagittarius–0° Capricorn): The twenty-first mansion is called the Wasteland (*al-baldah*). It rules the letter *sh* (ش). When the Moon alights in this mansion, an indeterminate spirit descends from it. Avoid most pursuits.

THE TWENTY-SECOND MANSION (0° Capricorn–12° 51′ Capricorn): The twenty-second mansion is called the Slaughterer's Joy (*saʿd al-dhābiḥ*). It rules the letter *t* (ت). When the Moon enters this mansion, a mixed spirit descends from it. It is not suitable for any pursuits, benevolent or malevolent.

THE TWENTY-THIRD MANSION (12° 51' Capricorn–25° 43' Capricorn): The twenty-third mansion is called the Voracious Auspice (*saʿd bulʿ*). It rules the letter *th* (ث). When the Moon alights in it, a spirit of an indeterminate nature descends from it. It is suitable for nothing. There is no point in trying to do anything in it, benevolent or malevolent.

THE TWENTY-FOURTH MANSION (25° 43' Capricorn–8° 34' Aquarius): The twenty-fourth mansion is called the Most Fortunate (*saʿd al-suʿūd*). It rules the letter *kh*. When the Moon alights in it, a fortunate, virtuous spirit descends from it and assists endeavors and benevolent deeds; it is of a balanced nature. Do in it whatever good deeds you wish.

THE TWENTY-FIFTH MANSION (8° 34' Aquarius–21° 26' Aquarius): The twenty-fifth mansion is called the Auspice of Tent-Poles (*saʿd al-akhbiyyah*). It rules the letter *dh*. When the Moon alights in it, a fortunate spirit descends from it. It is associated with all praiseworthy deeds. Work in it for love, friendship, and affection.

THE TWENTY-SIXTH MANSION (21° 26' Aquarius–4° 17' Pisces): The twenty-sixth mansion is called the First Spout (*al-fargh al-muqaddam*). It rules the letter *ḍ* (ض). When the Moon is in it, an auspicious spirit descends from it. It is associated with all good works. Do in it whatever you wish.

THE TWENTY-SEVENTH MANSION (4° 17' Pisces–17° 9' Pisces): The twenty-seventh mansion is called the Second Spout (*al-fargh al-muʾakhkhar*). It rules the letter *ẓ* (ظ). When the Moon alights in it, an indeterminate spirit descends from it. Ways and efforts are blocked in it.

THE TWENTY-EIGHTH MANSION (17° 9' Pisces–0° Aries): The twenty-eighth mansion is called the Rope (*al-rishā*).[16] It rules the letter *gh* (غ). When the Moon alights in it, a good, praised, pleasant spirit descends from it. It is especially suitable for pursuing knowl-

16 Also known as the Belly of the Fish (*baṭn al-ḥūt*).

edge. Prayers are certainly answered, and righteous deeds shall bear fruit.

ESOTERIC REFLECTIONS

REFLECT, MY BROTHER, on the benefits that God has placed in the letters. Through them, the divine utterance[17] has been put to paper; and, through them, the names of God are turned towards various uses. Through them, the divine speech may be understood. This inner meaning is a spirit descending from the mansions.

Similarly, the Qur'an has verses promising divine mercy and divine torment. The verses about mercy are angels bringing good fortune to the happy, and the verses about punishment are angels bringing misfortune to the condemned; the same can be said for the verses portending heaven and hell. This is what is meant by an "indeterminate" or "mixed" spirit—its being "mixed" pertains to the human being, and what the human being deserves, not the angels. The angels have no shortcoming; they are absolutely good. Human beings can embody both pure good and pure evil without any inherent contradiction, as expressed by the phrases *al-qāʾim* ("the upstanding") and *al-kāfir* ("the one who hides the truth"). "Mixed good" can also describe a faithful person who sins, as God says: "Others confess to their sins. They have intermingled good deeds and evil deeds. Perhaps God will incline towards them" (Qur'an 9:102).

This is the axis which the secrets of the letters wheel around. They continually orbit around it, revealing their compound natures, until the day they appear. The same for each mansion, spirit, and letter gathered in the whole point in forty days.[18] The same is true for the remaining mansions. Therefore, the final letters are spiritual letters which combine felicities and misfortunes; were it not for this letter-wise distinction and celestial cycle, the human being would

17 The Qur'an, or divinely revealed scriptures in general.

18 The meaning behind "forty days" here is elusive, but perhaps some readers will grasp what he intends through deep contemplation.

never have been able to distinguish the causes of fortune from the causes of misfortune, or the way this is intermixed or left out—and all of that has been poured into the nature of man.

THE LETTERS AND THE ELEMENTS

SINCE THESE MANSIONS have been spread across the twelve zodiacal signs to display the divine wisdom, twelve letters are grouped into six syllables. These are the letters in *lā ilāha illā Allāh* (there is no god but Allah):

ل ا إ ل ه إ ل ا ا ل ل ه

These letters number twelve, like the zodiacal signs, and are divided among them. Just as the zodiacal signs are fixed and mutable (*thābit* and *munqalib*), similarly, these letters are fixed and mutable.[19] The positive ones (*ithbāt*) are fixed, and the negative ones (*nafī*) are mutable—they go from existence to the non-existence which they originated from. The mysteries of these whirling letters are associated with the celestial sphere of the Moon, for the Moon is closer than anything else to the Earth, although the letters are closer to us than the Moon, for they are instilled in each and every one of us as part of our human nature. Since the letters associated with the mansions have already been mentioned, there is no need to repeat this. And everything increases while the Moon is waxing and decreases when the Moon is waning. Thus is the divine wisdom and decree. Do you not see how darkness and its opposite wax and wane?

God placed in the seven twinkling, orbiting planetary bodies—which have already been discussed—the secret of guidance. The Qur'an speaks of God "making the angels as messengers" (35:1) and "placing a representative (*khalīfah*) on earth" (2:30). The power of these seven bodies derives from the inner mysteries of the syllables of *lā ilāha illā Allāh*, which extend from the sacred celestial realms.

19 Astrological terms reflecting the nature of the signs.

Now, I would like to discuss the elemental qualities of the letters. These are the letters which are hot, moist, cold, and dry:

Hot letters: *alif*, *ṭ*, *m*, *t*, *sh*, and *dh* (ذ ش ف م ط ه ا)
Moist letters: *b*, *w*, *y*, *n*, *s*, *t*, and *ḍ* (ض ت س ن ي و ب)
Cold letters: *j*, *z*, *k*, *s*, *f*, *th*, and *ẓ* (ظ ث ف س ك ز ج)
Dry letters: *d*, *ḥ*, *l*, *ʿayn*, *r*, *kh*, and *gh* (غ خ ر ع ل ح د)

This is because fire combines heat and dryness; air combines moisture and heat; water combines moisture and cold; and earth combines dryness and cold. They also produce the four humors: yellow bile, blood, phlegm, and black bile.[20] Yellow bile has the nature of dry fire; blood has the nature of air, with moist heat; black bile has the nature of earth, being cold and dry; and phlegm has the nature of water, cool and moist. The eye can see the effects of this. For instance, some of the names suppress fever when written. These are the cool, dry names, like *ʿadl* (the Just) and *shadīd* (the Powerful); they are placed in a square with seven columns and seven rows. Some of the names ward off the cold, and these are the ones related to yellow bile, which burns; they have a square which you can see below. Understand and be guided!

ش	خ	ر	ع	ل	ح	د
ر	ع	ل	ح	د	ش	خ
ل	ح	د	ش	خ	ر	ع
د	ش	خ	ر	ع	ل	ح
خ	ر	ع	ل	ح	د	ش
ع	ل	ح	د	ش	خ	ر
ح	د	ش	خ	ر	ع	ل

20 *Ṣafrāʾ*, *dam*, *balgham*, and *sawdāʾ*, respectively.

PRESCRIBED ACTS FOR EACH DAY'S PLANETARY HOURS

Sunday

The first hour[21] is ruled by the Sun. Do acts pertaining to love, acceptance, and visiting kings and judges. It is suitable for wearing new clothing.

The second hour is ruled by Venus. It is a terrible hour. Do nothing at all.

The third hour is ruled by Mercury. Travel, and write things aimed at gaining affection, love, acceptance, and similar things.

The fourth hour is ruled by the Moon. Do not buy or sell anything then; it is good for nothing.

The fifth hour is ruled by Saturn. Do works pertaining to separation, hatred, enmity, and the like.

The sixth hour is ruled by Jupiter. Petition kings for what you need.

The seventh hour is ruled by Mars. Do nothing.

The eighth hour is ruled by the Sun. Strive to fulfill all your needs; it is good for all maters and is extremely fortunate.

The ninth hour is ruled by Venus. Inscribe talismans and the like for journeying, inspiring people's affections towards you, and instilling affection between people's hearts.

The tenth hour is ruled by Mercury. Do whatever you will, for this hour is praiseworthy.

The eleventh hour is ruled by the Moon. Make talismans, seals (*khawātim*), and similar things in it, for it is a good hour.

The twelfth hour is ruled by Saturn. Do nothing, for this hour is unfortunate. It is good for nothing except inflicting harm.

21 "Hour" here refers to the planetary hour, or the length of time attained by dividing the length of the day (the time between sunrise and sunset) into 12 portions. It is longer in the summer, shorter in the winter, and 1 hour at the equinox when the daytime is 12 hours long.

Monday

The first hour is ruled by the Moon. It is good for love, binding people's tongues, and attracting people's hearts towards you.

The second hour is ruled by Saturn. Travel and pursue your needs.

The third hour is ruled by Jupiter. Marry, write books, and go to trials at court.

The fourth hour is ruled by Mars. It is suitable for malicious works such as provoking bloodshed, inflicting headaches and nosebleeds, and causing illness and destruction.

The fifth hour is ruled by the Sun. Pursue your needs, attract hearts and kindle love and the passions.

The sixth hour is ruled by Venus. Pursue your needs, bind tongues, and attract hearts.

The seventh hour is ruled by Mercury. Make talismans and other things.

The eighth hour is ruled by the Moon. Marry and reconcile two angry foes.

The ninth hour is ruled by Saturn. Do works pertaining to separation, relocation, hatred, and the like.

The tenth hour is ruled by Jupiter. Do works pertaining to acceptance, love, and binding tongues.

The eleventh hour is ruled by Mars. Inscribe talismans and the like to spark enmity, hatred, and bloodshed.

The twelfth hour is ruled by the Sun. It is suitable for binding tongues and for instilling affection.

Tuesday

The first hour is ruled by Mars. Do works aimed at causing hatred, corruption, bleeding, hatred, and disease.

The second hour is ruled by the Sun. Do not do anything in it, ever.

The third hour is ruled by Venus. Propose to women and marry.

The fourth hour is ruled by Mercury. Inscribe talismans and the like to attract customers and to promote buying, selling, and trade.

The fifth hour is ruled by the Moon. Do not do anything in it, for it is deeply inauspicious.

The sixth hour is ruled by Saturn. It is suitable for binding and causing things like illnesses and eye diseases.[22]

The seventh hour is ruled by Jupiter. Do whatever you wish along the lines of inspiring affection and love.

The eighth hour is ruled by Mars. Do whatever you wish along the lines of provoking bloodshed, disease, and such.

The ninth hour is ruled by the Sun. Solemnize marriage contracts with women, and do works to kindle love and the passions.[23]

The tenth hour is ruled by Venus. Do not do anything in it, for it is an unfortuitous hour.

The eleventh hour is ruled by Mercury. It is suitable for impeding journeys and keeping someone from marrying.

The twelfth hour is ruled by the Moon. It is suitable for workings sparking hatred, corruption, relocation, evil, divorce, divorce, and the like.

Wednesday

The first hour is ruled by Mercury. Do workings for acceptance and love.

The second hour is ruled by the Moon. Do not do anything in it, for it is inauspicious.

The third hour is ruled by Saturn. It is suitable for workings aimed at causing things like illness, bleeding, and dehydration.

22 "Binding" (*ʿaqd*) can be used to refer to any act to prevent someone from doing something, such as "binding the tongue" to prevent a person from speaking, or binding a man to cause impotence. While binding may be conducted in various ways, Chapter 113 of the Qur'an refers to the folk magic common in the time of the Prophet Muhammad whereby people would tie knots in ropes and blow on them to work malefica; therefore, this chapter is sometimes recited for protection from evil.

23 In the Islamic tradition, the formal agreement of marriage—that is to say, the religious marriage—is sometimes performed before the actual wedding as a sort of legalized engagement period. Here, "marriage contracts" refers to the marriage contract rather than the actual wedding.

The fourth hour is ruled by Jupiter. Do any good deeds you wish, for it is an excellent hour.

The fifth hour is ruled by Mars. Beware of quarrelling with people during this hour. Do malefic works, since it is an evil hour.

The sixth hour is ruled by the Sun. It is suitable for travelling over land and sea. Do any good works that you wish.

The seventh hour is ruled by Venus. Do in it whatever you wish, for it is a highly efficacious hour.

The eighth hour is ruled by Mercury. It is suitable for curing colic and writing wards against things like the evil eye.

The ninth hour is ruled by the Moon. Do not do anything during this hour; it is vile.

The tenth hour is ruled by Saturn. It is good for visiting kings and noblemen.

The eleventh hour is ruled by Jupiter. It is good. In it, write magical squares for approaching judges, for legal matters, and for similar things.

The twelfth hour is ruled by Mars. Work any malefica you wish—such as for separation, hatred, and bloodshed.

Thursday

The first hour is ruled by Jupiter. Do works to attract prosperity and customers, and to be accepted by people.

The second hour is ruled by Mars. Do not draw blood during it.[24] Do works involving binding and bloodshed.[25]

The third hour is ruled by the Sun. Do not travel in it. Inscribe talismans and the like for acceptance, love, and affection.

The fourth hour is ruled by Venus. Do workings for things like love and marriage.

The fifth hour is ruled by Mercury. Solemnize marriage contracts.

The sixth hour is ruled by the Moon. Journey over land and sea. Do

24 For instance, cupping (*hijāmah*), a treatment used in Islamic traditional medicine.

25 Another version says not to do works involving binding or bloodshed. The reader is free to choose!

any benevolent work you wish.

The seventh hour is ruled by Saturn. Avoid courtrooms during it. It is suitable for meeting with scholars and clerical officials (*aṣḥāb al-qalam*, lit. "men of the pen").

The eighth hour is ruled by Jupiter. Do all good deeds.

The ninth hour is ruled by Mars. Meet with rulers and princes, and carry out destructive works.

The tenth hour is ruled by the Sun. Petition rulers, princes, soldiers, and dignitaries for what you need.

The eleventh hour is ruled by Venus. Inscribe talismans and the like for love and acceptance.

The twelfth hour is ruled by is ruled by Mercury. Do nothing in it, ever.

Friday

The first hour is ruled by Venus. Do workings to kindle the passions and women's love, and to attract women. Work also to reconcile an estranged husband and wife.

The second hour is ruled by Mercury. Make all kinds of talismans.

The third hour is ruled by the Moon. Do nothing in it, ever.

The fourth hour is ruled by Saturn. It is suitable for drying up things like fountains and wells.

The fifth hour is ruled by Jupiter. Inscribe talismans and the like aimed at acceptance and love.

The sixth hour is ruled by Mars. It is suitable for work causing destruction and bloodshed, as well as penning talismans and similar things for attracting women.

The seventh hour is ruled by the Sun. Inscribe talismans and the like to make sultans accept you, and to fulfill your needs.

The eighth hour is ruled by Venus. Do workings to inflame passions and affections; propose to women and marry.

The ninth hour is ruled by Mercury. Do other types of workings and deeds; they shall succeed.

The tenth hour is ruled by the Moon. Do works aimed at separation or relocation; they shall quickly succeed.

The eleventh hour is ruled by Saturn. Work for nothing apart from drying up waters, springs, and wells.

The twelfth hour is ruled by Jupiter. Travel to take care of your needs, and pursue any goal you wish.

Saturday

The first hour is ruled by Saturn. Do any works that you wish pertaining to acceptance and love. For Saturn only rules one auspicious hour, and that occurs at sunrise when Saturday is the first day of the lunar month, and the crescent Moon was sighted the night before. If Saturday falls on the last day of the lunar month, do other sorts of malefic works. Understand, and be guided! We have clarified things to you and shown you the way.

The second hour is ruled by Jupiter. Inscribe talismans and the like to make peace between people.

The third hour is ruled by Mars. Do works provoking hatred and any other malefica.

The fourth hour is ruled by the Sun. Inscribe talismans and the like to take audience with kings and their spokesmen, and to obtain what you need from them.

The fifth hour is ruled by Venus. There is absolutely no good in it.

The sixth hour is ruled by Mercury. Inscribe talismans and the like to improve hunting.

The seventh hour is ruled by the Moon. There is no good in it; do no written workings in it.

The eighth hour is ruled by Saturn. Do workings to cause things such as illness, blood loss, and nosebleeds.

The ninth hour is ruled by Jupiter. Do any good deeds you please; they shall be accomplished.

The tenth hour is ruled by Mars. Do malevolent workings, such as those aimed at causing disease.

The eleventh hour is ruled by the Sun. Do workings for acceptance and reconciling spouses.

The twelfth hour is ruled by Venus. Meet with kings, viziers, and dignitaries.[26]

The zodiacal signs and the elements

Know that whoever understands the appropriate times for deeds, benefic or malefic, shall attain any goal they wish, for it is the foundation of knowledge and the gate to knowledge. Here, I have illuminated for you what people have said about this subject to make workings easier for you.

I have also made this chart for you so you can know which zodiacal signs are fiery, earthy, airy, and watery. If the Moon is in a fiery sign, do fiery workings; the same with the other signs. Understand what has reached you. This is the chart:

Aries	Taurus	Gemini	Cancer
Leo	Virgo	Libra	Scorpio
Sagittarius	Capricorn	Aquarius	Pisces
FIRE	EARTH	AIR	WATER

If someone comes to you seeking assistance—on any day—write his name, the name of his mother, and his goal in unconnected letters. Count the letters associated with the elements and see which element predominates, then carry out their request when the Moon is in a sign that matches the element. This will lead to success.

How to determine which sign of the zodiac the Moon is in

This would have been particularly helpful before computers and calculators—and, of course, on cloudy nights.

26 The recommendations for the eleventh and twelfth hours seem to be flipped, in that love workings are traditionally associated with Venus, and kings are traditionally associated with the Sun. This page is also missing from two of source texts consulted here; it possibly could have been different in those editions.

Count how many days have passed of the Arabic month, double it, and add five. Then, beginning with the sign that the Sun is in, count by fives around the zodiac. When you can no longer subtract five, that is the sign that the Moon is in. And God knows best.

The enigmatic names (iḍmār) of angels associated with the letters

> Since the names here are untranslatable, and are akin to barbarous names, they have been provided in transliteration from the original form. In cases of uncertain pronunciation, the short vowel *a* may be inserted between the letters.

When you have resolved to perform a working, count up the total numerical value of the letters of name of the seeker, the target, and that day. Then keep subtracting thirty until you are left with a number below thirty. The remainder of the letters are the *iḍmār* for that working. People imbued with the secrets of the names cannot abandon the *iḍmār*, even for a blink of an eye; this constitutes the largest part of the working.

The following are enigmatic names of the hidden angelic servants (*iḍmār*) of the letters. The enigmatic name of the angel ruling over the letter *alif* is Halṭaṭaghiyāʾīl, and the enigmatic name of these letters is *hadhayūn shalhaṭāyā ṣamḥalashaf.*

Letter	Enigmatic name (*iḍmār*)
alif	*h-d-h-y-w-n sh-l-h-ṭ-a-y-a ṣ-m-ḥ-l-sh-f*
b	*h-y-l-kh m-d-m-kh*
j	*ṣ-h-a-y-n-ḥ n-sh-l-ṭ-k m-h-k-w-d-h*
d	*y-j-ṭ-k-y-l*
h	*h-sh-ṭ-ʿ*
w	*m-h-k-w-d-h sh-l-t-m-w-kh b-r-a-kh*
z	*s-ʿ-d-w-y-n h-ṭ-l-ṭ-m m-h-ṭ*

Letter	Enigmatic name (*iḍmār*)
ḥ	*k-t-l-a ṭ-l-kh ṭ-y-kh*
ṭ	*sh-m-h-ṭ m-l-sh-y-ḥ ṭ-m-h*
y	*m-f-y-ʿ h-k-h-f sh-w-n-y-dh-kh*
k	*sh-ʿ-w-w-d h-m-y-ṭ-a m-d-m-kh*
l	*ʿ-f-m-a-r-h ʿ-f-ʿ-y-ṭ ṭ-h-m-s ṣ-l-w-m*
m	*m-d-b-ḥ k-l-y-l*
n	*sh-f-y-ʿ w-l-kh-m y-h-y-ṭ*
s	*j-m-ṭ-ʿ-ṭ-ʿ ʿ-l-ṭ-r-j-y-m*
ʿ	*l-ḥ-ṭ-y-m ʿ-n b-w-a-r-z*
f	*k-y-ṭ-m r-z-ṭ-sh d-h-q-y-k*
ṣ	*m-sh-ʿ-w-d-ʿ ṣ-h-y-sh*
q	*ʿ-d-ʿ-ṣ-r ṭ-l-j-y-a-sh*
r	*sh-ṭ-y-f k-h-y-l d-y-n-w-m*
sh	*l-k-ṭ-f m-h-f-a-gh-l*
t	*sh-m-ʿ-f-y-l ṭ-w-sh y-a-n-w-kh*
th	*ʿ-m-w-ṭ-y-a-r w-a-k-sh h-f-y-ṭ*
kh	*h-h-k-y-n-j h-m-h-l-j-l*
dh	*ʿ-l-k-h-ṣ ṣ-h-d-ʿ s-h-l-ṭ*
ẓ	*y-w-kh r-w-kh a-h-m-w-sh*
ḍ	*y-w-kh r-w-kh a-h-m-w-sh*
gh	*s-ʿ-l-ṭ-f k-l-k-f-f h-y-w-ṭ*

Know that *ẓ* and *ḍ* have the same *iḍmār*.

These are all of the *iḍmārs*, and God knows best.

Chapter 3

THE TWENTY-EIGHT LUNAR MANSIONS

This chapter draws on two main traditions and definitions of the lunar mansions. First, al-Buni discusses the lunar mansions as twenty-eight equal segments of the sky, which include specific stars and constellations but which are not wholly defined by them, similar to how the twelve signs of the tropical zodiac demarcate twelve equal segments of the sky, and include specific stars and constellations but are not wholly defined by them. This approach to the mansions would have been used in esoteric and occult work. Historically, it developed outside the Arabian Peninsula. While, before the advent of Islam, some Arab tribes used the concept of lunar mansions, the twenty-eight equal lunar mansions became normalized throughout the Arab and Islamic world after expansion of Islam through increased contact with other cultures and their astrological traditions. Therefore, the worldview here is a synthesis of classical Arab-Islamic astrology and astronomy with other, older worldviews.

After that, the author addresses the constellations and stars native to the Arabian Peninsula before the time of Islam. These asterisms are more strongly associated with practical matters, such as timing journeys and predicting rains; they also include ancient Arab star lore. Although associated with the lunar mansions, these asterisms predate the equal division of the sky into twenty-eight mansions and so do not neatly fall into the lunar mansions, although they are associated with them. Since, prior to the era of Islam, the Arabian Peninsula lacked cultural unity, there are also varying definitions on what comprises an asterism, or even the name of a star. Some stars or asterisms are also referred to as "rain-stars" (*anwāʾ*). When reading this section, it should be remembered that the stars today are no longer in the positions that they were over a thousand years ago; for instance, in al-Buni's era, the North Star did not actually mark the north pole. Furthermore, some of the star lore he cites traces back to truly ancient times, hinting at the positions of the stars well before recorded history.

Deducing which lunar mansion the Moon is in

KNOW—MAY GOD MAKE you and me obedient towards Him—you can deduce which lunar mansion the crescent moon will be in each month. On the last day of the Arabic month, the Sun and Moon are in the same mansion. Then, at the end of that day,[1] the crescent Moon will appear. This will also be in the first, second, or third part of the Julian month; and the first or second half of the Julian month. Using the diagram and the lunar mansion of the crescent Moon as a base guide, count the number of days of the lunar month that have passed, and you shall find which mansion the Moon is in.

For example, say that the crescent Moon appears on the first night in the mansion called the "Two Signs" (*al-sharaṭayn*), while seven days of the Arabic month have elapsed. We want to know the mansion that the Moon will be in on that day, so we count forward seven mansions from the Two Signs (*al-sharaṭayn*), and arrive at the Forearm (*al-dhirāʿ*). Thus, we know that the Moon shall be in the Forearm (*al-dhirāʿ*). That is how it is done.

Here is a diagram; know and be guided!

1 That is, at sunset; in the Islamic lunar calendar, days begin at sunset. However, planetary days (such as Mars day or Venus day) begin at sunrise, not at sunset the night before. Throughout this book, al-Buni juggles several calendars.

The spirits and natures of the mansions

While al-Buni will subsequently embark on a description of the stars corresponding to each mansion, and some of the lore, these snippets based on other sources were included here to help contextualize the mansions and their Arabic names in the mind of the reader.

This and the following section on the mansions contain small diagrams of the asterisms associated with the mansions. Exoterically, they map important stars in the mansions; the later chapter of commentary also suggests some esoteric uses of them. Because the average pre-modern reader—especially an astronomer or astrologer wielding an astrolabe—would have been more familiar with the night sky than the average urbanite today, these asterisms would just have been shorthand. Since different manuscripts of the *Sun of Knowledge* vary widely in how the asterisms are drawn, the asterisms which best matched the descriptions of the mansions have been selected. Note that some of the asterisms here differ from those in the next section; this can also be seen in light of the varying cultural traditions that fed into the construction of the twenty-eight lunar mansions, and the disagreement over what constituted lunar mansions, or, indeed, specific constellations, in earlier eras. Also, some of the asterisms are identical, even though the mansions differ in appearance. The illustrations of the mansions here render the asterisms unnecessary, since they map out the lunar mansions clearly, but the asterisms have been included because they are part of the original text.

THE TWO SIGNS *(al-sharaṭayn)*
The first mansion, 0° Aries to 12° 51' Aries

The Two Signs are the two stars representing the horns of Aries. This mansion is also known as the Butting of the Ram (*al-naṭḥ*), a star in Aries.[2]

Its stars look like this: ✷✷
It rules the letter *alif* (ا).

2 Descriptions of the constellations or stars associated with the lunar mansions that have been included in the commentary on the translation have been taken largely from Abu ʿAli ibn al-Hatim (10th century AD), *De Imaginibus Caelestis*, and Edward William Lane, *Lane's Lexicon.*

The Two Signs is fiery and ill-omened but suitable for workings pertaining to women. When the Moon enters this mansion, a spirit descends towards the royalty and sparks hatred, bloodshed, and anger among them. During this time, the wise used to seclude themselves and avoid doing things. Some have said that they dreamt of frightening things which unsettled their temperament. It is best to abstain from sleep and keep silent, unless it is absolutely necessary to say something. Do not craft anything in it. If you must do something, work malefic acts against those who deserve it.

Whoever is born while the Moon is in this mansion shall be evil and depraved.

Its incense is black pepper and blackseed. And God knows best.

THE BELLY (*al-baṭīn*)

The second mansion, 12° 51′ Aries to 25° 43′ Aries

Al-baṭīn is the belly of the Ram. It is a diminutive form of *baṭn*, "belly," and hence means "little belly." It is marked by three small, barely shining stars in a tight equilateral triangle. *Al-bāṭin* ("the Inner" or "the Hidden") is also one of the names of God, and the nature of this mansion lends itself well to esoteric pursuits.

Its stars look like this: ✷ ✷ ✷
It rules the letter *b* (ب).

The Belly (*al-baṭīn*) is hot and moist. When the Moon alights in it, by the permission of God, a virtuous, temperate spirit descends to the earth.[3] It is suitable for deeds pertaining to men, as opposed to women. It is suitable for making talismans, alchemy, and great works. It is also suitable for beginning studies and making seals (*khawātim*), drawings and amulets (*naqsh*), and numerical sigils (*ruqūm*), as well as treating ailments through exorcism, spiritual healing, and medicine. It is also a good time for keeping an enemy at bay.

Whoever is born while the Moon is in this mansion will live a happy, guided life, blessed and beloved by creation. Its incense is aloeswood, saffron, and mastic. And God knows best.

3 In the classical Islamic tradition, as in some ancient Greek works, ethical ideas were comprised of balance—for instance, balancing traits of anger and cowardice to find a happy medium. Thus, balance is a virtue to aspire to.

THE MANSION OF THE PLEIADES (*al-thurayā*)
The third mansion, 25° 43' Aries to 8° 34' Taurus

> *Al-thurayā* is the Arabic name for the seven sisters of the Pleiades and also literally means "the abundant little ones" or "dewdrops." It is said to have been named such either because it consists of many stars, or because it predicted abundant rain. The Pleiades was the subject of copious ancient Arabic poetry and rhyme, some of which survives today.

Its stars look like this: 
It rules the letter *j* (ج).

When the Moon enters the Mansion of the Pleiades (*al-thurayā*), a spirit characterized by both heat and cold descends from this mansion. During it, make talismans, do works which assist women, and distill cooling medications. It marks success for travellers and those angling for extra profits. It is good time to meet with or write to kings, marry, and buy slave-girls and retainers (*mamālīk*). Everything that is devised and fashioned in it shall flourish and prosper, for, in it, the Moon is in equilibrium without the Sun.[4]

4 Traditionally, the Sun is in a fortunate position in Aries, and the Moon in Taurus; this mansion spans both. This may be because the solar influence can be perceived of as overly hot. The Moon, especially in Vedic culture where much of the lunar mansion lore comes from, sees the Moon as the ultimate benefic

Whoever is born while the Moon is in this mansion shall live a happy life. They shall abhor evil and embrace piety. They shall hate wickedness, love the righteous, and mingle with scholars.

Its incense is flaxseed and blackseed. And God knows best.

THE FOLLOWER (*al-Dabarān*)

The fourth mansion, 8° 34' Taurus to 21° 26' Taurus

> *Al-Dabarān* means "the follower" and is the Arabic name for the star Aldebaran, also known as the "eye of Taurus." The mansion is described as a red star with two small stars.

Its stars look like this: 

It rules the letter *d* (د).

The Follower (*al-dabarān*) is associated with the element of earth and is ill-omened. When the Moon alights in it, a spirit descends spreading enmity, hatred, and corruption throughout the lands. During that time, beware of seeking needs or beginning new things.

---

balance. Furthermore, the Moon would be especially well-situated here since the traditional degree of exaltation of the moon is 3° Taurus.

Do not make talismans, and do not fashion crafts. Everything done in it shall be ruined. It is only suitable for burying the dead, burying treasures, hiding secrets, digging wells, and crossing rivers. It is good for nothing else.

Whoever is born while the Moon is in this mansion shall be hated and forsaken.

Its incense is sweet pomegranate peel and frankincense.

THE HAIR-WHORL *(al-haqʿah)*
The fifth mansion, 21° 26′ Taurus to 4° 17′ Gemini

> This mansion is marked by the three small stars of Orion forming the head of Gemini.

Its stars look like this: 
It rules the letter *h* (ه).

This mansion is both auspicious and inauspicious. When the Moon alights in it, distill and develop poisons. Do not work with the Sun or the Moon. Do not plant crops, wear new clothes, or marry in it, for that shall not bode well. Do not engage in any spiritual workings during this time.

Whoever is born while the Moon is in this mansion will enjoy the latter years of his life, but not the early years.

Its incense is aloeswood,[5] frankincense, benzoin, and mastic. And God knows best.

THE LEANING STARS *(al-hanʿah)*
The sixth mansion, 4° 17’ Gemini to 17° 9’ Gemini

> This mansion is marked by the three stars between the two feet of Gemini. In English, Alhena is another name for the star Gamma Gemini, near the left foot of Pollux. While al-Buni holds that they were named as such because they look like they are leaning towards each other, they have also been described as looking like a mark on the neck.

Its stars look like this: * * * * *
It rules the letter *w* (و).

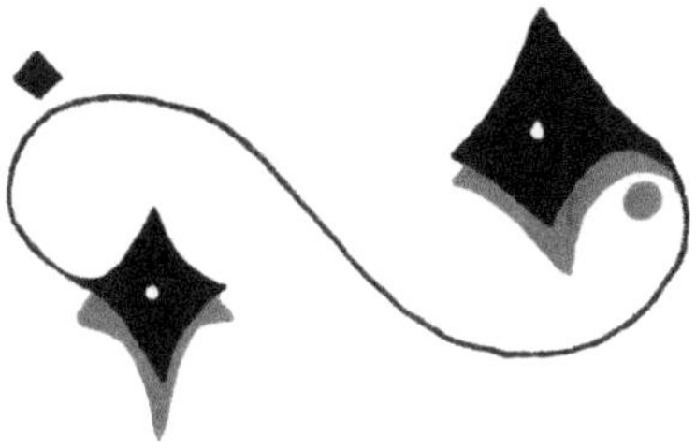

It is fortunate. When the Moon alights in it, do workings for affection and love. Burn sweet incense. Visit kings and notables and be open to their power, wealth, and circumstances. It is also a good time to spend time with noblemen and brethren. Start workings to fulfill your wishes, marry, take medication, buy slave-girls and horses, and plant trees. Build buildings, measure weights, travel,

5 *Nidd*, which can also refer of a blend of incenses, including aloeswood, ambergris, musk, and frankincense.

and buy and sell; all of that will go quite well.

Whoever is born while the Moon is in this mansion will live a happy life and die as a martyr.

Its incense is burdock and mugwort seed. And God knows best.

THE FOREARM (*al-dhirāʿ*)

The seventh mansion, 17° 9′ Gemini to 0° Cancer

Al-Dhirāʿ is the "forearm" of Leo and consists of two stars.

Its stars look like this: ✷✷
It rules the letter z (ز).

It is characterized by the element of air, and is fortunate and yielding. When the Moon alights in it, a virtuous spirit descends to the earth. It is suitable for spiritual healing, beginning studies, virtuous deeds, gathering in houses of worship, and meeting with scholars and the pious. Make talismans and amulets (*nārinjīyāt*).[6] Visit kings, and communicate with noblemen and brethren.

Whoever is born while the Moon is in this mansion shall be fortunate, guided, and blessed.

6 *Nārinjīyāt* can refer to illusions, sleight of hand, white magic, spellwork, or counter-spells.

Its incense is nettle and flax seed.

THE NOSE-TIP (*al-nathrah*)
The eighth mansion, 0° Cancer to 12° 51′ Cancer

> *Al-Nathrah* is marked by three stars—or, rather, two stars and a nebula—which form the nose and nostrils of Leo.

Its stars look like this: ✷ ✷ ✷
It rules the letter ḥ (ح).

It is cold, of mixed fortune. When the Moon alights in it, an angry spirit descends to the earth provoking enmity, hatred, ruptures, and similar things. It is suitable for making talismans appropriate to that, and for imprecating against enemies, criminals, transgressors, and foes. Do not do any works related to the Sun or Moon, or visit kings. Do not begin fashioning implements of war or take council for war, for this mansion is despicable. It is only suitable for destructive works, as we have mentioned.

Whoever is born in it will be unfortunate.

Its incense is costus and pomegranate peel. And God knows best.

THE TWINKLING EYES (*al-ṭarfah*)

The ninth mansion, 12° 51’ Cancer to 25° 43’ Cancer

> The eyes of Leo, represented by two small stars. In English, Alterf is another name for the star Lambda Leo.

Its stars look like this: ✷ ✷

It rules the letter ṭ (ط).

It is inauspicious and characterized by the element of water. When the Moon alights in it, a spirit similar to the one from the previous mansion descends to the earth. Do not construct talismans in it, do not make anything, and do not visit kings. Love is not found during this time, nor is wisdom wrought. Do not recite oaths (*qasam*). It is better to be alone rather than with others. It is wretched for all acts.

Whoever is born in it will be unfortunate.

Its incense is aloeswood and saffron. And God knows best.

THE FOREHEAD (*al-jabhah*)

The tenth mansion, 25° 43’ Cancer to 8° 34’ Leo

This mansion is the forehead of Leo. It is represented by four stars, two of which symbolize the forehead, and two of which symbolize the heart.

Its stars look like this: ✱ ✱ / ✱ ✱
It rules the letter *y* (ي).

It is cold and both fortunate and unfortunate, but more inclined towards wholesome works. When the Moon alights in it, begin workings for affection and similar things. Visit kings, and seek what you need. Treatments will be well-tolerated by the ill. It is suitable from moving from place to place. However, it is unsuitable for tailoring or wearing new clothes.

Whoever is born in it shall be clever and dexterous, fortunate and blessed; however, they shall be somewhat inclined towards trickery and deceit.

Its incense is myrtle seed and saffron. And God knows best.

THE MANE (*al-zubrah*)
The eleventh mansion, 8° 34' Leo to 21° 26' Leo

This mansion forms the mane of Leo and referring to two shining stars inside Leo. It has been suggested that, in ancient times,

> these stars were near the mane of Leo but, due to stellar precession, today, they are situated more towards its haunches. It is also known as the Two Ribs or the Two Piercings (al-kharatān), the latter interpretation indicating where it might have been speared.

Its stars look like this: ✷ ✷ ✷ ✷ ✷
It rules the letter *k* (ك).

It is hot and dry. When the Moon alights in it, perform spiritual healing, make talismans, treat diseases, and medicate chronic illnesses. It is also suitable for buying, selling, and visiting kings and chieftains or official heads. It is suitable both for travelling and sojourning, great works, and donning new clothes.

Whoever is born during it shall be beloved by the people but shall have a trickish, cunning streak.

Its incense is sweet pomegranate peel, nothing else. And God knows best.

THE WEATHER-CHANGE *(al-ṣarfah)*
The twelfth mansion, 21° 26′ Leo to 4° 17′ Virgo

> *Al-Ṣarfah* marks the tail of Leo. It is the name of a star which is called "the Weather-Change" because warmth departs when it rises and cold departs when it sets.

Its stars look like this: ✷
It rules the letter *l* (ل).

It is of an earthen and fiery nature. When the Moon alights in it, an auspicious spirit descends to the earth. It is suitable for middling works. Do not craft things, treat illnesses, or engage in spiritual workings. Do not visit kings. Make implements of war, bear weapons, and ride horses.

Whoever is born in it shall have a vile nature. That person shall hate the people, and the people shall hate him. None shall love him—and God knows best.

Its incense is nutmeg.[7] And God knows best.

THE HOWLING DOGS *(al-ʿawwā)*
The thirteenth mansion, 4° 17′ Virgo to 17° 9′ Virgo

> *Al-ʿAwwā* consists of five stars like the letter alif with the tail chopped off, as if they are dogs howling behind Leo. It is said that they are called this because when they rise or set, they bring severe cold.

Its stars look like this: ✷✷✷✷✷
It rules the letter *m* (م).

7 An alternate version lists *nidd* and saffron, *nidd* being either aloeswood or a blend of incenses, including aloeswood, ambergris, musk, and frankincense.

It is hot, dry and of mixed fortune. When the Moon alights in it, a spirit sinks to the earth which inflames passions and makes men fall in love with women and couple with them. It is suitable for embarking upon studies and learning all things. Do not craft precious stones, for it is unsuitable for that. Do not fight enemies, dispute, prosecute, or visit kings. It is suitable for wearing new clothes and tailoring clothes.

Whoever is born in it shall be fortunate, be they male or female.

Its incense is frankincense. And God knows best.

THE SKY-RAISER (*al-Simāk*)
The fourteenth mansion, 17° 9′ Virgo to 0° Libra

The name *al-Simāk* is used for two bright stars, Arcturus ("the Spear-Bearing Sky-Raiser," *al-simāk al-rāmiḥ*) and Spica ("The Unarmed Sky-Raiser," *al-simāk al-aʿzal*, also known as *al-sunbulah*). The Spear-Bearing Sky-Raiser had a nearby star which was seen as his spear, whereas the Unarmed Sky-Raiser did not. The name Sky-Raiser is said to have come from the impression that, when they were at their height, these stars appeared to hold up the sky the way that a pole holds up a tent.

Its stars look like this: ✷
It rules the letter *n* (ن).

It is earthen and dry. When the Moon is in it, a spirit begetting enmity and evil sinks to the earth. It is appropriate for mixing deathly poisons and everything destructive. It is unsuitable for starting benefic works, buying, selling, or bartering.

Whoever is born in it will be an unpopular, lying, unfortunate tale-bearer.

Its incense is frankincense and indigo.[8] And God knows best.

THE SHROUDED (*al-ghafr*)

The fifteenth mansion, 0° Libra to 12° 51' Libra

> The Shrouded (*al-ghafr*) consists of three small, obscure stars which shine little. Ghafr means to cover, hide, or wrap up; the name comes from the dimness of the stars, as if they are covered.

8 Another version has wild rue, or *ḥarmal*, in place of indigo. *Ḥarmal* is popularly burned for protection from evil spirits, and one can see how that could be done to dispel the evil spirit associated with this mansion. Additionally, *ḥarmal* also has psychedelic properties and has sometimes been used to induce visions. This may also relate to the rather extreme nature associated with this mansion.

In terms of star lore, an explanation for why the Shrouded was fortunate is because it was far from the Lion's claws and teeth, and far from the Scorpion's sting. So, despite lying between two dangerous creatures, it rests safely.

Its stars look like this: ✷ ✷ ✷

It rules the letter *s* (س).

It is of an airy nature and auspicious. When the Moon alights in it, a spirit descends that begets love, amicability, ease, and benevolence from kings. It is suitable for cures and antidotes to deathly poisons which dispel their harm. It is suitable for preparing precious stones, spiritual healing, making talismans, and whatever else is harmonious with that.

Whoever is born in it will be unfortunate, treacherous, and deceitful.

Its incense is frankincense, nothing else. Know, and be guided!

THE CLAW (*al-zubānā*)

The sixteenth mansion, 12° 51′ Libra to 25° 43′ Libra

Al-Zubānā are the claws of Scorpio.

Its stars look like this: ✷ ✷

It rules the letter *ʿayn* (ع).

It is airy and of both auspicious and inauspicious fortune. When the Moon alights in it, a spirit of opposites descends to the earth, so act accordingly. Whoever wears new clothes will suffer a dog bite, will be slandered by his enemies, and endure a painful bodily injury.

Whoever is born in it will be fortunate in all he does.

Its incense is mugwort seed and chamomile,[9] and God knows best.

CROWN (*al-iklīl*)

The seventeenth mansion, 25° 43' Libra to 8° 34' Scorpio

> The word *iklīl* can be used for a king's crown, an athlete's head-garland, or a bride's tiara. It is marked by three shining stars.

Its stars look like this: 

It rules the letter *f* (ف).

9 Another source says the incense is mugwort seed and nothing else.

It is of mixed fortune, both auspicious and inauspicious. When the Moon alights in it, a spirit descends from it which urges malice, unrest, corruption, and hatred. Nefarious things are done, as well as un-nefarious things. Do not travel or marry in it. Do not buy slaves and do not plant fruit trees or crops, for they shall not thrive. Neither tailor nor wear new clothing in it, nor dispute, nor prosecute in court, nor petition for your needs.

Whoever is born in it, be they male or female, will be miserable and blamed.

Its incense is pepper, saffron, and aloeswood.[10] And God knows best.

THE HEART (*al-qalb*)
The eighteenth mansion, 8° 34' Scorpio to 21° 26' Scorpio

> *Al-Qalb* is the heart of Scorpio. It is marked by a red star between two small, shining stars. According to an old saying, "When the heart of Scorpio rises, winter comes like the dog." It portended vehement, cold winds.

Its stars look like this: 
It rules the letter ṣ (ص).

10 Alt. *'ūd nidd, nidd* being either aloeswood or a blend of incenses, including aloeswood, ambergris, musk, and frankincense.

It is fortunate and watery. When the Moon alights in it, a spirit descends from it which rectifies what was corrupted previously. It is suitable for buying weapons, war equipment, and livestock; veterinary medicine; felling trees; farming; ploughing; digging up buried things; curing animals; taking purgatives; blood-letting; and cupping.

Whoever is born in it will be unfortunate, be they male or female, and shall have a trickish streak.

Its incense is myrobalan leaf (*waraq al-ihlīlaj*). And God knows best.

THE STINGING TAIL (*al-shawlah*)

The nineteenth mansion, 21° 26' Scorpio to 4° 17' Sagittarius

> Al-Shawlah is the tail of Scorpio. It is marked by two stars beneath which is a third, shining star.

Its stars look like this: 

It rules the letter *q* (ق).

It is characterized by fortune interwoven with misfortune. When the Moon alights in it, a spirit descends to earth from it which vacillates between evil and good. It is suitable for tying and unbinding, making and breaking agreements, and whatever deeds are of an ambivalent nature. It is unsuitable for sewing new clothing, making talismans, or performing spiritual healing. Seclusion is preferable.

Whoever is born in it will be a despicable, blameworthy, slanderous, depraved liar.

Its incense is pomegranate peel and mastic.

THE OSTRICHES *(al-naʿāʾim)*
The twentieth mansion, 4° 17′ Sagittarius to 17° 9′ Sagittarius

> The Ostriches (*al-naʿāʾim*) are nine stars of Sagittarius, four of which are in the Milky way; they are said to be as if they are drinking from the Milky Way. The remaining are said to have been returning from drinking from the Milky Way.

Its stars look like this: 
It rules the letter *r* (ر).

It is fiery, fortunate, and dazzling. When the Moon alights in it, a spirit descends to the earth which purifies hearts and urges love, good fortune, and happiness. All done in it will end up well. It is suitable for crafting precious stones. In it, embark upon the study of matters of wisdom and religion. Make talismans, build buildings, plant trees, and don new clothes; whoever dons them shall remain happy and joyous until they wear out.

Whoever is born in it shall be blessed, happy, and successful in all endeavors.

Its incense is frankincense and mugwort. And God knows best.

THE WASTELAND (*al-baldah*)
The twenty-first mansion, 17° 9′ Sagittarius to 0° Capricorn

It consists of six stars of Sagittarius; when the Sun enters it, it portends the shortest day of the year.

Its stars look like this: 
It rules the letter *sh* (ش).

It is fiery and unfortunate. When the Moon alights in it, a spirit descends which strives for enmity, hatred, separation, and evil. Only strive for those ends. Beware of making talismans or working with precious gemstones. Do not perform spiritual healing, farm, plant, travel, mix with kings, marry, buy slaves, barter, wear new clothes, or do any works at all.

Whoever is born in it shall be a wretched swindler.

Its incense is spikenard (*sunbul*) and aloeswood.[11] And God knows best.

THE SLAUGHTERER'S JOY (*sa'd al-dhābiḥ*)
The twenty-second mansion, 0° Capricorn to 12° 51' Capricorn

> This mansion is marked by two stars which shine little; they appear a forearm's distance apart. They are named such because one appears as if it is a sheep about to be slaughtered by the other. They are said to be in the horns of Capricorn.

Its stars look like this: 
It rules the letter *t* (ت).

11 *'Ūd nidd*, *nidd* being either aloeswood or a blend of incenses, including aloeswood, ambergris, musk, and frankincense.

It is of an earthen nature and of mixed fortune, tending towards the nefarious. When the Moon alights in it, a spirit descends which strives for hatred, enmity, and rupture; nothing done in it shall work out well. Kings become enraged. People regret after buying and selling unless they are very nitpicky. It is suitable for good works, digging things up, and farming. In it, secret and buried things are dug up, and secrets are hidden.

Whoever is born in it, be they male or female, shall be handsome, blessed, covetous towards this world, and deceitful.

Its incense is safflower (*ʿuṣfur*). And God knows best.

THE VORACIOUS AUSPICE (*saʿd balʿ*)

The twenty-third mansion, 12° 51′ Capricorn to 25° 43′ Capricorn

> This mansion consists of two obscure, equal stars. They take their name from the impression that one is about to swallow the other. Saʿd means "fortunate" or "auspicious." Sometimes a third star is also mentioned.

Its stars look like this: 

It rules the letter *th* (ث).

It is of mixed essence and fortune. When the Moon alights in it, a spirit which works evil and good descends to the earth. It is suitable for buying slaves, retainers, and livestock; speaking with shaykhs and the elderly; sowing crops; crossing rivers; flowers; digging wells; and heavy labor. It is also suitable for going on outings, and hosting and preparing banquets.

Whoever is born in it shall be upright and blessed.

Its incense is chamomile (*bābūnaj*). And God knows best.

THE MOST FORTUNATE (*saʿd al-suʿūd*)
The twenty-fourth mansion, 25° 43ʹ Capricorn to 8° 34ʹ Aquarius

> It consists of two stars, one in the left shoulder of Aquarius, the other in the tail of Capricorn. Some sources also refer to a solitary bright star. A less esoteric reason why this mansion was named such is that when it rose at sunset, it heralded rain; when it set at sunset, it heralded a reprieve from hot sandstorms.

Its stars look like this: 
It rules the letter *kh* (خ).

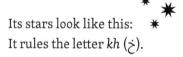

It is of an earthen and airy nature. When the Moon alights in it, a spirit descends which erases the effects of what came before.[12] It is suitable for all deeds. Therefore, in it, begin acts for things such as love, affection, and reconciling hearts. Perform spiritual healing; make talismans; and meet with kings, chiefs, and dignitaries. Perform in it works for love, as you wish; they shall blossom to fruition.

Whoever is born in it, be they male or female, shall be blessed and love the righteous.

Its incense is aloeswood and mastic, and God knows best.

THE AUSPICE OF TENT-POLES (*saʿd al-akhbiyah*)

The twenty-fifth mansion, 8° 34′ Aquarius to 21° 26′ Aquarius

> It is marked by four stars in the shape of a triangle whose middle is the fourth star. Akhbiyah can refer to tent-poles or holes where things are hidden, and it is also said that is called such because, when it rises, scorpions and serpents emerge from their holes.

Its stars look like this: 

It rules the letter *dh* (ذ).

12 That is, the previous inauspicious mansions.

It is of an airy and unfortunate nature. When the Moon alights in it, a spirit descends to the earth stirring up separation, sedition, hatred, division, and war. Deeds done in it do not reach fruition; or, if they do come to completion, they do not work out well. Do not treat illnesses or perform spiritual healing. Neither make talismans nor perform alchemy (*kīmiā*) or natural magic (*sīmīyā*).

Whoever is born in it shall be wicked and faithless.

Its incense is frankincense, astragalus (*ʿanzarūt*), and pepper. And God knows best.

THE FIRST SPOUT (*al-fargh al-muqaddim*)
The twenty-sixth mansion, 21° 26′ Aquarius to 4° 17′ Pisces

> The asterisms associated with this and the next mansion form two bucket-spouts, associated with the bucket of Aquarius, the water-bearer. The image is that of a leather bucket, attached to a well. A wooden crossbar at top keeps the bucket open, thereby forming a forward and backward spout. This is why the asterisms appear in the shape of a square, and include Pegasus and Andromeda.

Its stars look like this: 
It rules the letter *ḍ* (ض).

It is of an airy and fortunate nature. When the Moon alights in it, a spirit descends which inflames love and lusts and makes people susceptible to affection. It is suitable for alchemy, spiritual healing, engraving talismans, and natural magic (*sīmīyā*). Beneficial medicines are prepared in it, and poisoning is cured. In it, visit kings, chiefs, and dignitaries.

Whoever is born in it shall have a good life.

Its incense is frankincense, blackseed, and saffron. And God knows best.

THE SECOND SPOUT (*al-fargh al-mu'akhkhir*)
The twenty-seventh mansion, 4° 17' Pisces to 17° 9' Pisces

> *Al-Fargh al-mu'akhkhir*, also known as *al-fargh al-thānī*, is the second bucket-spout. It consists of two stars.

Its stars look like this: 
It rules the letter ẓ (ظ).

It is watery and fortunate. When the Moon alights in it, a spirit descends which works ill deeds, similar to what happens in other inauspicious mansions. Refrain from war, meeting with enemies, disputing, or bloodshed. It is suitable for blood-letting, cupping, and workings to cause bleeding and to prevent men and women from having intercourse. It is also suitable for visiting baths, cutting the hair and nails, and taking beneficial medicine.

Whoever is born in it will be a wicked, miserable traitor.

Its incense is pepper and cinnamon. And God knows best.

THE ROPE (*al-rishā*)
The twenty-eighth mansion, 17° 9' Pisces to 0° Aries

> *Al-Rishā* is the rope of the bucket. It is also known as the Belly of the Fish (*baṭn al-ḥūt*). It is a group of many stars, in the form of a fish, in the navel of which is a bright star. It has also been described as the drapery around Andromeda. Although al-Buni does not mention this, this mansion is also—unsurprisingly—considered auspicious for casting enchantments for fishing. In English, Alrescha is another name for the star Alpha Piscium.

✶ ✶ ✶
✶   ✶
Its stars look like this: ✶ ✶ ✶
It rules the letter *gh* (غ).

It is of a watery and fortunate nature. When the Moon alights in it, a spirit descends to the earth which sets things aright. In it, make talismans and do good deeds. Work with precious stones and gem-talismans, and perform spiritual healing. All that is done in it shall go well. It is suitable for travelling, marriage, wearing new clothes, moving from one place to another, and mingling with judges and officials.

Whoever is born in it shall be blessed.

Its incense is blackseed. And God knows best.

Which lunar mansions correspond to which signs of the zodiac

¶ The Second Spout (*al-fargh al-muʾakhkhar*), the Rope (*al-rishā*), and one-third of the Two Signs (*al-sharaṭayn*) are in Aries.

¶ Two-thirds of the Two Signs (*al-sharaṭayn*), the Belly (*al-baṭīn*), and two-thirds of the Mansion of the Pleiades (*al-thurayā*) are in Taurus.

¶ One-third of the Mansion of the Pleiades (*al-thurayā*), the Follower (*al-dabarān*), and the Hair-Whorl (*al-haqʿah*) are in Gemini.

¶ The Leaning Stars (*al-hanʿah*), the Forearm (*al-dhirāʿ*), and two-thirds of the Nose-tip (*al-nathrah*) are in Cancer.

¶ One-third of the Nose-tip (*al-nathrah*), the Twinkling Eyes (*al-ṭarfah*), and two-thirds of the Forehead (*al-jabhah*) are in Leo.

¶ One-third of the Forehead (*al-jabhah*), the Mane (*al-zubrah*), and the Weather-Change (*al-ṣarfah*) are in Virgo.

¶ The Howling Dogs (*al-ʿawwāʾ*), the Sky-Raiser (*al-simāk*), and one-third of the Shrouded (*al-ghafr*) are in Libra.

¶ Two-thirds of the Shrouded (*al-ghafr*) the Claw (*al-zubānā*), and two-thirds of the Crown (*al-iklīl*) are in Scorpio.

¶ One-third of the Crown (*al-iklīl*), the Heart (*al-qalb*), and the Stinging Tail (*al-shawlah*) are in Sagittarius.

¶ The Ostriches (*al-naʿāʾim*), the Wasteland (*al-baldah*), and two-thirds of the Slaughterer's Joy (*saʿd al-dhābiḥ*) are in Capricorn.

¶ One-third of the Slaughterer's Joy (*saʿd al-dhābiḥ*), the Voracious Auspice (*saʿd al-balʿ*), and two-thirds of the Most Fortunate (*saʿd al-suʿūd*) are in Aquarius.

¶ One-third of the Most Fortunate (*saʿd al-suʿūd*), the Auspice of Tent-Poles (*saʿd al-akhbiyah*), and the First Spout (*al-fargh al-muqaddim*) are in Pisces.

And God knows best.

The stars in the lunar mansions

This section marks a transition to a discussion of observational astronomy and star lore. This and the remainder of the chapter address the locations, rising, and setting of the asterisms associated with the mansions, rather than the theoretical construct of twenty-eight equal mansions.

Note that the zodiacal constellations are no longer where they were in ancient times, which has led to today's discrepancy between the constellations of the tropical zodiac, and the demarcations of the actual zodiacal signs. The stars associated with the lunar mansions have also drifted over the years. Additionally, in the ancient Arabic tradition, some of the constellations, such as Leo, were much larger than they were in al-Buni's time. Therefore, discussions like this resolve the complexities of layering multiple traditions.

I did not discuss this previously.

THE TWO SIGNS (*al-sharaṭayn*) is the first mansion which consists of two, separated stars, one of them to the south and the other to the north. They are named that because they signify the coming of rains. These two luminaries mark the two horns of Aries and are also called "the Butting" (*al-nāṭiḥ*). When they are overhead, the eye adjudges them to be about ten arm-spans apart. A small star near the Sky-Raiser (*al-simāk*) sometimes precedes them.

It looks like this: ✷✷✷.

THE BELLY (*al-baṭīn*) consists of three small bright stars in an equilateral triangle. They form the belly of Aries. It is small, for many stars make up the ram of Aries; they mark only its belly. The Pleiades are its hindquarters, and the Two Signs (*al-sharaṭayn*) are its horns.

It looks like this: ✷✷✷

THE PLEAIDES (*al-thurayā*) consists of seven stars, six of which are bright and one of which is small and hidden. People test their eyesight by looking for it. The name *al-thurayā* comes from *al-tharwah*, which means "dewy and drizzly."[13] It goes by other names as well, such as *al-najm* ("the Star"), even though it is made up of several stars.

13 It also means "abundance" or "wealth," but al-Buni has focused on it being dewy and drizzly.

Some scholars have said that "by the Star when it sets" (Qur'an 53:1) alludes to the Pleiades, since the Arabs called the Pleiades "the Star" although it is formed of multiple stars. The Messenger of God also spoke of it as the Star; he said, "When the Star rises, pestilence dies off from fruit trees." By "the Star," he meant the Pleiades. The Pleiades are also called *al-ʿunqūd* and *al-qadam*. This couplet has been passed on:

When the Pleiades display themselves at night
    The sharp-sighted see seven stars
Atop Mount Hiraʾ
    Like a pearl bracelet encircling a wrist.

It looks like this: 

THE DYED PALM (*al-kaff al-khaḍīb*)[14] is outstretched towards one of the fish of Pisces, along with the Amputated Hand (*al-jazmā*), which is beneath the Two Signs (*al-sharaṭayn*).[15] The Impeder (*al-ʿayyūq*, Capella) is a large, brilliant, reddish star, shining alongside the Milky Way. Trailing behind it, according to some of the learned, are three stars called the Flags (*al-aʿlām*). Although they are not part of the mansions of the Moon, we have mentioned them here because they are near the Pleiades (*al-thurayā*).

The Impeder is said to have been named such because Pleiades and Alebaran were in love, which is why Aldebaran was following her. However, the Impeder prevented the two from meeting. The image of the Pleaides connected to two outstretched hands is well-established in pre-Islamic Arabian star lore.

14 Presumably dyed with henna; the star Beta Cassiopeiae.

15 According to ancient stories, her hand was amputated because she had contracted leprosy.

THE FOLLOWER (*al-dabarān*; that is, Aldebaran) marks the hind end of Aries. Some say that it is called the Follower (*al-dabarān*) because it trails behind the Pleiades. Others say that it is marked by five stars in Taurus which are called *shāmah* and look like this: *⁑***. Others say that that it is marked by the single red star called Aldebaran; it is also called the Mountain (*al-ʿatīq*) because it resembles a great mountain.

Before it are some small stars called the Young Camels (*al-nawq al-ṣighār*, they Hyades).[16] Altogether, they look like a cow's head, and are behind the Pleiades (*al-thurāyā*).

☾

THE HAIR-WHORL (*al-haqʿah*) consists of three stars, near each other. They form the head of Gemini and are like three fingers held together. They look like this: ✳✳✳.

Some say they are the ring of stars next to the animal by Orion's leg. Ibn ʿAbbās—may God be pleased with him—said about a man who divorces his wife the number of the stars in the sky: "It is enough that he divorces her the number of stars of the Hair-Whorl in Gemini (*haqʿat al-Jawzāʾ*)." They shine brilliantly.[17]

☾

THE LEANING STARS (*al-hanʿah*): It consists of five separate stars; namely, two large stars between which are three small stars and which look like: ✳✳✳✳✳.

They are called *al-hanʿah* because each of them is leaning towards its neighbor, and the verb *hanaʿa* means "to lean" or "to incline towards."

☾

THE FOREARM (*al-dhirāʿ*): It is called the Forearm because it is the foreleg of the lion. It consists of two gleaming stars. Some say

16 Also called *al-qalāṣ*.

17 This is a reference to the provision in Islamic law that a man may not divorce and remarry his wife more than three times.

there is a third, small star between the two, as if they are the lion's claws. The eye adjudges them to be a stride's-distance apart. There are actually two forelegs, one outstretched and the other folded under. The outstretched one is above the Sky-Raiser (*al-simāk*). The brighter one is called the Weeping Star (*al-shiʿrā al-ghumayṣāʾ*, Procyon) because she was unable to cross the Milky Way and reach her mate, and so she cried until she went blind. Others say that she cried because she was unable to reach the star Suhayl (Canopus, her brother).

> In fact, astronomical models indicate that Sirius or al-Shi'ra al-abur crossed over the Milky Way, while Procyon or al-Shi'ra al-ghumaysa did not. About fifty-thousand years ago, it was on the other side of the Milky Way, but, due to stellar precession and its relatively near distance to the Earth, it "crossed over." So it is possible that in this story are traces of truly ancient sky lore.

THE NOSE-TIP (*al-nathrah*): It consists of two stars, a hand-span apart. It in is a white splotch, like a white cloudlet cut off from the billows of clouds. It is the tip of the nose of the lion. Some say that it is comprised of three stars and that it looks like this: ✷✷✷, and that it is between the mouth of the lion and its nostrils. It is also called "the nose of the lion."

THE TWINKLING EYES (*al-ṭarfah*) consists of two stars preceding the Forehead (*al-jabhah*). They are the eyes of the lion; the eye adjudges them to be a whip's-distance apart. It looks like this: ✷✷✷.

THE FOREHEAD (*al-jabhah*) consists of four stars which mark the upper back or nape of the neck of the lion, one of which is a shining star to the south.[18] Each pair of stars is about a whip's-distance apart. They are also called the Star of the Lion[19] and rise after the Twinkling Eyes. They look like this: ✱✱ ✱✱.

☾

THE MANE (*al-zubrah*): It consists of two stars on the upper back of the lion where his mane flows. They are about a stride's-distance apart and look like this: ✱✱.

☾

THE WEATHER-CHANGE (*al-ṣarfah*): It is a lone star, facing the Mane. Some say it is the Heart (or Penis) of the Lion.[20] In any case, it is called the Weather-Change because it foretells the end of the cold season and the beginning of the hot season, or the end of the hot season and the beginning of the cold season.

☾

THE HOWLING DOGS (*al-ʿawwāʾ*): It consists of five stars, which are said to demarcate the haunches of the lion. They look like this: ✱✱✱✱✱.

☾

THE SKY-RAISER (*al-simāk*): Two different, brilliant stars are called the Sky-Raiser: the Unarmed (*al-simāk al-aʿzal*; Spica) and the Spearman (*al-simāk al-rāmiḥ*; Arcturus). However, the Spearman is not part of the lunar mansions.

This mansion is demarcated by two stars which are said to be the lion's hind-paws or shins.

The Spearman is named as such because there is a star near him

18 Possibly Regulus, known in Arabic as the Heart of the Lion.

19 *Nawʾ al-asad*, *nawʾ* denoting the stars used to predict seasonal changes and rain.

20 Al-Buni writes it as *qalb al-asad*, "the Heart of the Lion," the name of Regulus. However, it has been argued that this was an error introduced into the manuscript and that it should be *qanb al-asad*, "the Penis of the Lion," which was also mentioned in star lore. Given that Regulus is associated with the previous mansion, this makes sense. See E.W. Lane, *Lane's Lexicon*, s.v. *q-n-b*.

which is as if it is his spear. The Unarmed is named as such because it is alone, without any nearby stars; therefore, it has no spear. They are called the Sky-Raisers because they appear to be holding up the sky. Each star looks like this: ✷.

Behind the Spearman is a star called the Beggar's Bowl (*qaṣʿah al-masākīn*; the Northern Crown) and a star called the Lion's Rump (*ʿajuz al-asad*)

The Unarmed (Spica) separates the northern from the southern stars.[21]

THE SHROUDED (*al-ghafr*): It consists of three small stars which the Moon enters and which are part of Libra. They are named as such because they appear as if they are the hairs of the lion's tail hanging down. They look like this: ✷✷✷.

THE CLAW (*al-zubānā*): It consists of two bright stars which mark the two claws of Scorpio the scorpion. They look like this: ✷✷.

THE CROWN (*al-iklīl*) consists of four stars, like so: ✷✷✷✷. Some say that they mark the head of Scorpio, with three of them forming a crown on its head.

THE HEART (*al-qalb*) is the heart of the scorpion. It is a luminous star with two other stars, and looks like this: ✷✷✷.

THE STINGING TAIL (*al-shawlah*) consists of two separate stars, sometimes called "the scorpion's stars" (*najmat al-ʿaqrab*); and they look like this: ✷✷. Some say that they are the tail of the scorpion, which the scorpion has raised, as if he is brandishing it

21 Lit. the Yemeni versus the Syrian stars.

(*shā'ilah*). Others say that they are away from the Milky Way, as if they drank from it and left.

☾

THE OSTRICHES (*al-naʿā'im*): It consists of nine stars, some of which are drinking from the Milky Way and others which have already drunk their fill and left.[22] They have also been likened to a wooden post atop a well which a pulley and rope would be attached to.

☾

THE WASTELAND (*al-baldah*): It consists of six stars of Sagittarius the archer. They set with the Sun on the shortest day of the year. Some say that the Wasteland is a cleft between two eyebrows. It looks like this: ✷✷✷✷✷✷.

☾

THE SLAUGHTERER'S JOY (*al-dhābiḥ*) consists of two stars, an arm-span apart. Next to each star is a dimmer star. Each pair looks look like a person about to slaughter an animal, hence the name.

It looks like this: ✷✷ / ✷✷

☾

THE MOST FORTUNATE (*saʿd al-suʿūd*) is a single, brilliant star bringing prosperity. It looks like this: ✷.

☾

THE VORACIOUS AUSPICE (*saʿd balʿ*) is also a single star, like an open mouth about to swallow something. It looks like this: ✷.

22 There is a gap in the manuscript here; this description was taken from Ibn Hatim, *De Imaginibus Caelestis* and *Lane's Lexicon*.

THE AUSPICE OF TENT-POLES (*saʿd al-akhbiyah*) consists of three stars arranged as if they are a cooking-trivet. Then, there is a fourth star beneath the three. They look like this: ✱✱✱✱. However, some people say that this mansion has only two stars.

The other Auspices. Other people mark ten asterisms called *saʿd* ("auspice"), including six which the Moon does not pass through. The four which the Moon passes through are: the Most Fortunate, the Slaughterer's Joy, the Auspice of the Tent-Poles, and the Voracious Auspice. The other six are: the Auspice of the Kingdom, the Auspice of the Livestock (or the Obscure), the Auspice of the Dove, the Auspice of the Skillful, and the Auspice of the Rain.[23] Each of these asterisms called a *saʿd* is formed of two stars an arm-span apart; they are in a uniform layout.

THE FIRST AND SECOND SPOUTS (*fargh al-muqaddam* and *fargh al-muʾakhkhar*): Each of them consists of two stars, five arm-spans apart, as the eye sees, like they are spouts of the bucket of Aquarius. They are spoken of together as the Two Spouts (*al-farghān*).

THE ROPE (*al-rishā*): It consists of many small stars in the shape of a fish. Some call it the Belly of the Fish (*baṭn al-ḥūt*). In its middle is a bright star which the Moon crosses.

These are the mansions of the Moon. The Moon passes through them every month. Each night, the Moon is in one of them. Between sunrise and sunset, fourteen mansions wheel overhead; the same for the time between sunset and sunrise. Dawn is greeted by two mansions. Each rises in the east and sets in the west. If a person is praying while facing Mecca, the mansions will rise to their left and

23 The sources were unclear and variant on the exact spelling of the names of the last six auspices.

set to their right—of course, with variance in different regions. The Sun also passes through these mansions.

The rain-stars

Scholars of ancient Arabian cosmology and lore agree that the *anwā'* were stars that the tribes of the Arabian Peninsula used to predict rain and other seasonal matters; since different tribes were in different regions, there were sometimes some differences. Some tribes also used their own lunar mansions, which, perhaps, travelled to the Arabian Peninsula through trade contacts with India. Eventually, these stars and mansions were integrated into the system of twenty-eight equal lunar mansions.

However, al-Buni's brief remarks suggest that some people shied away from this concept. This may be because, in some early Islamic texts, there is a tension between people who held that the rain-stars were independent actors, versus those who attributed all acts to God. That is, did the stars themselves bring the rain, or did they simply mark when God sent the rain? This is not dissimilar to the debates that arose in later Islam and Christianity over the astrological role of the planets: were the planets independent actors, or simply reflecting the will of God? Furthermore, since the rain-stars were integrated into the equal-mansion system, there may have been a desire to give the equal-system precedence over the ancient star lore.

KNOW THAT THE Arabs called these mansions *anwā'* (sing. *naw'*) because when the westernmost one set, the easternmost one would rise. Some people also hold that they were called *anwā'* because when one of their stars would set in the west, its companion-star would rise in the east at sunrise, each night for thirteen days. This would continue throughout the year, except in the case of the Forehead (*al-jabhah*), when it would take fourteen days.

However, I personally have not heard of the word *anwāʾ* used in this context except in these discussions. The Arabs used to attribute the rain, wind, cold, and heat to them. Thus, ʿUmar ibn al-Khattab, may God be pleased with him, said, "Our rain comes in this-or-that rain-star (*nawʾ*)."[24]

When the mansions rise

The Two Signs (*al-sharaṭayn*) rises on the nineteenth day of April (*Naysān*). On that day, the Sun enters the Crown (*al-iklīl*).

The Belly (*al-baṭīn*) rises when one night remains of April.

The Pleaides (*al-thurayā*) rises on the thirteenth day of May (*Ayyār*). Then it hides beneath the horizon for fifty days, and reappears at sunrise. When it is overhead at sunset, cold weather intensifies, and pestilence dies off from fruit-trees. The Prophet said, "When the Pleiades rises, pestilence dies off."

The Follower (*al-dabarān*) rises on the sixteenth of May.

The Hair-Whorl (*al-haqʿah*) rises on the eighth of June (*Ḥazīrān*).

The Leaning Stars (*al-hanʿah*) rises on the twenty-first of June.

The Forearm (*al-dhirāʿ*) rises on the fourth of July (*Tammūz*).

The Nose-tip (*al-nathrah*) rises on the seventeenth night of July, when Sirius[25] rises.

The Twinkling Eyes (*al-ṭarfah*) rises on the first night of August (*Āb*).

The Forehead (*al-jabhah*) rises on the fourteenth night of August.

The Mane (*al-zubrah*) rises on the twenty-ninth of August.

The Weather-Change (*al-ṣarfah*) rises on the eighth of September (*Aylūl*).

24 ʿUmar ibn al-Khattab (584–644 AD), the second caliph to rule the nascent Muslim empire.

25 *Al-shiʿrā al-ʿabūr*, the One who Crossed Over—that is, who crossed over the Milky Way to be with her brother Suhayl (Canopus), leaving their sister, the Weeping Star (*al-shiʿrā al-ghumayṣāʾ*; Procyon) on her own. Legend has it that Suhayl fled for his life after a disaster on his wedding night.

The Howling Dogs (*al-ʿawwā*) rises on the nineteenth night of September.

The Sky-Raiser (*al-simmāk*) rises when two nights remain of September.

The Shrouded (*al-ghafr*) rises on the twelfth of October (*Tishrīn al-Awwal*).

The Claw (*al-zubānā*) rises on the twenty-fifth of October.

The Crown (*al-iklīl*) rises on the eighth of November (*Tishrīn al-Thānī*).

The Heart (*al-qalb*) rises on the twenty-first of November.

The Stinging Tail (*al-shawlah*) rises on the third of December (*Kānūn Awwal*).

The Ostriches (*al-naʿāʾim*) rises on the sixteenth of December.

The Wasteland (*al-baldah*) rises on the twenty-ninth of December.

The Slaughterer's Joy (*saʿd al-dhābiḥ*) rises on the eleventh night of January (*Kānūn Thānī*).

The Most Fortunate (*saʿd al-suʿūd*) rises on the sixth of February (*Shubāṭ*).

The Auspice of Tent-poles (*saʿd al-akbiyah*) rises on the eighteenth of February.

The Voracious Auspice (*saʿd balʿ*) on the twenty-sixth of February.

The First Spout (*al-fargh al-muqaddim*) rises when two nights have passed in March (*Ādhār*).

The Second Spout (*al-fargh al-muʾakhkhar*) rises on the fourteenth of March.

The Rope (*al-rishā*) rises on the fourth of April (*Naysān*).

And God knows best.

How the lunar mansions are divided among the four seasons

This refers to which mansion the Sun is in, and which mansion is rising at sunrise or setting at sunset along with the Sun.

Know that the mansions are divided as follows:

SPRING: The Two Signs, the Belly, the Pleaides, the Follower, the Hair-Whorl, the Leaning Stars, and the Forearm.

SUMMER: The Nose-tip, the Twinkling Eyes, the Forehead, the Mane, the Weather-Change, the Sky-Raiser, and the Howling Dogs

AUTUMN: The Shrouded, the Claw, the Crown, the Heart, the Stinging Tail, the Ostriches, and the Wasteland

WINTER: The Most Fortunate, the Slaughterer's Joy, the Auspice of Tent-Poles, the Voracious Auspice, the First Spout, the Second Spout, and the Rope.

Each season has seven mansions.

The ancient Arab rhyming proverbs about the lunar mansions

This section relates a selection of early Arabic rhyming proverbs about the stars associated with lunar mansions figured into daily life.

It is related that our teacher, al-Kindi, may God have mercy upon him, said that the Arabs used to say:[26]

> When the Two Signs (*al-sharaṭayn*) rises, the day and night are equal,[27] trees grow green shoots, cities prosper, neighbors are kind to each other, and beggars sleep everywhere.
>
> When the Belly (*al-baṭīn*) rises, debts are paid.
>
> When the Pleaides (*al-thurayā*) rises at night, give your shepherd a cloak; when it rises at dawn, give him a water-skin.
>
> When the Follower (*al-dabarān*) rises, crops scorch, and streams dry up.
>
> When the Hair-Whorl (*al-haqʿah*) rises, people scout for food.
>
> When the Leaning Stars (*al-hanʿah*) rises, gird your stomachs.[28]
>
> When the Forearm (*al-dhirāʿ*) rises, the Sun unveils its rays, and mirages glisten everywhere.
>
> When the Nose-tip (*al-nathrah*) rises, the bee rejoices at plenty, but cows give not a drop to drink.

26 The text gives a line of transmission of this as being Abu Mansur al-Khawlani from al-Mughni from Abu Muḥammad al-Manawi. It is typical for classical Islamic texts to provide a person-to-person chain going from teacher to student or copyist, as it provided a means of authenticating a text before the era of mass printing.

27 This is because, in the first century BC, the stars of *al-sharaṭān* marked the beginning of spring. However, due to stellar precession, that was no longer true by the time of al-Buni. Still, the association of *al-sharaṭān* with spring persists. And, in any case, the rising of the tropical zodiacal sign of Aries along with the mansion of the Two Signs still marks the beginning of spring.

28 An alternate text says, "Strength falters."

When the Twinkling Eyes (*al-ṭarfah*) rises, hosting guests becomes a delight.

When the Howling Dogs (*al-ʿawwā*) rises, nomads settle, and the breeze is pleasant.

When the Sky-Raiser (*al-simmāk*) rises, waters are thronged.

When the Shrouded (*al-ghafr*) rises, travellers return.

When the Claw (*al-zubānā*) rises, everyone is preoccupied with looking after his family.

When the two Spouts (*farghān*) rise, along with the Vulture (al-nasr; Vega), streams overflow at every bridge.

When the Crown (*al-iklīl*) rises, excuses fail.

When the Heart (*al-qalb*) rises, every difficulty eases.

When the Stinging Tail (*al-shawlah*) rises, old men rush to urinate.

When the Ostriches (*al-naʿāʾim*) rises, the cold hits everything standing.

When the Wasteland (*al-baldah*) rises, you eat wheat-butter gruel—and this is made by scraping the bottom of the barrel.[29]

When the Most Fortunate (*saʿd al-suʿūd*) rises, green shoots grow, skins soften, and no one likes to sit in the sun.

29 The text adds that another version says that "you eat *jaʿdah*, a well-known plant."

When the Slaughterer's Joy (*al-dhābiḥ*) rises, dogs guard their owners.

When the Auspice of Tent-Poles (*saʿd al-akhbiyah*) rises, people like to wear cloaks.

When the Voracious Auspice (*saʿd balʿ*) rises, the baby camel walks, and earth glistens.

When the First Spout (*al-fargh al-muqaddim*) rises, serve and do not regret.

When the Second Spout (*al-fargh al-muʾakhkhir*) rises, hasten and do not delay.

When the Fish (*al-samakah*) rises, it is possible to travel, and thorns catch on things.[30]

These are some of the ancient rhymes of the Arabs. We have mentioned them to wrap up our discussion of the mansions. And God knows best.

30 The text clarifies that this occurs with the thorns of the *saʿdān* plant.

Chapter 4

THE TWELVE SIGNS OF THE ZODIAC AND THE PLANETS

KNOW—MAY GOD BLESS you and me with obedience towards Him—that God said about the twelve zodiacal signs and twenty-eight mansions:

> And We made the zodiacal signs (*burūjan*) in the heavens, and adorned them to the beholders.
>
> (QUR'AN 15:16)

> Blessed be He who placed in the heavens the zodiacal signs (*burūjan*), and placed therein a lamp and a shining Moon.
>
> (QUR'AN 25:61)

> By the sky, filled with the zodiacal constellations (*burūj*).
>
> (QUR'AN 85:1)

> And We measured out mansions (*manāzil*) for the Moon.
>
> (QUR'AN 36:39)

Burj ("zodiacal sign," "constellation"; also "tower," "castle") is the singular of *burūj*. *Burj* also means "castle" and sometimes "stronghold." For instance, the Qur'an uses that word to mean "stronghold" in the expression "though you be in lofty towers" (4:78). Al-Hasan al-Basri, may God's mercy be upon him, said: "*Burūj* speaks of castles in the sky, just as there are castles on earth."[1] Other scholars say that the verse "blessed be He who placed in the heavens the zodiacal signs (*burūjan*)" refers to the places that the seven planets travel though, and that they are the twelve zodiacal signs; namely: Aries, Taurus, Gemini, Cancer, Leo, Virgo, Libra, Scorpio, Sagittarius, Capricorn, Aquarius, and Pisces.

Aries and Scorpio are the domiciles (*bayt*)[2] of Mars. Taurus is the domicile of Venus. Gemini and Virgo are the domiciles of Mercury. Cancer is the domicile of the Moon. Leo is the domicile of the Sun. Pisces is the domicile of Jupiter. Capricorn and Aquarius are the domicile of Saturn.

This is how the constellations are divided between the four elements. Each element is associated with three signs, and is called a "triplicity" (*muthallathah*). Aries, Leo, and Sagittarius are the fire triplicity; Taurus, Virgo, and Capricorn are the earth triplicity; Gemini, Libra, and Aquarius are the air triplicity; and Cancer, Scorpio, and Pisces are the watery triplicity.

Qur'anic exegetes disagree over what the word *burūj* means in these verses. Some say they are castles in the sky, as evinced by the expression "though you be in lofty towers" (Qur'an 4:78). Some say that *burūj* refers to stars. Some say that it refers to lights or lamps. And still others say they are the gates to the heavens, which is another expression for the Milky Way.

My view matches that which has been related from Ibn ʿAbbas,[3] may God be pleased with him—that the *burūj* are what are commonly known as the twelve zodiacal signs, and that God divided them into groups of four and triplicities. That is, they are divided among the seven planets, as we have already mentioned. Different peoples call them different names, in their own languages, but they agree on what is meant.

1 Al-Hasan al-Basri (c. 642–728) was a famous Islamic scholar, exegete, and mystic.
2 *Bayt* means "house." In traditional astrology, a planet is considered to be strongest when it is in its own sign. "Domicile" is commonly used in traditional Western astrology.
3 An early Muslim famous for providing explanations of the Qur'an.

THE CONSTELLATIONS OF THE ZODIAC

ARIES THE RAM (*al-ḥamal*), the first sign: It consists of thirteen stars, five of which lie outside the main form. They form the figure of a ram (*kabsh*). Its head faces west, and its tail end faces east; it is gazing backwards such that its muzzle rests upon it back. It includes the stars of the Two Signs (*al-sharaṭayn*) which form one of the mansions of the Moon.

TAURUS THE BULL (*al-thawr*), the second sign: It consists of thirty-three stars, eleven of which lie outside the main form. It depicts the silhouette of the front half of a bull with its head hanging down, looking back towards the Butting of the Ram (*al-naṭḥ*, the first lunar mansion). At its navel, it is split into two halves, the front facing east, and the rear facing west. Its stars include those in the lunar mansions called the Pleaides (*al-thurayā*) and the Follower (*al-dabarān*).

GEMINI THE TWINS (*al-jawzā'*, also *al-tawa'mān*), the third sign:[4] It consists of eighteen stars, seven outside the main form. It depicts two standing children, one of whom has placed his hand on the shoulder of the other. Their heads and the other stars of the constellation are to the north and east, following the path of the Milky Way. Their legs face west.

CANCER THE CRAB (*al-saraṭān*), the fourth sign: It consists of seven stars, four of which lie outside its main form. It faces east, with its hind side facing west and south, following the Twins, as if they are both inclining south towards the Milky Way.

4 When two or more names for the same sign are listed, it is because the author himself has mentioned them.

LEO THE LION (*al-asad*), the fifth sign: It consists of twenty-seven stars, eight of which lie outside its main form. It stands upright, and includes the brilliant star Regulus (*qalb al-asad*, lit. "heart of the lion").

VIRGO THE MAIDEN (*al-ʿadhrā*) or the Grain-Spike (*al-sunbulah*), the sixth sign: It consists of twenty-six stars, six of which lie outside the main form. It depicts a maiden with two wings. Her skirt brushes the ground, and her head is upon the star marking the Weather-Change (*al-ṣarfah*). The bright star Spica (*al-simmāk al-aʿzal*, "the unarmed sky-raiser") rests on her left shoulder.

LIBRA THE SCALES (*al-mīzān*), the seventh sign: It consists of eight stars. It depicts a set of scales, like the name says. Nine additional stars lie outside it.

SCORPIO THE SCORPION (*al-ʿaqrab*), the eighth sign: It consists of twenty-one stars, three of which lie outside of the main form. It depicts a complete scorpion, standing tall.[5] One of its stars is the bright star Antares (*qalb al-ʿaqrab*, lit. "the heart of the scorpion").

SAGITTARIUS THE ARCHER (*al-qaws*, also *al-rāmī*), the ninth sign: It consists of twenty-one stars which follow behind the stars of the Scorpion. It depicts a creature which is half-man half-horse—its body up until the shoulder is a horse, and then, after that, it is a man. He has drawn his bow and is leaning forward in the saddle.

CAPRICORN THE GOAT (*al-jaddī*), the tenth sign: It consists of twenty-eight stars. The front half depicts a goat, and the rear half depicts a fish up until its tail.

5 Sources vary between "complete" and "tall" (*tāmm* versus *qām*); however, both descriptions are apt.

AQUARIUS THE WATER-BEARER (*al-dālī* or *al-dalw* and also *sākib al-mā'*, "the water-pourer"), the eleventh sign: It consists of forty-two stars, three of which are outside the main form. It depicts a man standing, his hands held out. In one hand is an overturned jug. He is spilling the water towards his feet while water flows from atop to the south.

PISCES THE FISH (*al-ḥūt*), the twelfth sign:[6] It consists of thirty-four stars, four of which lie outside its main form. It depicts two fish; the tail of one joins the tail of the other.

Altogether, these constellations include three-hundred stars, although some people say they include three-hundred forty stars. Note that some people define the zodiacal constellations differently. They say that Aries and Taurus are zodiacal constellations, but that Gemini is a star overhead in the sky; they say it is called *al-jawzā* because it is in the middle of the sky, and the word *jawz* denotes the middle of a thing.[7] Then they identify Cancer as a zodiacal constellation, but do not mention Leo. Virgo too is a zodiacal constellation, but some people do not mention Libra. They identify Scorpio as a zodiacal constellation, and similarly Sagittarius. They observe that Capricorn is near a star by the north pole which one can use to find the direction for prayer (*al-qiblah*, i.e. the direction towards Mecca).

THE LANDS RULED BY EACH SIGN OF THE ZODIAC

Know that Aries rules Babylon, Persia, and Azerbaijan.

Taurus rules Hamedan and the Kurds.

6 A *ḥūt* is a rather large fish, such as a whale. For instance, the Qur'an speaks of Jonah being swallowed by the *ḥūt*. Of course, zodiacal constellations are by nature large.

7 Like the middle of an empty desert, or the nut inside a shell.

Gemini rules Gorgan, Gilan, and Sufan.

Cancer rules China and eastern Khorasan.

Leo rules the Turks, the Tatars, and those adjacent to them.

Virgo rules the Levant, as well as the Tigris, the Euphrates, and the lands between the two.

Libra rules the Roman lands stretching towards Africa, Egypt, Ethiopia, and Sudan.

Scorpio rules the Hijaz [the Western Arabian Peninsula], Yemen, and the neighboring regions.

Sagittarius rules the territory from Baghdad to Isfahan.

Capricorn rules Kerman, Oman, Bahrain, and India.

Aquarius rules the territory from Kufa to the Hijaz.

Pisces rules Tabaristan and Alexandria. It also shares rulership over the Roman lands, the land between the Tigris and the Euphrates, the Levant, and Egypt.

These are some of the inhabited lands; we have mentioned them to round off our discussion on the signs of the zodiac.

THE FOUR SEASONS

Perhaps the most valuable thing the reader can take from this section is that, throughout the centuries, people have not agreed on what to call the seasons. Fortunately, an astronomical definition of the beginning of a season solves the dispute.

The subject of the four seasons returns in Chapter 8, in which al-Buni presents evocations to the rulers of the four seasons.

AUTUMN (*rabīʿ*). People call it different names. The Arabs called it *rabīʿ* because rains came then. Others call it *kharīf* because fruit are harvested then. It begins when the Sun enters Libra.[8]

WINTER (*shittā*). It begins when the Sun enters Capricorn.

SPRING (*ṣayf*).[9] It begins when the Sun enters Aries. Commonfolk also call it *rabīʿ*.

SUMMER (*qayḍ*). It begins when the Sun enters Cancer. Commonfolk also call it *ṣayf*.

THE FOUR WINDS

The north wind (*rīḥ al-shamāl*) blows from the north pole.

The east wind (*ṣabā*) blows from the place where the Sun rises on the equinox.

Next is the west wind (*al-dabūr*). The Arabs held that the west wind disturbed the clouds, drove them across the sky, and blew them lower. Then, if they encountered the eastern wind, they would pile on top of each other until they became a dense mass.

The south wind (*janūb*) blows against the north wind, just as the west wind blows against the east wind. And God knows best.

8 Today, *rabīʿ* is generally used for spring.

9 Today, *ṣayf* is generally used for summer; *qayḍ* also has the meaning of an extremely hot part of summer. Perhaps the uses of the seasons here reflect a climate which is better characterized by two seasons—hot and cold—rather than four seasons.

ISLAMIC NARRATIONS ABOUT THE SEVEN HEAVENS

The Qur'an speaks of "seven heavens" and "seven earths" but does not specify what is meant by those phrases. These narrations attributed to the Prophet Muhammad and early Muslims are intended to shed light on the question of "what are the seven heavens"?

We have already discussed how the ancients envisioned the celestial realm. This is what religious scholars[10] have to say about the heavens.

It is related from Ibn ʿAbbas—or [his father] al-ʿAbbas ibn ʿAbd al-Muttalib:[11]

We were with the Prophet in a place called al-Bathaʾ, and a cloud passed by. The Prophet said, "Do you know what this is?"
We said, "A cloud."
He said, "And rainclouds."
We said, "And rainclouds."
He said, "Clouds, or the highest heavens (*ʿanān*)."[12]
We said, "And the highest heavens?" and then fell silent.
The Prophet said, "Do you know how far the heavens are from the earth?"
We said, "God and His Messenger know best."
He said, "They lie five hundred years' distance apart; each level of the heavens is five-hundred years high. In the seventh heaven, there is a sea whose depth is the same as the distance between

10 Literally *mutasharriʿīn*, "people who make Islamic law."
11 One of the manuscripts has "Ibn ʿAbd al-Malik" in place of "Ibn ʿAbd al-Muttalib"; this is a clear error insofar as Ibn ʿAbbas and his father are well-known historically due to being close relatives of the Prophet Muhammad as well as early Muslims. However, the scribe can be forgiven, as it is a painstaking task to copy such a lengthy book.
12 *ʿAnān* has a dual meaning of "clouds" and "the highest heavens."

> the heavens and earth. Then, above them, are eight [angels in the form of] goats. The distance between each of their hooves and knees is the same distance as there is between the heavens and the earth. And God is above that. None of the deeds of the children of Adam are hidden from God."[13]

This can be proved by the verse: "God is the one who created the seven heavens and, like them, seven earths" (Qur'an 65:12). Thus, each is fourteen-thousand years wide; everything in the heavens—the divine veils, the throne, and the seat of divinity—equals the distance that the children of Adam would travel.[14] However, angels speed through the heavens in a single hour—some of them in a single moment. Similarly, Satan can dart to the earth just like an angel in the heavens.[15]

Abu Rakid[16] relates from ʿAli:[17]

> ʿAli was asked, "How far are the heavens from the earth?"
> He said, "The distance of an answered prayer."
> Someone asked him, "How far is the east from the west?"
> He said, "A day's travel."

Thaʿlabi relates from Ibn ʿAbbas:

> Each year, the Sun rises in one of three-hundred sixty apertures (*kuwwah*); it only rises in that aperture on that day of the year, and then it will have to wait until the next year.

The Sun provides many benefits and illustrates many truths. There is but one Sun, yet it illuminates the whole world. Similarly,

13 A similar narration is found in the famous book of Prophetic narrations called *Sunan Ibn Majah*.
14 *Ḥujub*, *kursī*, and *ʿarsh*, respectively.
15 The printed version says that Satan can get to the earth faster than the angels; this is what is found in the primary manuscript used.
16 Or Rakah.
17 ʿAli ibn Abi Talib (599–661 AD), the fourth Muslim caliph and a central figure in Islamic spirituality; most Sufi lineages trace back to him.

the Creator—exalted be He!—is one, and administers the whole world. Second, although the Sun is far from us, its light is near; similarly, God is far from the creation in terms of His divine essence, but near when answering prayers. Third, no one is deprived of its light. Similarly, God provides for everyone without depriving anyone. Fourth, eclipses illustrate to us that we will be resurrected after death, just as nightfall tells us of its darkness. Fifth, the clouds shade it, just as committing sins obscures a person from attaining true knowledge of God.

As for its benefits, they are copious. First, it is a lamp for the world; God says, "And God made it a shining lamp" (Qur'an 71:16). Second, it dries provisions and ripens fruits without requiring any extra effort or trouble. Third, it travels from east to west to benefit people. Fourth, it never stops in any one place, lest it harm any creatures. Fifth, during winter, it is in its lowest constellations; and, during summer, it is in its highest constellations—this, for the benefit of the world. Sixth, it never shines in the same spot as the Moon, lest sunlight and moonlight clash.

You might argue, "But it is in the fourth celestial sphere,[18] and the heavens do not shield it; rather, the clouds shield it." Should you say that, I would reply, "The heavens are composed of a subtle, delicate essence, whereas the clouds are thick and heavy, because they rise from the earth."

18 Here, referring to the mediaeval celestial or planetary spheres, rather than the "seven heavens."

A PARABLE FROM THE PROPHET MUHAMMAD ABOUT THE MOON

Abū Hurayrah relates:[19]

Some people asked the Prophet, "Will we be able to see our Lord on the Day of Resurrection?"
He said, "Do you have any difficulty seeing the full Moon when it is not covered by any clouds?"
They said, "No."
He said, "Do you have any difficulty seeing the Sun when it is not covered by any clouds?"
They said, "No."
He said, "Thusly you will see God."[20]

You might ask why he is making a parable out of both the Sun and the Moon when Sun shines brighter and never wanes. Were you to ask that, I would reply in two ways. Firstly, since the light of the Sun overwhelms people's eyes, they cannot gaze upon it directly. Therefore, it eludes them; they cannot reach their goal. However, the Moon is different, for eyes can behold it. Secondly, the moonlight was diminished for the sake of God,[21] who made it to be such. For when Gabriel spread his wings across the Moon, its light faltered. His heart broke since, before that, the light of the Moon had rivalled the light of the Sun. Therefore, God compelled the Moon to do two things. First, He made it mark the first day of every month for the people of the world. Second, He instructed His prophet—

19 Abu Hurayrah (603–681) was a companion of the Prophet Muhammad to whom many Prophetic narrations are ascribed. He is said to have acquired his nickname (which means "Father of the Kitten") due to having a kitten he was particularly fond of.

20 This is also related in a book of narrations attributed to the Prophet Muhammad called *Ṣaḥīḥ al-Bukhārī*. The first sentence was not included in the text here but was included to contextualize the excerpt.

21 Literally *al-ḥaqq*, "the Truth"; another name for God.

may the peace and blessings of God be upon him—to use it as a parable for the greatest and highest of matters.

If you were to argue that God says in the Qur'an, "Sight comprehends God not, but God comprehends all sight" (6:103), I would reply that we are not claiming that eyes can "comprehend" God, in the sense of encompassing Him. Rather, what it means for something to be "comprehended" is to be captured by the gaze. Otherwise, the Creator—exalted be He—cannot be materialized.

The Moon has many benefits. Among them are that it is a lamp for creation at night, and that our prophet Muhammad wrought a miracle through it: "The Hour has drawn nigh, and the Moon has been split in two" (54:1).[22] God apportioned mansions for it so that we would be able to measure time, and He erased ninety-nine parts of its light, as in the verse: "So We effaced the sign of the night, and made the sign of the day, giving sight" (Qur'an 17:12). Were it not for that, people would have left their dwellings night and day, and no one would have known whether it was night or day. And the Commander of the Faithful, ʿAli ibn Abi Talib, said: "Sleeping naked beneath the Moon begets leprosy, and when a garment is washed and hung under the Moon, it frays and shows signs of wear."[23] And God knows best.

THE KNOWN STARS AND CONSTELLATIONS[24]

As elsewhere in the book, the Arabic names of the stars and constellations have been translated into English, with the Arabic transliteration and corresponding English names in parentheses. However, in cases where the English (or sometimes Lat-

22 This is referring to a miracle attributed to the Prophet Muhammad, in which some people challenged the Prophet to perform a miracle, so he raised his hand and the Moon split in two.

23 This saying is not attributed to ʿAli ibn Abi Talib in any other prominent extant sources. ʿAli ibn Abi Talib (599–661 AD), the fourth Muslim caliph and a central figure in Islamic spirituality; most Sufi lineages trace back to him.

24 The preceding paragraph was omitted since it is just a sequential list of the twenty-eight lunar mansions.

inate) names parallel the Arabic names—such as in the case of Triangulum and "the Triangle"—no translation has been given in the parentheses. In a few places, the standard English names were used for clarity, such as in the case of the North Star.

GOD SAYS: "He it is Who has made for you the stars, that you might be guided by them amid the darkness of land and sea" and "By the stars, you are guided" (Qur'an 6:97 and 16:16). And it is narrated from Saʿid ibn Jubayr that Ibn ʿAbbas—may God be pleased with him—said, "Astronomy (*ʿilm al-nujūm*) offers enormous benefits that most people miss out on." He was referring to observational knowledge of the stars, not the significance attached to them. People agree that the light of the Moon arises from the light of the Sun; however, they disagree about where the light of the stars come from. Does it also come from the Sun, or somewhere else?

There are one-thousand twenty-two known stars. They include the following.

THE NORTH STAR ("the Goat Kid," *najm al-jaddī*): It is the best star to use to find the direction of prayer;[25] it lies near the north pole.[26] Around it is a ring of stars, like the wheel of a hand-mill. Nearby are the two stars known as the TWO CALVES (*al-farqadān*, the Little Dipper asterism): PHERKAD and KOCHAB.[27] A bright star faces them. Between those stars and that bright star are three stars above, three stars below, wheeling around the North Star; they do not move from their places. The North Star is the axis of this wheel

25 The *qiblah*; the direction towards Mecca.

26 A thousand years ago, Polaris was not quite as close to the north pole as it is today. The author notes another view that there is another star closer to the north pole.

27 Pherkad is also known as Gamma Ursae Minoris, and Kochab is also known as Beta Ursae Minoris. The English name Kochab is derived from the Arabic *kawkab* (meaning "star" or "planet"). Pherkad comes from *farqad* meaning "calf."

and points towards the north pole. Nearby, the DAUGHTERS OF THE BIER (*banāt naʿsh*, the Big Dipper) cycle around the North Star and the pole.

> The stars of the Big Dipper were called the Daughters of the Bier because the square part of the dipper was envisioned as a bier (*naʿsh*); the three daughters (*banāt*) of the deceased followed behind it. A similar depiction is also used for the Little Dipper, which is referred to as the Daughters of the Smaller Bier.

Some say that the axis of this wheel does indeed demarcate the pole, and that the North Star indicates it when there is no Moon. However, when the Moon is bright, only someone with eyesight as sharp as iron can see it.

SUHA (Alcor) is to its side. It is a faint star which people can use to test their eyesight. The North Star, which is used to find the direction of prayer, is one of the Daughters of the Smaller Bier (Little Dipper). The Smaller Bier is comprised of the Two Calves[28] in front, then the other daughters, and finally the North Star. Suha is a faint star in the Greater Bier (Big Dipper). It is mentioned in the proverb: "Show her Suha, and she shows me the Moon."[29]

How to find the direction of prayer (*qiblah*) via the North Star: If you are in Syria, place it behind your back. If you are in Iraq, place it opposite your right ear. In Egypt, place it behind your right side. Although it is quite high, you will be facing the door to the Sacred House, where Abraham stood.[30] When your back is to the Two

28 *Al-farqadān*, Pherkad and Gamma Ursae Minoris.

29 Meaning, to try to explain something to someone who doesn't get it, since the Moon is so much brighter than Alcor. See also E.W. Lane, *Lane's Lexicon*, s.v. *s-h-w*.

30 The "Sacred House" refers to the Kaʿbah in Mecca which is faced by Muslims during prayer. The complex of the Kaʿbah contains a stone called the "station of Abraham" which is said to retain an imprint of Abraham's footprint; this is what is being referred to in the text.

Calves[31] or the Greater Bier (the Big Dipper), you will be facing the Kaʿbah in Mecca.

The Two Calves are two shining stars near the pole. The Daughters of the Bier consists of seven stars, four of which form the bier, and three of which are the daughters. The same with the Daughters of the Lesser Bier (*naʿsh ṣughrā*). Neither the Sun nor the Moon reaches the north pole.

The south pole is marked by the rising of SUHAYL (Canopus), which can only be seen from the Arabian Peninsula.[32] Suhayl is by the south pole, and rises from the place where the south wind blows from.[33] Then it travels west, marking the direction of prayer, then sets. It is a lone, unusually red star; because it is so low on the horizon, it seems to pulsate. It is one of eight stars which rise to the left of the direction of prayer. It is visible in all of the Arab regions of Iraq and the Levant, but cannot be seen in the Byzantine lands. There are ten-odd days between the day that it rises in the western Arabian Peninsula (the Hijaz) and when it rises in Iraq. Some call Suhayl the "star of the Arabs" (*najm al-ʿarab*).[34] As a saying goes, when Suhayl rises, one is not safe from floods.

Know that of these one thousand twenty-two stars, three hundred and twelve stars are in twelve constellations which lie along the path of the Sun; those are the twelve zodiacal constellations. There are also three-hundred sixty stars in twenty-one constellations north of the ecliptic; they include the GREAT BEAR, the LITTLE BEAR,[35] the DRAGON (*al-tinnīn*; Draco), and others. There are

31 *Al-farqadān*; Pherkad and Kochab.

32 Occasionally, especially in mediaeval works, Canopus is known in English as Soheil or Suhel. It is not visible in mid-to-northern latitudes but would have been visible in North Africa and the Arabian Peninsula.

33 Suhayl effectively marked the direction of south in the Arabian Peninsula since it rarely rose very high in that latitude, so it would be like a beacon pointing southwards. Because of this, Suhayl rose and set fairly quickly, and thus became metaphorical for someone who was unreliable. One side of the Kaʿbah in Mecca was aligned with Suhayl, and this is why it could be used to determine the direction of prayer.

34 Possibly, this is because of its role in ancient Arab sky lore, its use by Arab tribes in tracking seasons, and its visibility in the Arabian Peninsula.

35 Here, al-Buni refers to the Big and Little Dipper as the Greater and Lesser

also three-hundred sixteen stars in fifteen constellations south of the ecliptic. However, people rely on the parans when there is an observable arch between the stars. Apart from the stars that we already mentioned, most astronomers disagree on their names or how they should be constellated. Abu Muhammad ʿAbd al-Jabbar, known for his book *Insights into the Fixed Stars* (*al-Basrah fi al-Kawakib al-Thabitah*), says:

> The northern stars include the Little Bear, which depicts a bear standing and stretching its tail. It consists of seven stars. The Arabs called it the Daughters of the Lesser Bier (*banāt naʿsh al-ṣughrā*). Four of its stars form the Bier (*naʿsh*); they are in the shape of a square. There are three stars at its tail. At the end is the North Star, which guides a person towards the direction of prayer. Altogether, there are eight stars, seven of which form the Dipper. They are the stars observed near the north pole.

My view is that this should also include the Great Bear. That is, it should include twenty-seven stars, eight of which are outside the constellation. It should also include the seven stars that the Arabs identified as the Greater Bier—four in its body, and three in its tail, one of which the Arabs called the LEADER (*al-qāʾid*; Alkaid). Then come the stars called the SHE-KID (*ʿanāq*; Mizar) and the BLACK HORSE (*jawn*; Alioth); near the She-Kid is the faint star called Suha.

The northern constellations also include the following.

THE DRAGON (*al-tinnīn*), which is composed of thirty-one stars and depicts an enormous, powerful serpent with many curves. Its head is marked by four stars in a tilted square; the Arabs called those stars the CAMEL-MOTHERS (*al-ʿawāʾidh*). The Dragon also demarcates a specific part of the sky, and a *tinnīn* is a gargantuan serpent.

Bears, rather than the Daughters of the Bier.

THE BEGGAR'S BOWL, which is also called the NORTHERN CROWN (*al-iklīl al-shamālī*). The Beggar's Bowl is known as such because it consists of a ring of eight stars; it is behind the SPEAR-BEARING SKY-RAISER (Arcturus).

THE KNEELER (*al-jāthī*; Hercules), who is upon his knees. It is made up of twenty-nine stars, including the stars of Lyra (*al-salbāq*). Some call it the Lyre (*al-lūzā*) or the Byzantine Cymbals (*al-ṣunj al-rūmī*).

THE TURTLE (*al-salaḥfāh*), which has ten stars, including the bright star called the Vulture (*al-nasr al-wāqi*ʿ; Vega).[36]

THE HEN (*al-dajājah*; Cygnus) has seventeen stars, two of which lie outside of the main image of the constellation. Most its stars lie in the Milky Way, near the Vulture.

THE QUEEN (*dhāt al-kursī*; Cassiopeia) which depicts a woman sitting on a throne with her feet dangling; she is inside the Milky Way. In this constellation lies the star called the DYED PALM;[37] it is in the middle of the back of the throne and is also known as the CAMEL-HUMP (*sanām al-nāqah*).

PERSEUS (*barshāwus*), also known as the BEARER OF THE GHOUL'S HEAD (*ḥāmil ra*ʾ*s al-ghūl*). It consists of twenty-six stars, three or six of which lie outside the main form; the most accurate view is that three stars lie outside the main form. It depicts a man standing on his left foot, his right foot upraised. His right hand is above his head, and in his left hand is the severed HEAD OF THE GHOUL (*ra*ʾ*s al-ghūl*; Algol).

36 In modern Arabic, *nasr* often denotes an eagle; "vulture" would have been a more appropriate earlier usage. This impression was also preserved in the mediaeval Latin rendering of the name as Vultura Cadens. In ancient Egypt, it was also depicted as a vulture, and in India, as both an eagle and a vulture. The English name Vega is a Latinization of *al-wāqi*ʿ, "alighting."

37 Beta Cassiopeiae.

THE CHARIOTEER (*mamsak al-ʿinān*; Auriga) consists of fourteen stars. It depicts a man standing. In one hand, he holds a whip; and, in the other, the reins, behind the IMPEDER (*ʿayyuq*).[38]

THE SNAKE-CATCHER (*al-ḥayyā*; Ophiuchus) consists of twenty-four stars, five of which lie outside the main form. It depicts a standing man who has grabbed a snake with his hands. Then there is the actual SNAKE (*al-ḥawā*; Serpens), which consists of eighteen stars, and which has raised its head and tail above his head.

THE ARROW (*al-sahm*; Eridanus), consists of five stars, like the beak of the HEN and the FLYING VULTURE (*al-nasr al-ṭāʾir*; Altair).

THE EAGLE (*al-ʿuqāb*; Aquila) consists of nine stars, six of which lie outside the main form. It includes the FLYING VULTURE (Altair) because its wings are outstretched.

THE DOLPHIN (*al-dulfīn*; Delphinus) consists of ten stars grouped behind the FLYING VULTURE (Altair). It depicts a sea-creature resembling an opened water-skin; not all astronomers have mentioned it in their catalogues. A *dulfīn* is an animal which lives in the sea and which saves people who are drowning.

THE PIECE OF THE HORSE (*qitʿat al-faras*, Equuleus) consists of four stars. They are said to depict the front of a horse, behind the stars of the Dolphin.

PEGASUS (*al-faras al-akbar*) has two wings. It consists of twenty stars in the shape of a horse. It has a head and forelegs, but does not have its hindlegs or hindquarters.

ANDROMEDA (*andrūmīdā*), also known as the Chained Woman (*al-marʾah al-musalsalah*) consists of twenty-two stars and depicts

38 Theta Aurigae.

a woman standing with her hands outstretched. On her hand is a chain; some say that the chain is on her feet.

TRIANGULUM (*al-muthallath*) consists of four stars between Pisces and the bright star by the HEAD OF THE GHOUL (*ra's al-ghūl*; Algol).

All of these constellations are north of the ecliptic, and they include three hundred sixty stars.

The southern constellations are comprised of three-hundred twelve stars. They include the following.

CETUS (*qayṭus*), which has twenty-two stars and depicts a sea-creature with two legs and a fish's tail.

THE GIANT (*al-jabbār*; Orion) is made up of thirty-eight stars. It depicts a seated man with a staff in his hand. At his waist are his girdle and sword. It includes the bright red star BETELGEUSE (*al-jawzā'*).

ERIDANUS (*al-nahr*) is made up of twenty-four stars and resembles a very twisty river.

THE RABBIT (*al-arnab*; Lepus) consists of twelve stars beneath Orion's feet; they look as if they are a rabbit whose face is to the west and whose back is to the east.

CANIS MAJOR (*al-kalb al-akbar*) consists of twenty-eight stars, with eleven stars outside the constellation and trailing behind Orion, facing the SHIP (*al-safīnah*). It includes the bright stars Sirius (*al-shiʿrā al-ʿabūr*) and Mirzam.[39]

39 *Mirzam* was a term used for moderately bright stars; in this case, it refers to a star called *mirzam al-shiʿrā*, a bright star near Sirius which, in English, is also called Mirzam.

SIRIUS (*al-shiʿrā*) is the star which rises after Orion. When it rises, it portends intense heat. There are two stars called "Sirius"—the one who crossed over and the one who is weeping. The Arabs said that they were the sisters of Suhayl (Canopus).[40]

THE TWO MIRZAMS (*al-mirzamān*) are two stars accompanying Sirius and Procyon. One is in the same constellation as Procyon, and the other is in the lunar mansion called the Forearm (*al-dhirāʿ*).

CANIS MINOR (*al-kalb al-aṣghar*) consists of two stars. One is the Syrian Sirius (*al-shiʿrā al-shāmiyyah*) and the other is the WEEPING STAR (*al-ghumayṣā*; Procyon). They are both quite bright.

THE SHIP (*al-safīnah*; Argo Navis)[41] consists of forty-five stars congregated together in the south. They rise after Canis Minor. One of them is Suhayl (Canopus), the gleaming red star.

HYDRA (*al-shujāʿ*) consists of twenty-five stars, two of which lie outside its main form. It depicts an extraordinarily long, bendy serpent with its head resting upon the four stars of Pegasus. It extends long, from the claws of Scorpio to Cancer.[42] and is between Canis Minor[43] and the Heart of the Lion (Regulus).

THE GOBLET (*al-kaʾs*; Crater) consists of seven stars in a circle. They are by the back of Hydra and are also called the Dish (*al-bāṭiyyah*).

40 The "weeping Sirius" is Procyon; the one who crossed over is Sirius proper. See Chapter Three, the final section on the Forearm, for a brief discussion of these stars.

41 Argo Navis is an ancient name for this constellation, which was known to the Greeks, Egyptians, and Indians, and perhaps the Sumerians. However, in the era of modern seafaring, it proved to be too large to effectively navigate by, so it was split into the present-day constellations of Carina, Puppis, and Vela and declared obsolete.

42 The manuscript says *sharaṭayn*, which appears to be a mistaken transcription of *saraṭān* (Cancer).

43 Lit. *al-shiʿrā al-shāmiyyah*.

THE CROW (*al-ghurāb*; Corvus) consists of seven stars. It also called Spica's Throne (*ʿarsh al-simmāk al-aʿzal*) and *al-ḥibā*.

CENTAURUS (*qayṭūris*) consists of thirty-seven stars and depicts a creature that is half-horse, half-man. The front of it is human, and the back—onwards to its tail—is a horse. It has grasped the legs of the BEAST. The Arabs called it *shamārīkh*.

THE BEAST (*al-sabuʿ*; Lupus) consists of nineteen stars, gathered together behind the stars of Centaurus, south of Scorpio.

THE SOUTHERN CROWN (*al-iklīl al-junūbī*; Corona Australis) is made up of thirteen stars. It is shaped like a pinecone. The Arabs called it the Dome (*qubbah*).

THE SOUTHERN FISH (*al-ḥūt al-junūbī*) consists of eleven stars, six which are outside its main form. It depicts a great fish whose stars are to the south of Aquarius. Its head faces east, and its tail faces west.

THE MILKY WAY (*al-majarrah*) runs south of Scorpio.[44]

These are all the southern and northern stars. Or, rather, this is a brief selection of what has been catalogued about the well-known stars. The stars which are not well-known are extraordinarily many in number, and we shall discuss some of them someday in the future, God willing.

THE SIZES OF THE PLANETS

Know that the Sun is one hundred sixty and a half times larger than the Earth. The Moon is twenty-nine times larger, and the same with Venus, Mercury, and Mars. Jupiter is twenty-eight times larger than

44 Lit. *hirzāt al-ʿaqrab*.

the Earth, and Saturn is ninety-nine times larger than the Earth.[45]

Some scholars say orb of the direct influence of the Sun is fifteen degrees forward and backward; the orb of the direct influence of the Moon is twelve degrees forward and backward; the orb of the direct influence of Jupiter is nine degrees forward and backward; the orb of the direct influence of Saturn is the same; orb of the direct influence of Mars is eight degrees forward and backward; the orb of the direct influence of Venus is nine degrees forward and backward; and the same with Mercury. And God knows best.

Know that the smallest stars in the skies are either the same size as the world, or many times bigger. The prominent fixed stars, like Sirius, Spica, Vega, Altair, and Regulus—which number fifteen—are each ninety-four and a half times bigger than the world.

HOW LONG IT TAKES FOR THE PLANETS TO PASS THROUGH THE SKY

Know that the Moon passes through the sky in twenty-nine days and a bit less than a third of a day.

Mercury passes through the sky in less than twenty-eight days.

Venus passes through the sky in two-hundred twenty-four days and about a third of a day.

The Sun passes through the sky in three-hundred sixty-five days and about fourth of a day.

Mars passes through the sky in six-hundred and thirty days.

Jupiter passes through the sky in eleven years and three-hundred twenty days.

Saturn passes through the sky in twenty-nine years. And God knows best.

45 Similar factoids can be found in other classical sources, including al-Farghani's *On the Science of the Stars*.

HOW LONG THE PLANETS REMAIN IN THE ZODIACAL SIGNS

Know that the Moon abides in each zodiacal sign for two or three nights. Mercury abides in each of the zodiacal signs for fifteen days. Venus abides in each of the zodiacal signs for twenty-five days. The Sun abides in each of the zodiacal signs for a month. Mars abides in each of the zodiacal signs for forty-five days. Jupiter abides in each of the zodiacal signs for a year. Saturn abides in each of the zodiacal signs for thirty months.

THE EXALTATION (*SHARAF*) OF PLANETS

The exaltation, or *sharaf*, of a planet is the sign where, astrologically, it is considered to be particularly well-placed, but which is not its domicile or ruling sign.

Know that the Moon is exalted in Taurus. Mercury is exalted in Virgo. Venus is exalted in Pisces. The Sun is exalted in Aries. Mars is exalted in Capricorn. Jupiter is exalted in Cancer. Saturn is exalted in Libra.

THE MILKY WAY

The Milky Way is called the "lamp of the sky" since it is a thick group of stars, like a dome. It is also called the "gate to the heavens." The Arabs also called it "the mother of the stars" (*um al-nujūm*) because no other patch of stars in the sky is so densely populated.

THE DAYS ASSOCIATED WITH EACH PLANET

The Sun is associated with Sunday. The Moon is associated with Monday. Mars is associated with Tuesday. Mercury is associated with Wednesday. Jupiter is associated with Thursday. Venus is associated with Friday, and Saturn is associated with Saturday.

PLANETARY CONJUNCTIONS

A conjunction (*iqtirān*) occurs when a planet is in a sign and has another in its gaze,[46] and they meet in the same sign. God has decreed that planetary conjunctions exert effects; understand that.

When Saturn and Jupiter are conjunct, wars rage throughout the lands, and kingdoms fall. Similar things happen when Saturn and Mars are conjunct, and when Saturn and the Sun are conjunct.

When Saturn and Venus are conjunct, prices rise, and drought strikes.

When Saturn is conjunct Mercury, it bodes well for scholars and scribes.

When Saturn is conjunct the Moon, tyranny and injustice break out among rulers and judges.

When Jupiter is conjunct Mars, severe misfortunes break out throughout the world.

And God knows best.

THE PLANETS: THEIR NATURES AND RULERSHIPS

KNOW THAT THE Moon is of a cold, dry, feminine nature; its heat is accidental (rather than intrinsic) because it is lit from the light

46 Planets which can see each other or which are within each other's gaze (*naẓar*) are planets situated in a conjunction or one of the traditional astrological aspects (sextile, trine, square, or opposition). Here, the author is specifically speaking about conjunctions.

of the Sun. It rules spleen and the lungs, and is the lesser fortune.[47]

Mercury is said to be both masculine and feminine. Sometimes it is auspicious, sometimes inauspicious. It is balanced between hot and cold. It rules speech and writing.

Venus is feminine, auspicious, cold, and moist. She rules the humor of phlegm, the female genitalia, and the joints. She rules the passions, bridal crowns, composing melodies, singing, entertainment, fun, and laughter.

The Sun is masculine, hot, and dry. It rules the humor of yellow bile. It is a fortunate planet to have in an astrological aspect (*naẓar*), but unfortunate when in an astrological opposition. Its substance is gold. It rules the heart. It rules honor, status, happiness, joy, and kingship.[48]

Mars is feminine,[49] hot, dry, and inauspicious. It rules the humor of yellow bile, and its substance is copper.[50] Its preferred taste is bitter. It rules the head and the guts. It rules terminal diseases, killing, and miscarriage.[51]

Jupiter is masculine; of a temperate, balanced, airy nature; and fortunate. It rules the humor of blood. Its substance is tin, and it is associated with good-tasting things and the color white. It rules a calm spirit in the heart, generous gifts, devotion, exaltation, and authority.

Saturn is masculine, cold, dry, and shadowy. It rules black bile. Its substance is lead. Its preferred taste is bitter, and its preferred

47 Alternate text: The Moon rules laughter and adornment, along with the humor of phlegm.

48 An alternate text adds that it also rules learning.

49 This differs from the traditional characterization of Mars as masculine. It is possible that the author is conflating sect (that is, whether Mars is associated with day and night) with gender (a planet's association with masculinity or femininity), since Mars is associated with nighttime, and nighttime is considered feminine. Sometimes, in classical Arabic astrological works, gender and sect were intermixed; see Ibn Ezra.

50 An alternate text identifies its substance as iron.

51 Alternate text: It rules killing, women, and similar things.

color is black. It rules the male genitalia,[52] boldness,[53] uniqueness, isolation, force, and fatalism.[54]

Some people hold that these constellations, celestial spheres, and planets themselves cause effects to happen on earth, thereby governing the world. In support of this, they cite the Qur'anic verse which says: "By those which govern affairs" (79:5).

However, my view is as follows. It is related that after Enoch (Idris)—peace be upon him—visited the heavens, he told people of the constellations, stars, and other things. What has been related from him about this can be taken as truth. Therefore, there is no need to pay heed to what the religion has rejected. For it has been indubitably proven that the Creator—exalted be He—created and fashioned these celestial bodies.

As for "those which govern affairs," Ibn ʿAbbas said that some angels are tasked with apportioning sustenance, some are tasked with delivering rain, and some are tasked with moving the winds. Of course, the angels are creations of God, even if they also act as agents. Thus the angels only act as agents through the permission of God[55]—exalted and powerful be He! For God is omniscient, omnipotent, and wise. God's alone is the power and decree: "God's is the creation and the command; blessed be God, the Lord of the Worlds" (Qur'an 7:2).

52 *Madhākīr*; an anomalous plural of *dhakar*. See E. W. Lane, *Lane's Lexion*, s.v. *dh-k-r*.

53 *Jasārah*; it is possible that this is a copying error for *ḥasārah*, "loss."

54 Alternate text: It rules hatred, tyranny, force, and oppression.

55 That is, they act under instructions from God, not as independent agents.

Chapter 5
THE SECRETS OF *BISMILLĀH*

Bismillāh al-raḥmān al-raḥīm—"in the name of God, the Compassionate, the Merciful" is the opening verse of the Qur'an and also begins each chapter of the Qur'an but one. It is commonly uttered or written before important tasks and works. Here, al-Buni delves into the spiritual significance of this phrase, both in and of itself and in terms of the letters it is comprised of, and prescribes recitations of it for both spiritual and practical benefit. He also briefly explains how to employ the four archangels in the Islamic tradition to produce practical results. According to al-Buni, reciting *bismillāh al-raḥmān al-raḥīm* is at once pragmatic and salvific. More than the previous chapters, this chapter blurs the line between conventional theology, the mystical path, and practical occultism.

Since this phrase occurs copiously throughout this chapter, it will be broken down here for non-Arabic speakers and left untranslated in the text:

bi—in
ism—name
Allāh—God
al—the
raḥmān—Merciful
al—the
raḥīm—Compassionate

The words *raḥmān* and *raḥīm* come from the same word root as "womb" (*raḥm*), symbolizing a sort of motherly care from the divine.

Know—may God help us be obedient towards Him and understand the secrets of His names—that whoever comprehends the secrets which God instilled in *bismillāh al-raḥmān al-raḥīm* shall not burn in the Fire; whoever inscribes *bismillāh al-raḥmān al-raḥīm* and its square shall not burn in the Fire.[1] Religious scholars concur that *bismillāh al-raḥmān al-raḥīm* should precede all important works; this mimics the Qur'an. According to Abu Hurayrah,[2] the Prophet Muhammad said: "Any important matter which is not preceded by *bismillāh al-raḥmān al-raḥīm* is severed at its outset"[3]—meaning that it will be blessed little and bear little fruit. Additionally, it is related[4] that one hundred forty divine scriptures descended from the heavens. Seth[5] alone received sixty scroll's-worth; Abraham received thirty; and Moses received ten, prior to the Torah. Then came the Torah, the Gospel, the Psalms, and the Criterion.[6] The true meanings of all of

1 "Fire" (*al-nār*) here is lightly ambiguous; while, in this context, it speaks of the fire of hell, it could also be taken to mean that a person who bears *bismillāh al-raḥmān al-raḥīm* prepared and inscribed in the right form would be secure from physical flames.

2 Abu Hurayrah (603–681) was a companion of the Prophet Muhammad to whom many Prophetic narrations are ascribed. He is said to have acquired his nickname (which means "Father of the Kitten") due to having a kitten he was particularly fond of.

3 The word here used for "severed" is *ajdham*, which can also be used for amputating a limb; for instance, in the case of leprosy. Al-Buni adds that there are two alternate versions of this narration, using the word *aqṭaʿ* and *abtar*, both of which mean "cut off." Regardless of the latter word in the narration, the import is the same.

4 From the Prophet Muhammad, or early Muslims.

5 Seth, the son of Adam. In some Islamic spiritual traditions, including Twelver Shiʿism, Seth is treated as one of the inheritors of the spiritual lineage of the prophets linking Adam to the later prophets. Abraham and Moses figure heavily in the Qur'an, which emphasizes the continuity of the message of the Qur'an with that of the Abrahamic prophets.

6 The Qur'an speaks of the revelation of the Criterion (*furqān*), such as in 25:1. It is generally taken as a synonym for the Qur'an, although the Qur'an also uses

these scriptures are encapsulated in the Criterion, the meanings of the Qur'an are encapsulated in the first chapter,[7] the meanings of the first chapter are encapsulated in the phrase *bismillāh al-raḥmān al-raḥīm*, and the meanings of *bismillāh al-raḥmān al-raḥīm* are encapsulated in the letter *b*—which holds the secrets of what was and what was not, and what will be and what will not be.[8]

It is narrated:

> When *bismillāh al-raḥmān al-raḥim* descended, the divine throne trembled, and the nineteen angels guarding hell[9] said, "Whoever recites this shall never enter hell."

Bismillah al-raḥmān al-raḥīm consists of nineteen letters,[10] which is the same as the number of the angels guarding hell—may God save us from it!

---

the phrase in the context of divine revelations received by Moses and Aaron. The idea behind the word *furqān* is that the divine scripture draws a dividing line distinguishing between things, such as truth and falsehood.

7 Surah al-Fatihah, the first chapter of the Qur'an.

8 This expression reminiscent of a quotation attributed to ʿAli ibn Abi Talib, probably spuriously: "Know that all of God's secrets are in the divine scriptures, and all of the secrets of the divine scriptures are in the Qur'an. All of the secrets of the Qur'an are in the first chapter, and all of the secrets of the first chapter are in *bismillāh al-raḥman al-raḥīm*. All of the secrets of *bismillāh al-raḥmān al-raḥīm* are in the *b*, and all of the secrets of the *b* are in the dot beneath the letter *b*—and I am the dot which is beneath the letter *b*." While the earliest written source of this quotation may be in *Kitab Durr al-Munazzam fi al-Sirr al-Aʿzam* by Muhammad ibn Talhah al-Shafiʿi (available in manuscript form), a discussion of it along with the esoteric overtones of the Arabic letter *b* can be found in Henry Corbin, *Temple and Contemplation* (n.l.: Routledge, 2013), 90. Note that this sentence and portions of the introduction are absent from the Feyzullah Efendi Madrasa manuscript.

9 The Qur'an refers to nineteen guardians of hell known as the *zabāniyah*; for instance, in 96:18. Christian Lange suggests the Arabic word *zabāniyah* may derive from the Syriac word *shabbāyā*, used for angels who conduct the souls of the dead, or frightening demons. Puzzling over the significance of the number nineteen, he proffers his best guess that it could represent the sum of the twelve signs of the zodiac plus the seven traditional planets. See Christian Lange, *Paradise and Hell in Islamic Traditions* (New York: Cambridge University Press, 2015), 64–65.

10 Nineteen Arabic letters: *b-s-m-alif-l-l-h-alif-l-r-ḥ-m-n-alif-l-r-ḥ-y-m*. The words *Allāh* and *raḥmān* are two of the few Arabic words to have implied

> It is also narrated from Jabir—may God be pleased with him:[11] When bismillāh al-raḥmān al-raḥīm descended from the heavens, the clouds fled eastward, the winds stilled, the seas stirred, the animals hearkened to God, the malevolent spirits (shayāṭīn) were pelted in the heavens, and the indomitable Lord swore: "Whenever My name is pronounced over an ill person, they shall be healed; whenever My name is pronounced something, it shall be blessed."

And Ibn Masʿud[12]—may God be pleased with him—says:

> Whoever wants to be saved by God from the nineteen angels of hell should recite this phrase copiously.

Bismillāh al-raḥmān al-raḥīm consists of nineteen letters; each letter saves a person from one of the angels of hell. Reciting it copiously bestows upon a person an aura of awe and grandeur on a person, in both the celestial and terrestrial worlds. Through *bismillāh al-raḥmān al-raḥīm*, Solomon, the son of David, upheld his kingdom;[13] whoever writes it a hundred times and bears it shall awe people's hearts.

It is narrated from ʿAbd Allah ibn ʿUmar, may God be pleased with him:

---

long vowels; that is, in the Qur'anic script, there is no separate *alif* in the middle of *Allāh* or *raḥmān* to denote the inner vowel sound *ā*.

11 Jabir ibn ʿAbd Allah al-Ansari (d. 697), a particularly long-lived companion of the Prophet Muhammad.

12 ʿAbdullah ibn Masʿud (c. 594–653), a companion of the Prophet Muhammad.

13 The text literally says *qā'im* meaning "standing upright," "managing," or "upholding." This could be referring to King Solomon's rule overall, or the Qur'anic account of King Solomon, which says that, after he died, he remained standing upright leaning on his staff, and the jinn continued laboring for him until worms ate through his staff and he fell: "When We decreed death for Solomon, naught showed them his death but an earth-creature nibbling on his staff. When he fell, the jinn saw clearly that he had died. Had they known the unseen, they would not have tarried in humiliating punishment" (34:14).

> If a person desperately needs something from God, they should fast on Wednesday, Thursday, or Friday. Then, on Friday, they should bathe, attend the mosque, and give charity. After performing the Friday noontime congregational prayers, they should say, "O God! I ask you by your name, *bismillāh al-raḥmān al-raḥīm*—God, there is no God but He, the Living, the Subsisting! Neither slumber overtakes Him, nor sleep. To him belongs everything in the heavens and earth. Who can intercede with God except by His leave? He knows what lies before them and behind them, but they embrace no part of His knowledge, save what He wills. The divine seat embraces the heavens and the earth. Protecting them tires Him not. He is exalted, magnificent.[14] By the One before whom faces and voices fall humble, and hearts tremble, I ask You to bless our master Muhammad, his family, and his companions, and to do for me this-or-that."

At that point, one should state one's need. He also used to say:

> Do not teach this to the foolish, let they invoke God's wrath against each other, and their prayers be answered.

It is narrated that the Prophet said:

> The distance between *bismillāh al-raḥmān al-raḥīm* and God's Greatest Name[15] is like the distance between the white of an eye and the pupil.

And also:

> Nothing lies between the malevolent spirits[16] and human beings apart from *bismillāh al-raḥmān al-raḥīm*.

14 Qur'an 2:255, known as the Throne verse.
15 *Al-ism al-aʿẓam*, mentioned in the next section.
16 *Shayāṭīn*.

Wondrous facets of the word Allāh

Allāh is the Arabic word for "God" and has been used by people of all faiths—including Jews, Christians, Muslims, and adherents to the pre-Islamic traditions—to refer to the primary force of divinity. It cannot take a plural form; for demiurges, multiple gods, or deities, *ilāh* (pl. *ālihah*) is used instead.[17] It consists of the prefix *al-* ("the") and *ilāh* ("God"). In this section, al-Buni ponders on some of the unique features of this word. He also mentions the Greatest Name of God (*al-ism al-aʿẓam*), which is said to be a secret name of God known only to the prophets and the spiritual elite; whoever utters it can work miracles. According to some Islamic traditions, the Greatest Name is made up of seventy-three letters; sometimes it is said to be hidden in various invocations. Generally, *Allāh* is not considered to be the greatest name, and, later, al-Buni indicates that the Greatest Name is something else, although he hints at a parallel here.

Bism ("in the name of") is the hidden, implicit name hinting that, beyond it, lies the Greatest Name, which is *Allāh*, for the Greatest Name is the Name of Majesty.[18] *Allāh* is the axis around which the other divine names revolve; the other divine names flock back to it. The name *Allāh* is like a flag flying above the other names, for if someone asks you, "Who is the Merciful?" you will reply "*Allāh*!" The other divine names are appended to *Allāh*, thereby demonstrating God's majesty and loftiness.

The word *Allāh* (*alif-l-l-h*) has an especially unique feature, which the other divine names do not share. If you remove the *alif*, you will be left with *lillāh* (*l-l-h*, "to God"). If you then remove the *l*, you will be left with *lahu* (*l-h*, "to Him"). If you then remove the *l*, you will be left with *hu* (*h*, "He," often recited in Sufi rituals). Therefore, each letter of the word *Allāh* stands on its own, upholding the

17 Allāh was also not the name of the Moon god, despite the many pamphlets saying this.

18 The "Name of Majesty" is an expression used for the word *Allāh*.

meaning of the entire word. The same cannot be said for the other divine names; if you remove one of their letters, the entire word falls apart. So this is the Greatest Name whose letters never falter. Nobler than all the other names, it shows that the divine essence is honorable and ever-fixed in its might and perpetuity.

The divine name *Allāh* has an additional distinction: it demonstrates the uniqueness of the divine essence, lordship, and godhood. Since *alif* is the first of the letters, the first of the numbers, and the first of the digits, God is unique in His essence and singular in number. It also hints at the unity and uniqueness of the divine secret which all of creation humbles itself before. The word *Allāh* ends with the letter *h*; this also points to the singularity of divinity, for no other divine name ends with *h*. It is as if God is telling us, in His own voice: "I am the First and the Last; I am the manifest and the hidden."

After *Allāh* follows *raḥmān*. God says: "Say, call upon God (*Allāh*) or call upon the Merciful (*al-raḥmān*)—whichever name you call upon, to God belong the most beautiful names" (Qur'an 17:110). Therefore, while you are free to beseech God by saying "O God!" or "O Merciful One!," it is better to say "O God (*Allāh*)!," for this name encompasses the attribute of mercy—although all the divine names are honorable. However, if you wish to implore God's mercy, you can invoke, "O Merciful!" However, the name *Allāh* is deemed to be the most specific. This name is Syriac,[19] and carries the intrinsic meaning of "bringing things from non-being into being." It has other meanings as well, which can be discovered through meditation and contemplation, for they have been barred from the foolish, lest they use this knowledge to commit abominable or forbidden acts and thereby earn divine wrath, similar to Balʿura, whom God tempted into disobedience—may God protect us from that![20] O God, keep us from employing Your names to disobey You.

19 Syriac, or pseudo-Syriac, names and terms are often used in Arabic magic and esotericism, although not in conventional Islamic theology and practice. They are often recognizable due to their utter unpronouncability.

20 Balʿam ibn Baʿura is said to have been an ascetic man who, due to his prayers and piety, had been gifted knowledge of God's Greatest Name, through which

THE FOUR ARCHANGELS

THE NAME *ALLĀH* has four letters: *a-l-l-h*.[21] These four letters represent the four elements, the four cardinal directions—east, west, north, and south—and the four archangels: Jibrā'īl, Mīkā'īl, Isrāfīl, and 'Azrā'īl.[22] Jibrā'īl is responsible for delivering the divine scriptures to the prophets, and for bestowing might and victory. Through him, God smote the ancients.[23] Isrāfīl is responsible for blowing the trumpet heralding the end of the world and the beginning of the Resurrection. In fact, he shall sound three blows: to terrify, fell, and resurrect the creatures. God says:

> On that day, the trumpet shall be blown, and all in the heavens and earth shall fear. (Qur'an 27:87)

> The trumpet shall be blown, and all in the heavens and earth shall fall faint, except for those whom God wills. Then the trumpet shall sound again, and—behold!—they shall stand upright, looking about. (Qur'an 39:68)

Therefore, each blow of the trumpet will be separate.

'Azrā'īl is the angel who grasps people's souls upon death, thereby curbing tyrants, the godless, and the haughty. However, he brings joy and ease to the faithful, for he delivers them to their Lord, whereupon they rejoice at the divine presence, salvation, and forgiveness awaiting them.

---

any prayer would be answered. However, he was tempted either by women or by wealth to misuse this name, thereby committing great wrongs. There are various stories of how this happened—for instance, being bribed to pray against Moses and his people—but the message is the same. He is said to be referred to in Qur'an 7:176, although the Qur'an does not give details.

21 Readers unacquainted with the Arabic language have probably noticed by now that short vowels are not usually written in Arabic, similar to Hebrew.

22 Jibrā'īl corresponds to Gabriel, Mīkā'īl corresponds to Michael, and 'Azrā'īl corresponds to Azrael. It is not clear whether the angel Isrāfīl corresponds to any angels in the Judaeo-Christian tradition, although Isrāfīl might correspond to Raphael, Uriel, or Seraphiel.

23 Noah's flood, etc.

Mikā'īl is responsible for providing all creatures their daily bread, replenishing their strength, and keeping them alive. Not even a single sesame-seed falls on its own accord; rather, this happens through the auspices of the angels assigned to it. Jibrā'īl has angelic assistants beyond count, with specific rituals and recitations[24] corresponding to them.

Each of these four archangels is associated with a specific day. Jibrā'īl is associated with Monday, since it is cold and moist. Isrāfīl is associated with Thursday, since it is hot and moist. ʿAzrā'īl is associated with Saturday, since it is cold and dry, and since he is associated with dust, death, and dissolution. Mīkā'īl is associated with Wednesday, since it is a blend of the four elemental natures. Each of these four archangels also has a specific magic square. Jibrā'īl has a nine-by-nine square, Isrāfīl has a four-by-four square, ʿAzrā'īl has a three-by-three square, and Mikā'īl has an eight-by-eight square.

These are their squares:

ʿAZRAʾĪL'S SQUARE—SATURN

4	9	2
3	5	7
8	1	6

24 *Adhkār* and *aʿmāl*.

ISRĀFĪL'S SQUARE—JUPITER

8	11	14	1
13	2	7	12
3	16	9	6
10	5	4	15

JIBRĀʾĪL'S SQUARE—THE MOON

45	49	35	57	25	65	15	73	5
4	44	48	34	56	24	64	14	81
80	3	43	47	33	55	23	72	13
12	79	2	42	46	32	63	22	71
70	11	78	1	41	54	31	62	21
20	69	10	77	9	40	53	30	61
60	19	68	18	76	8	39	52	29
28	59	27	67	17	75	7	38	51
50	36	58	26	66	16	74	6	37

MIKĀʾĪL'S SQUARE—MERCURY

39	55	30	14	44	60	17	1
63	47	6	22	52	36	9	25
12	28	49	33	7	23	62	46
20	4	41	57	31	15	38	54
29	13	40	56	18	2	35	51
5	21	64	48	10	26	59	43
42	58	19	3	37	53	32	16
50	34	11	27	61	45	8	24

Know—may God make you and me obedient towards Him—that these squares are extremely effective at attaining whatever you want. Anyone who uses them will find them to be very accurate in accomplishing their aims. So fear God, always, no matter what frame of mind or situation you are in.

To use one of these four squares, write its seal after writing its numbers and checking it. Then add your goal; you shall attain whatever you seek.

To use the nine-by-nine square [associated with the Moon and Jibraʾil], inscribe it on a white piece of paper or a shining, unspoiled piece of silver. Do this at sunrise on Monday, during the hour of the Moon. If your aim is benefic, inscribe it while the Moon is waxing—even better if the Moon is exalted or fortunate, free from any afflictions. If your aim is not so benefic—for instance, you wish to take vengeance against enemies or smite oppressors—then inscribe it while the Moon is waning, combust,[25] and applying to a conjunction with Saturn or Mars. But beware not to do this against the undeserving! 'Tis better to forgive; God says: "Forgiveness is nearer to reverence... Whoever pardons someone and sets matters aright shall find their reward with God" (Qur'an 2:237; 42:40). If your goal is benefic, incense it with a sweet-smelling incense; if your goal is malefic, incense it with a foul-smelling incense. Then, see what zodiacal sign the Moon is in. If it is in an air sign, hang it in the air.[26] If it is in a fire sign, burn it in fire. If it is in a water sign, set it adrift into water, or bury it near water. If you wish to set it adrift, seal it in a watertight Persian reed sealed with wax, and recite the following invocation over it. If the Moon is in an earth sign, then bury it in the ground beneath the target's doorstep—or your doorstep, if you want it to act upon yourself. Even if you are seeking something enormous, you will see a response.

If your aim is benefic [alternate: for any aim], recite this invocation over it:

> In the name of God, the beneficent, the merciful (*bismillāh al-raḥmān al-raḥīm*). O God! I beseech You through Your beautiful names, all of which are praised and glorious. Whenever they befall something, it falls humble. Whenever goodness is besought through them, it transpires. Whenever misfortunes are averted through them, they disappear. And I beseech You through Your perfect words: were all the trees on earth pens, and all the seas ink—and even if seven seas of ink were added to them—the words of God would never run out; God is mighty, wise.[27] O Sufficient, O Guardian! O Kind, O Subtle! O Sustainer, O Loving! O Opener, O Expander! O Honorable, O Bestower, O Open-handed! O Magnanimous, O Bounteous! O Giver, O Granter! O Merciful,

25 That is, quite close to the Sun.

26 For instance, from a tree.

27 Qur'an 31:27. As a side note, this verse has been employed in the Indonesian esoteric tradition—which synthesizes the Arab-Islamic tradition with local and other customs—to induce astral projection; God knows best.

> O Compassionate! O Needless, O Savior! O Benevolent, O Freer from Need! O Merciful, O Compassionate, O Needless, O Savior! O Kind, O Benevolent, O Generous, O Blesser, O Beauteous, [O Avenger]![28] O God, free me from what you have prohibited through what You have permitted.[29] Free me free me from disobeying You through obeying You. Render me needless of all others but You through Your grace, O most merciful of the merciful! I beseech you through Your majestic name. There is no god but God: the mighty, the merciful, the compassionate. He is the subtle, the tremendous; the knower, the kind; the pardoner and the forgiver. He bestows security. [Alternate: He bestows security, dispels fear, and plucks the souls.][30] He answers prayers, is near, hears all, and is quick in response—the honorable, the mighty, the glorious, the benevolent, the kind!

Know that whoever bears these names[31] shall enjoy an impeccable character and manners. They shall be generous, honorable, and sympathetic to others. Indeed, they shall witness the mysteries of the divine name "the Subtle" (*al-laṭīf*). Others shall embrace them easily and praise them for their outward and inward characteristics, for hidden in this lies God's Greatest Name. Whenever God is invoked by this name, He responds; whenever He is besought by it, He gives. It is one of the greatest and loftiest ways to remember God.

If you persist in reciting these names, amazing secrets shall be revealed to you. You shall quickly attain whatever you seek, including prosperity. If you make a habit of reciting them at midnight,

28 *Yā kāfī yā walī, yā ra'ūf yā laṭīf, yā razzāq yā wadūd, yā fattāh yā wāsi', yā karīm yā wahhāb yā bāsiṭ, yā dhā al-ṭawl ya dhā al-faḍl al-'aẓīm, yā mu'ṭī yā mughnī, yā raḥmān yā raḥīm, yā ghanī yā mughīth, yā ḥannān yā mannān, yā jawād yā mun'im, ya muḥsin.* "O Avenger" (*yā muntaqim*) is omitted from the sources which do not specify that this invocation is only for benefic acts.

29 For instance, through lawfully earned wealth, free me from the temptation to steal.

30 As before, "plucking the souls" (*al-mumīt*) is not in the version aimed at benefic acts. In the context of the text, it may be more appropriate for plucking the souls of tyrants.

31 An alternate version adds: "and recites them."

you shall witness wonders—to the extent of your aspiration—for reciting them continually unlocks hidden secrets. It simply is not possible to recite them continually without glimpsing matters in the celestial and astral worlds. The realms of the angels, humans, and jinn shall be at your disposal, along with the imaginal realm.[32] For these are the perfect words; they work wonders.

The *divine name "the Sufficient" (al-kāfī)*: If you recite this name with a particular wish in mind, your wish shall be fulfilled from a direction you never dreamt of. If a person who feels weak and who aspires for more recites this name, God shall uplift them without any undue effort or loss. If you lose something and then recite this name,[33] your lost item shall be returned to you.

The Pardoner (al-ʿafw): Reciting this name dispels pains and sorrows.

The *Kind (al-raʾūf)*: This is what the fearful and sorrowful recite. When they recite this name, they shall find tranquility and security, and their fear shall subside. Should a person commit to reciting this name continually—to the point that they seclude themselves, abstain from food, and are overwhelmed by a spiritual beatitude (*ḥāl*)—and then touch fire, they shall not be harmed. Should they blow over a boiling pot, it will cease to boil—by the permission of God. However, that person should also recite the names "O Forbearing" and "O Benevolent" (*al-ḥalīm* and *al-mannān*), and say: "O Forbearing! O Benevolent! O Kind!" (*yā ḥalīm, yā raʾūf, yā mannān*).

If you must face someone whom you fear will harm you, write these three names on the first Monday of the month during the hour of the Moon. Then, when you come face-to-face with that person, God will extinguish that person's malice towards you on sight. Reciting these names continually also frees a person from overwhelming lusts and appetites.

32 *ʿĀlam al-taṣwīr.*
33 Alternate: "who recites 'the Sufficient, the Gatherer' (*al-kāfī al-jāmiʿ*)."

THE VIRTUES OF *BISMILLĀH AL-RAḤMĀN AL-RAḤĪM*

NOW, LET US return to our discussion about the virtues of *bismillāh al-raḥmān al-raḥīm*. For when these words descended, the angels in the heavens rejoiced, and the divine throne trembled. Thousands upon thousands of angels trailed after *bismillāh al-raḥmān al-raḥīm*, and it but strengthened their firm faith. At its descent, the celestial spheres moved, and kings humbled themselves. *Bismillāh al-raḥmān al-raḥīm* was written across Adam's forehead five-hundred years before he was created, and was inscribed upon Jibrāʾīl's wing the day he descended to Abraham and said: "In the name of God, O fire! Be coolness and safety for Abraham."[34] *Bismillāh al-raḥmān al-raḥīm* was inscribed on Moses' staff in Syriac; had it not been, it would not have parted the sea. *Bismillāh al-raḥmān al-raḥīm* was inscribed on Jesus' tongue, when he spoke in the cradle;[35] he used to speak it when raising the dead, who sprung back to life through the permission of God. And *bismillāh al-raḥmān al-raḥim* was engraved upon Solomon's ring.[36]

The unique merits and facets of *bismillāh al-raḥmān al-raḥīm* are as follows.

The *Qur'an.* It begins each chapter of the Qur'an.

Seeking aims and desires, and trade. A person who recites it seven-

34 An allusion to Qur'an 21:68–69, which tell of how Abraham's people tried to cast him into a raging fire. At that time, according to the Islamic tradition, Jibrāʾīl came to him and offered to save him, but Abraham declined and said he would put his full faith in God alone; therefore, the fire was commanded to cool for Abraham.

35 An allusion to Qur'an 19:27–34, which says: "Then [Mary] brought [Jesus] to her people. They said, 'O Mary! You have brought an amazing thing! O sister of Aaron, your father was not an evil man, nor was your mother unchaste. Then she pointed to him. They asked, 'How can we speak to a child in the cradle?' He [Jesus] said, 'Truly, I am a servant of God. God has given me the Book and made me a prophet. He has blessed me wheresoever I may be...'" Note that, according to the Qur'an, Mary gave birth to Jesus alone in the desert, rather than in Bethlehem.

36 Al-Buni goes into further detail about Solomon's ring, which he used to control the jinn, later in the book.

hundred eighty-six times (its numerical value) for seven days with a specific intent in mind will attain good or avert evil—whichever they seek—or sell their merchandise, for goods circulate through the permission of God.[37]

Protection from Satan, theft, death, and calamity. Reciting it before sleeping one-hundred and twenty-one times will draw down divine protection. God will protect you from Satan, theft, and sudden death; all misfortunes shall be averted.

Protection from oppressors. Should a person come face-to-face with an oppressor and recite *bismillāh al-raḥmān al-raḥīm* fifty times, that oppressor will become submissive towards them. God will cast fear of the reciter in the oppressor's heart, thereby saving the reciter from danger.

Curing pain. If a person who is in pain recites it one-hundred times for three days, God shall alleviate their pain—with the permission of God.

Provision. If a person recites it three-hundred times at sunrise, while facing the sunrise, and then sends blessings upon the Prophet Muhammad[38] one hundred times, God shall grant them provision and sustenance in ways they could never have imagined. This will continue, until God has fully freed them from any need; however, for that to happen, they must recite this regularly.

These are some of the facets and merits of *bismillāh al-raḥmān al-raḥīm*, so understand them! Further virtues of it are as follows.

Freeing prisoners. A prisoner who recites it one thousand times each day and night shall be freed, even if they were condemned to death.

Wishes and desires. On Friday, while the imam of the mosque is giving a sermon[39] from the pulpit and uttering prayers,[40] if you re-

37 Seven-hundred eighty-six is the sum of the letters of *bismillāh al-raḥmān al-raḥīm*. While the numerological use of the Arabic letters has largely fallen out of circulation, 786 persists as shorthand among Muslims for *bismillāh al-raḥmān al-raḥīm*.

38 For instance, one formula used for this is *allahummā ṣallī ʿalā Muḥammadin wa āl-i Muḥammad* ("O God! Bless Muhammad and the family of Muhammad").

39 *Minbar*.

40 *Duʿāʾ*; that is, spoken prayer, not the ritual prayer accompanied by bodily

cite it one-hundred thirteen times with a secret wish in mind, then raise your hands and beseech God, God shall grant you what you wish, through His grace.

Love. If you want someone to love you, recite it over a cup of water seven-hundred eighty-six times, then give it to your beloved to drink. He or she shall love you ardently, especially if he or she is lawful to you.[41]

Curing dim-wittedness. If a dim-witted person drinks this water at sunrise for seven days, they shall gain their wit and remember all that they hear.

Rain. If you recite it when rain is falling sixty-one times with the intent that God will make it rain somewhere else, God shall make it rain there that very day—even if you be in the east and the place be in the west.

Dreams and spiritual mysteries. If you recite it after the dawn prayer for forty days with a pure intent and humble heart, God shall infuse your heart with profound secrets. In your dreams, they shall see all that happens in the world. For this, you should recite it two-thousand five-hundred times each day, and abstain from eating any sort of meat or animal products. You shall see wonders. Furthermore, concealing these secrets will help you to better attain what you desire.

Know, my brother—may God make me and you obedient towards Him—that I have only explained these virtues of *bismillāh al-raḥmān al-raḥīm* so that they may help in obeying God. God is your guardian; God suffices; and God protects.

Approaching kings; status and honor. If you are desperately in need of something or about to approach a king, fast on Thursday, then break the fast with raisins or dates, nothing else.[42] Pray the sunset prayers and recite *bismillāh al-raḥmān al-raḥīm* one-hundred and twenty-one times. Then, when you go to bed, continue reciting it without

movements.

41 For instance, husband and wife.

42 An alternate version says "oil and dates" (*zayt* instead of *zabīb*).

counting until sleep overtakes you. When you wake up on Friday, pray the dawn prayer and recite *bismillāh al-raḥmān al-raḥīm* the same number of times as you did after the sunset prayer. Then write it the aforementioned number of times on a piece of paper with ink made of musk, saffron, and rosewater; and incense it with musk and ambergris. By God—and there is no god but He!—anyone who carries this paper, man or woman, shall become in the eyes of the people like the full Moon when it is shining bright. They shall attain status and dignity, be respected and obeyed. Everyone who sees them shall love them and do whatever they need; love for them will be cast into people's hearts. This is how it is written:[43]

ب س م ا ل ل ه ا ل ر ح م ن ا ل ر ح ي م
b-s-m-a-l-l-h-a-l-r-ḥ-m-n-a-l-r-ḥ-y-m

Write it a hundred and twenty-one times.

Prosperity. Or, it can be written normally[44] one-hundred and twenty-one times upon a gazelle-skin parchment with ink made of musk, saffron, and rosewater; then incensed with costus, storax, and benzoin. If someone in a tight financial situation carries it, God shall open the door to bounty to them. If a debtor carries it, God shall pay off their debts, and it shall protect them from all sorts of calamities.

Childbirth. If it is written inside a glass goblet forty times, and then washed off with *zamzam*[45] water or fresh well water, and an ill person drinks that water, God shall cure them. If a woman in the midst of a difficult childbirth drinks that water, she shall give birth quickly, safe and unharmed.

43 Note that the letters are written in an unconnected form.
44 That is, with connected letters as it is usually written.
45 A spring in Mecca; the Qur'an says when Abraham left Hagar and their infant child in Mecca, they were suffering thirst, so God made it miraculously spring from the desert for her. It is believed to have continuously flowed since then, and to have curative powers.

Nightmares. If a child is having nightmares and it is written eleven or nineteen times, then attached to the child, the nightmares shall stop, by the permission of God.

Protection from spirits, and trade. If it is written upon a piece of paper thirty-five times and hung inside a house, neither any malevolent spirits nor jinn shall enter that house, and it will be very blessed. If it is hung in a shop, it will blossom with customers, profit, and goods; and God will blind the evil eyes of the envious to it.

Protection from misfortune. If it is written on the first day of the month of Muharram[46] on a piece of paper one hundred thirteen times and a person carries it, that person shall be secure from misfortunes, nor shall their family suffer misfortune, as long as that person lives.

Conception and childbirth. If a woman keeps losing her children or is barren, it can be written one-hundred thirteen times on the third day after her menses, and she should wear it. When her husband copulates with her, she shall conceive, by the permission of God. However, she should not take it off for sixty-one days; after that, she is free to keep wearing it or to take it off. She shall give birth to a healthy child and will not experience any discomfort or difficulty in her pregnancy, by the permission of God.[47] The same thing should be done by a woman who miscarries or loses her children; she will give birth to a living child, by the permission of God. This is tried and true, but it works best when done with a sincere intent.

Farming. If it is written on a paper one-hundred and one times and buried on a farm, the crops will be fruitful and will be protected from pestilence or danger.

Questioning in the grave. If it is written seventy times and placed beneath the body of a dead person who has been shrouded, that person shall be secure from the questioning of Munkar and Nakir,[48]

46 The first month of the Islamic lunar year.

47 The copyist in the Fayzullah Effendi manuscript adds that in some other manuscripts, it says that *bismillāh al-raḥmān al-raḥīm* should be written sixty-one times and that that this is more correct, but God knows best.

48 In Islamic belief, after a person goes to the grave, the angels Munkar and Na-

and it shall be a light for them until the day they are resurrected, God willing.

Fishing. If it is inscribed three times on a black lead tablet and placed in a fishing net, fish will flock towards it from every direction. Then, the fisherman will catch as many fish as his heart desires, through the blessings of this divine name, for it is the most beloved name to God, the exalted.[49]

Poisonous bites and stings. It may be written one time on a slip of paper and placed beneath the bezel of a ring, and that ring may be placed in buttermilk. If it is given to a person who has been stung or bitten to drink, and that person vomits it back up, the poison shall be expelled, by the permission of God.

If the letters are written in a disconnected manner and it is carried, it has great merits, for:

the letter *b* stands for God's splendor (*bahāʾ*)
the letter *s* stands for God's radiance (*sanā*)
the letter *m* stands for God's glory (*majd*) and kingdom (*malakūt*)
the letter *alif* stands for God's everlastingness (*azaliyyah*)
the letter *l* stands for God's subtlety (*luṭf*)
the letter h stands for "He is God—there is no God but He" (*huwa Allāh alladhī lā ilāha illā hu*)[50]
the letter *alif* stands for God's command (*amr*)
the letter *l* stands for God's rule (*lahu al-mulk*)
the letter *r* stands for God's kindness and mercy (*raʾūf* and *raḥīm*)
the letter *ḥ* stands for God's wisdom
the letter *m* stands for God's rule (*mulk*)
the letter *n* stands for God's blessings (*niʿmah*)

...and so on and so forth.

---

kir come to question them.

49 Al-Buni is speaking of *bismillāh al-raḥmān* in the singular—that is, as one name—even though the phrase is comprised of three names (*Allāh*, *al-raḥmān*, and *al-raḥīm*).

50 Alt. "guidance" (*hidāyah*).

Wealth. If the letter *b* from *bismillāh* is written alone, like this—ب—twenty-one times, and placed in a person's belongings or wealth, their holdings will multiply, for in it lies blessings and the power of growth.

Bites and stings. If a person is suffering from a bite or sting, it can be written this number of times, along with this verse written in disconnected letters:

Peace be upon Noah, throughout the worlds. (Qur'an 37:79)

س ل ا م ع ل ى ن و ح ف ي ا ل ع ا ل م ي ن
s-l-a-m-ʿ-l-y-n-w-ḥ-f-y-a-l-ʿ-l-m-y-n

The writing should then be washed off with water, and the water should be given to them to drink; they shall be cured then and there, by the permission of God.

Goodness and blessings. If someone writes it on a piece of paper and gazes at the letter *m* every day for forty days, while reciting "O God! King of the Kingdom! You grant kingship to whom You will, and seize kingship from whom You will. You elevate whom You will, and abase whom You will" (Qur'an 3:26), goodness and blessings shall come to them from directions that they cannot even fathom, due to what their hands hold.

Protection from tyrants. A person who must face a sultan or tyrant may write *al-raḥmān*[51] fifty times on a piece of paper and recite *bismillāh al-raḥmān al-raḥīm* over it one-hundred fifty times, then carry it on their person when standing before the sultan or tyrant. They shall be secure from their evil and incur no harm.

Spiritual vision and authority. If you recite it one thousand times every day, with a sincere intent and reverent heart, you shall see the angels and celestial spirits (*ruḥāniyyīn*). This should be done after fourteen days of fasting, ascetic practices, and purification. (Some people also say it should be recited one thousand times after each of the five daily prayers.) If you do this, you shall speak with the angels

51 Alt. *al-raḥmān al-raḥīm*.

and celestial spirits, and the angels and celestial spirits shall speak back. The angels and celestial spirits shall serve you and be at your beck and call, carrying out whatever you desire in this world, God willing.

Assistance from others. When seeking assistance from someone, write it in mixed-up, separated, shortened form like this:

ن م ح ر ل ا
n–m–ḥ–r–l–a

Also write the name of the target and the target's mother in separated, unconnected form. Carry it during an auspicious hour and meet the person in question; as soon as their eyes fall upon you, they will do anything you ask—even jump into a fire.

Escaped servants. If you have a servant who keeps running away, write *al-raḥmān* like so:

ا ل ر ح م ن
a–l–r–ḥ–m–n

seven times, along with the name of a servant who has fled. Bury it in your house beneath a heavy stone, and implore, "O God! I ask You by the right of *bismillāh al-raḥmān al-raḥīm*, and by the right of Your name *al-raḥmān*, that you keep this servant from slipping away, O Lord of the worlds!" The servant shall return and decide never to run away again nor leave the household he is in, God willing.

Irksome bugs and jinn. Inscribe *al-raḥmān* on a knife with a steel blade, then recite *al-raḥmān* over it three hundred thirty-one times. Use it to slaughter a rooster; lop off its head so it stumbles about headless. Then, bury its head beneath the threshold of your house; it will drive away all the pesky bugs and jinn.

An ointment. Alternatively, boil its head in good oil and store it in a flask. It will be a very beneficial ointment, excellent for easing pain and staunching excessive feminine bleeding.

Armor. A person who writes *al-raḥīm* two-hundred eighty-nine times[52] and carries it into battle [alt. on a battle-standard in battle] shall be untouched by weapons and unharmed. Whoever he meets in battle shall flee, God willing.

Headache. If a person is suffering from a headache, *al-raḥīm* may be written twenty-one times on a piece of paper and affixed to them; their headache shall subside, by God's will.

Epilepsy. If *al-raḥīm* is written on the palm of an epileptic, and recited into their ear seven times, they shall be cured that very moment, by the permission of God.

Love. If you engrave the blessed name *al-raḥīm* on seven almonds with a copper stylus or needle on Friday during Venus hour—that is, the first hour after sunrise—and recite the name *al-raḥīm* over the almonds the number of times equivalent to its numerical value, and feed them to your intended, he or she shall love you ardently, more than anyone else.

Courage. If it is written like this, in separated, mixed-up form:

م ح ي ا ر ل
m-ḥ-y-a-r-l

upon a piece of tiger or cheetah skin,[53] and a cowardly person carries it, his heart will embolden, and his courage will grow.

Facial paralysis. If it is written like this:

ر ل ا ي م ح
r-l-a-y-m-ḥ

upon a new mirror on Monday at sunrise, and a person suffering from facial paralysis gazes long into it, God shall cure that person.

Authority and respect. If this is written like this:

ا ل ر ح ي م
a-l-r-ḥ-y-m

52 Alt. one-hundred ninety times.

53 *Nimr aw fahd*; may also include the skin of a lynx, panther, or leopard.

upon a silver ring weighing two dirhams, and worn, God will grant the ring-bearer an aura of dignity, awesomeness, fearsomeness, and authority.

Deposing tyrants. Should you want to depose a tyrant or do away with haughty, heavy-handed miscreants, inscribe the following *bismillāh* square on a piece of lead, inserting the target's name in the appropriate place in the square. Incense it with asafoetida and red garlic, then bury it near a fire that kept continually alit. Beware—do not let the lead touch the fire, for it will kill and destroy the target,[54] and you will be held accountable for that on the Day of Resurrection! This is the square:

<target>	الرحيم	الرحمن	الله	بسم
بسم	<target>	الرحيم	الرحمن	الله
الله	بسم	<target>	الرحيم	الرحمن
الرحمن	الله	بسم	<target>	الرحيم
الرحيم	الرحمن	الله	بسم	<target>

The tyrant's name is inserted in the squares marked <target>. Then, recite over it:

> *Bismillāh al-raḥmān al-raḥīm.* O God, I beseech You by Your Greatest Name—and it is *bismillāh al-raḥmān al-raḥīm*—before which faces humble, necks bow, voices silence, and hearts tremble. I ask You, O God, to bless our master Muhammad and to exact what I need from <target>, the son[55] of <target's mother>. O God! If you know that he will abandon his ways, then guide him

54 So, basically, you put it in the fire.

55 *Fulān ibn fulānah.* This does not exclude the possibility of the form *fulānah bint fulānah*—"<target>, the daughter of <target's mother>"—but, admittedly, the majority of dictators are male.

to do that. But if You know that he will never change, then strike him down with Your anger and wrath. Destroy him, O Mighty, O Vanquisher! O Powerful, O Supreme—O Allah![56]

Repeat "O Allah!" six more times. Pronounce the entire invocation seven-hundred times, and the oppressor shall swiftly either be guided by God, or be annihilated. Fear God! God guides to what is right.

Love and respect. Write *bismillāh al-raḥmān al-raḥīm* in the middle of a circle eight times; around it, write the Qur'anic verse beginning with "Muhammad is the messenger of God."[57] Incense it with a sweet-smelling incense during an auspicious hour and then carry it on your person; people shall dignify, awe, and honor you. No one will be able to gaze upon you without loving you. People will incline towards you and seek friendship with you, including women. Fear God! God guides to what is right.

This is the circle:

56 *Yā qahhār, yā qādir, yā muqtadir, yā Allāh.*

57 Qur'an 48:29.

Happiness. Bismillāh al-raḥmān al-raḥīm may be written upon a gazelle-skin parchment while the Moon is rising in Pisces. Then, *bismillāh al-raḥmān al-raḥīm* should be recited the number of times equivalent to its numerical value over the parchment.[58] It may then be carried. Whoever carries it shall live a happy life and die as a martyr; the bearer of this parchment shall never find in themself anything they dislike.

THE FIRST CHAPTER OF THE QUR'AN

The first chapter of the Qur'an—Surah al-Fatihah—consists of seven verses and begins with *bismillāh al-raḥmān al-raḥīm*. This section provides an esoteric commentary on the first three verses of it.

In the name of God, the Merciful, the Compassionate (Qur'an 1:1). Know, O reader—may God make me and you obedient to Him—that *bism* alludes to the hidden name, *Allāh* is the Greatest Name, and *al-raḥmān al-raḥīm* is the divine self-disclosure, for God is Merciful (*raḥmān*) in this world and Compassionate (*raḥīm*) in the afterlife.

All praise be to God, the Lord of the worlds (Qur'an 1:2). This juxtaposes *bismillāh al-raḥmān al-raḥīm; bismillāh* faces *al-ḥamdu lillāh* ("all praise be to God"), *al-raḥmān* ("Merciful") juxtaposes *rabb* ("Lord"), and *al-ʿālamīn* ("worlds") juxtaposes *al-raḥīm* ("Compassionate").

Master of the Day of Judgment (Qur'an 1:3). Know that all of that is implied in this verse. "Judgment" (*dīn*) speaks of the external manifestation of God's lordship, for for God is the king, master, and sovereign[59] who bedazzles the intellects, lights, and subtleties on that Day through His attribute of kingship. Thus, He is the King of Kings, illuminating souls through His power and grandeur. He is the Mas-

58 That is, seven-hundred eighty-six times.
59 *Malik*, *mālik*, and *malīk*.

ter of the Day of Judgment. And He shall manifest His glory to those who paid heed and were uplifted in the worldly realm. Thus, He is the King of Kings. And He shall manifest His glory to those brought near His court, as said in the verse: "In the seat of honor with a most powerful King" (Qur'an 54:55).

Understand these subtle divine secrets! For all of this is found in *bismillāh al-raḥmān al-raḥīm*. The letter *b* is what links goodness to all realms of creation and the true divine kingdom. Uttering it with the tongue is a path of ascent which climbs ever upwards. However, *al-raḥmān al-raḥīm* leads the way down to the new beginning, just as *bismillāh al-raḥmān al-raḥīm* leads the way up to the first beginning. Thus, it contains the secrets of the beginning and the end. In it also lie the levels of monotheism, for *bismillāh al-raḥmān al-raḥīm* juxtaposes the confession of faith in God, and God juxtaposes God. In this lie the levels of the angels, which are juxtaposed with *al-raḥmān*, and the knowledgeable, who are juxtaposed with *al-raḥīm*.

Similarly, with respect to the fourfold worldly realm, as evinced in the verse: "Those whom God has graced: the prophets (*nabiyyīn*), the truthful (*ṣiddiqīn*), the martyrs (or witnesses, *shuhadā'*), and the righteous (*ṣāliḥīn*)—what an excellent fellowship!" (4:69) *Bism* in proportion to *Allāh* is with respect to the prophets; *Allāh* in proportion to *bism* is with respect to the truthful; God's compassion (*raḥmāniyyah*) in proportion to His mercy (*raḥīmīyyah*) is with respect to the levels of the prophets and the martyrs (or witnesses); and God's compassion with respect to His mercy is with respect to the righteous. Thus, the levels ascend, one after another, to *bismillāh al-raḥmān al-raḥīm*: the beginning of the cycle is *bismillāh al-raḥmān al-raḥīm*, and the end of the cycle is *bismillāh al-raḥmān al-raḥīm*. Through it manifest the secrets of man and jinn.[60] And how the worlds tremble at *bismillāh al-raḥmān al-raḥīm*!

60 Lit. *thaqalayn*, a Qur'anic phrase used to speak of mankind and jinnkind.

It is narrated:

> On the Day of Resurrection, anyone whose scroll of deeds contains *bismillāh al-raḥmān al-raḥīm* eight hundred times, and who had certain faith in God's lordship, shall be freed from the hellfire and brought into the eternal abode.

THE GOSPEL

According to Islamic belief, Jesus is a prophet and received a revealed scripture from God. However, this scripture is no longer present with us today. Occasionally, Islamic texts quote this original "Gospel," as this section does here. Al-Buni is not actually implying that this is in the New Testament as we have it today; Muslim authors then and now distinguished between the New Testament, as canonized by Christians, and the non-extant Gospel believed to have been revealed to Jesus.

Here, and throughout the next section, al-Buni speaks of *bismillāh al-raḥmān al-raḥīm* as the "writ of faith" (*āyat al-īmān*, in some sources written as *āyat al-amān*) provided by God to creation. *Āyah* means "sign of God" and is also used to refer to the verses of the Qur'an; both meanings are applicable here. *Īmān* and *amān* convey the meanings of safety, security, and also faith, the idea being that the sincere employment of *bismillāh al-raḥmān al-rāḥīm* protects a person in this world as well as in the hereafter.

The Gospel says:

> [God said:] "O Jesus! Let *bismillāh al-raḥmān al-raḥīm* open your prayers and scriptural readings. Whoever begins their prayers and scriptural readings with that shall have no fear of Munkar

> and Nakir.[61] If someone does that, when they die, God shall ease the pangs of death for them and rescue them from the tightness of the grave. God shall widen their grave as far as they can see, and raise them from their grave glowing and shining, with their face filled with a brilliant light. They shall be accounted leniently, and granted extra weight on their scales of deeds. The path shall be illuminated for them wholly, until they enter Paradise. Then, in the pavilions of the realm of the Resurrection, a voice shall proclaim for them felicity and forgiveness."
>
> Jesus said: "I am honored by this."[62]
>
> God said: "It is for you especially, and for those who follow you—who act as you do, and speak as you do. It will also be for Ahmad (Muhammad) and his followers after you."

Jesus told this to his disciples. However, eventually, after he was raised to heaven,[63] his disciples passed on. Others came who strayed and changed what he had taught. Therefore, God took away the "writ of faith" (*bismillāh al-raḥmān al-raḥīm*) from those who called themselves Christians and monks, and it remained only among those who truly adhered to the Gospel. This continued until God sent Muhammad as a prophet. Then, *bismillāh al-raḥmān al-raḥīm* was inscribed at the beginning of every Qur'anic chapter, book, treatise, and letter. God—the Lord of Might and Glory—swore that it would simply be impossible for a faithful person to utter it over something without that thing being blessed by it.

61 The angels who question the deceased in the grave, which can take on either a frightening or a welcoming form.

62 Alternate: "Jesus said: 'Who will this be especially for?'"

63 According to the Qur'an, Jesus was not killed on the cross but rather was raised to heaven, where he awaits until returning to earth during the end times.

SAYINGS OF THE PROPHET AND THE PIOUS

The Prophet said:

> When a truly faithful person recites *bismillāh al-raḥmān al-raḥīm*, the mountains shall glorify God along with him and seek forgiveness for him—even if he does not hear them glorifying God.[64]

The Prophet also said:

> When a person says *bismillāh al-raḥmān al-raḥīm*, Paradise says, "Here I am, at your service! O God, your servant has said *bismillāh al-raḥmān al-raḥīm*, so take him away from the fire and bring him to Your garden.

And:

> A group of my followers will come forth on the Day of Resurrection reciting *bismillāh al-raḥmān al-raḥīm*. On their scales of deeds, their good deeds shall outweigh their evil deeds.
>
> "Glory be to God," other nations shall exclaim. "Nothing outweighs the deeds of Muhammad's followers!"
>
> It shall be explained to them: "This is because they began speaking with three of the greatest divine names. Were these names to be placed in one pan of the scale, and the entirety of the heavens and 'earths' and everything lying between them to be placed in the other pan, these names would be heavier! These names are: *bismillāh al-raḥmān al-raḥīm*."

64 This is alluding to two concepts in the Qur'an: firstly, that the mountains used to glorify God with Solomon; and, secondly, that all of creation glorifies God, even if human beings cannot understand it. See Qur'an 17:44, 21:79, and 34:10.

Then the Prophet said [that God said]:

> I have made these names a shield against every calamity, a cure for every ailment, and a ward against Satan, the outcast. Through the blessings of these names, I have protected this nation from being swallowed up by the earth, calumny, metamorphosis, and drowning.[65] So, through these names, approach the Mighty and Generous.

It is related from al-Hasan al-Basri, may God have mercy upon him:[66]

> "And when you mention the name of your Lord alone to them in the Qur'an, they turn their backs in revulsion" (Qur'an 17:46)—This refers to *bismillāh al-raḥmān al-raḥīm.*
>
> "[God] enjoined the word of reverence upon [the faithful], they being more worthy of it and deserving of it" (Qur'an 48:26)—This was *bismillāh al-raḥmān al-raḥīm.*

However, some say this latter phrase was "there is no god but God." And he said:

> A person who writes this, reciting it reverently, shall be placed among those who are near God.

It is narrated from ʿIkrimah:[67]

> God was, when there was no other thing. So God created the light, then the Tablet, then the Pen. Then God commanded the Pen to march across the Tablet until the end of time, inscrib-

65 Expressions of divine wrath meted out to some of the ancients, according to the Qur'an.

66 Al-Hasan al-Basri (c. 642–728) was a famous Islamic scholar, exegete, and mystic.

67 ʿIkrimah (d. c. 636) was a companion of the Prophet Muhammad.

ing all that was and would be. The first thing that the Pen wrote was *bismillāh al-raḥmān al-raḥīm*. God made it a writ of faith, guaranteeing security for any of His creatures who recite it regularly. The inhabitants of the seven heavens and pavilions of Paradise—the cherubim, the righteous, and those glorifying God—all recite it.

The first thing revealed to Adam was *bismillāh al-raḥmān al-raḥīm*. He said, "Now, I know that my descendants shall never burn in the Fire if they keep up reciting this." After that, it rose back up to the heavens until the time of Abraham, whereupon it was revealed to Abraham when he was about to be catapulted into the blaze, but God saved him from that.[68]

Then it rose back up to the heavens until the time of Solomon. When it was revealed to him, the angels said: "Now the reign of Solomon is complete." God commanded him to proclaim to all the tribes of the Israelites, ascetics, and worshippers: "Whoever wishes to hear this writ of faith should come to Solomon, the son of David, in the prayer-niche of his father." They gathered around him, and Solomon stood, ascended the pulpit, and recited this writ of faith for them; it was *bismillāh al-raḥmān al-raḥīm*. When they heard it, they rejoiced, saying, "We testify that you are a true messenger of God, O son of David!"

Then it rose back up to the heavens until the time of Moses. When it descended to Moses, he used it to overpower Pharaoh, Qarun, Haman, and their forces.[69]

68 An allusion to Qur'an 21:68–69, which tell of how Abraham's people tried to cast him into a raging fire. At that time, according to the Islamic tradition, Jibra'il came to him and offered to save him, but Abraham declined and said he would put his full faith in God alone; therefore, the fire was commanded to cool for Abraham.

69 Qarun is identified as the biblical Korah. It is not clear whether Haman corresponds to a biblical figure. Haman was a supporter of the Pharaoh of Egypt and hence an enemy of Moses. Qarun was a wealthy man who rebelled against Moses. Both are mentioned in passing in the Qur'an.

> Then it was raised up to the heavens again until the time of Jesus. God revealed to him: "O son of Mary! Do you know what I have revealed to you?"
>
> Jesus said: "Aye, O Lord."
>
> God said: "I have revealed to you the writ of faith; it is *bismillāh al-raḥmān a-raḥīm*. Hold fast to reciting it—night and day, coming and going, sitting or standing, eating or drinking—always. For whoever comes to the Judgment Day with it written eight hundred times in their scroll of deeds shall be forgiven their sins."

Once, one of the righteous folk went to visit a pious shaykh, in hopes of receiving prayers and blessings. He found people had flocked around the man's door, waiting for him to come out. A rainbow had come out, with one end alighting upon his door. When the shaykh opened the door and stepped out, he put his foot upon the rainbow and said, "*Bismillāh al-raḥmān al-raḥīm.*" Then he walked up and over the rainbow until he stepped down the other side—with the people watching him all the while. The man who had come to visit the shaykh—and he was said to have been named al-Malihi—exclaimed, "Look how far ahead of us this man is, and we could also do this too, if God wills!" Then he dedicated himself to hard work and spiritual striving until he became one of the top spiritual elite.[70] They shaykh who had walked along the rainbow was ʿAbd Allah al-Rajraji, may God be pleased with him.

SCROLLS AND LETTERS

My brother, look at what lies in *bismillāh al-raḥmān al-raḥīm*! Listen carefully to this verse: "[The Queen of Sheba said:] This [letter] is from Solomon, and it [says]: '*Bismillāh al-raḥmān al-raḥīm*. Do

70 Lit. *al-afrād*; a person whose spiritual status is so high that they enjoy a special status with God and spiritual truths are unveiled to them. See Nikos Yiangou, "Transpersonal Dimensions in Islamic Spirituality," in *International Journal of Transpersonal Studies*, vol. 38, no. 2 (2019).

not exalt yourself before me, and come to me obediently'" (Qur'an 27:30-1).[71] How the Queen of Sheba obeyed! The writ of faith (*bismillāh*) entered and settled in her heart; all of that was due to the blessings of *bismillāh al-raḥmān al-raḥīm*. Thus there are secret ways it can be used to carry out acts, to attract people's hearts, or to physically bring people to you, for hearts and souls rejoice at it.

It consists of nineteen letters; they are reckoned as ten letters, when repeated letters are not counted more than once. They are as follows:

b–s–m–a–l–l–h–a–l–r–ḥ–m–n–a–l–r–ḥ–y–m

¶ The *m* is repeated thrice,
¶ the *l* is repeated four times,
¶ the *r* is repeated twice,
¶ the *a* is repeated twice,
¶ and the *b*, *s*, and *h* are unrepeated; nor are the *n* or *y*.

Therefore, there are six repeated letters:

a–l–r–ḥ–m–n

¶ The *m* is repeated three times.
¶ The *alif* is repeated three times.
¶ The *l* is repeated four times.
¶ The *r* is repeated two times.
¶ The *ḥ* is repeated two times.

Therefore, excluding repeated letters, the letters comprising *bismillāh al-raḥmān al-raḥīm* are:

b–s–m–a–l–h–r–ḥ–n–y

71 This verse tells of a letter which the Queen of Sheba receives from Solomon, which begins with *bismillāh al-raḥmān al-raḥīm*. This verse is also sometimes used to summon jinn.

The upshot of this is that *bismillāh al-raḥmān al-raḥīm* consists of ten letters, when repeated letters are not counted. The letter *b* acts as a conduit for conveying goodness. It is a cold letter; therefore, it always begins the "writ of faith" (*bismillāh*). The letter *b* is also one of the eternal letters persisting on the Day of Resurrection. There is a hidden secret behind this: the singular ones are from the divine essence. They point to the truth; they are from the Truth and travel from you to it.

Know that the scrolls revealed to Abraham, Noah, and Solomon all began with *bismillāh al-raḥmān al-raḥīm*. So too did the first revelation sent to the Prophet: "Read, in the name of your Lord who created..." (96:1-2). By beginning with the secret of the letter *b*, it hinted at the mysteries of divinity. They travel from you towards you, for they are the places where the hidden divine essence manifests, as when God said: "Through Me, you know Me." When God created the letter *b*, he created alongside it eighty-one angels glorifying and sanctifying God.

FURTHER VIRTUES OF *BISMILLĀH AL-RAḤMĀN AL-RAḤĪM* IN THE PROPHETIC TRADITION

Protection. The Prophet said:

> Whoever says "in the name of God, the Greatest" (*bismillāh al-aʿẓam*) three times upon awakening shall be protected from harm. Nothing on heaven or earth will harm them that day, and no calamity shall strike them that day, for God hears and knows all. And whoever says this three times at eventide shall be safe from harm until waking up the next day.[72]

Poison. It is said that Khalid ibn al-Walid[73]—may God be pleased with him—once drank lethal poison. The Byzantine emperor sent

72 The text notes that another version of this narration reads *fālij* ("paralysis") instead of *faj'ah* ("calamity"), and that a third version reads "nothing shall harm him" (*lā yuṣibhu shay'*).

73 Khalid ibn al-Walid (592–642) was a companion of the Prophet and a military

him a messenger, who bore a lethal poison and told him, "If what you swear is true—that no poison shall afflict a person who says these words—then drink this." So he clasped the poison in his hands, while the messenger, his companions, and other people were around him, and said, "*Bismillāh al-raḥmān al-raḥīm.*" Then he drank it, and stood up, unharmed.

Other versions of this account say that he said, "In the name of God with whose name none is harmed, neither on earth nor in the heavens; He is hearing, knowing." After that, he drank the poison, but, by the power of God, it did not harm him, apart from making him sweat. So see, my brother, how this noble name protects people from being harmed by poison!

Protection. Through this noble name, Noah's ark sailed forth. Through it, Abraham was saved from Nimrod's fire, which God made cool and safe for him. Through it, you shall be safe whether you remain at home or venture outside, for the Prophet said:

> When you enter and leave your home, say, "In the name of God, we enter and leave, and in God we trust."

Also say *bismillāh al-raḥmān al-raḥīm* when locking the door, for Satan will not unlock a lock which *bismillāh* is recited over. He will not get near you if you say "*bismillāh*, and upon the path of the Messenger of God" before going to sleep.

Protection from leprosy. The Prophet said, "Ritual ablutions [before prayer] are incomplete if someone does not say *bismillāh*," and "Whoever eats with a leper and says "in God I trust' shall not be harmed."[74] ʿUmar ibn al-Khaṭṭāb did this. When a man who had leprosy was there, ʿUmar brought out food and invited him to eat with him, saying, "In the name of God in God I trust."

Curing the evil eye. This name cures the [evil] eye. Strike the afflicted person's chest with your hand and say: "*Bismillāh.* O God,

---

commander.

74 The text notes that this latter narration has been transmitted in the book of Prophetic narrations known as *Sunan Abi Dawud*.

remove this heat and suffering from him!" Also say *bismillāh al-raḥmān al-raḥīm* when you put your foot in the stirrups, intending to travel; no harm shall befall you.

Protection during travel. When a faithful person says *bismillāh al-raḥmān al-raḥīm*, Satan shrinks down to the level of a fly. The Prophet used to recite it over people who set out on a journey and wanted to bid farewell to him. He used to say, "When you mount your animals, say, 'In the name of God, and upon the path of the Messenger of God.'" The Prophet used to begin his journeys by saying: "In the name of God. I seek refuge with God from the travails of the open road..."—and the rest of the prayer is in the books of Prophetic narrations. He also told Talhah ibn ʿAbd Allah—when his hand was struck in the heat of battle, causing him to lose his fingers—"If you had said *bismillāh al-raḥmān al-raḥīm*, the angels would have lifted you up from the battle while the people were watching!"

Look at the blessings of this name—the angels raise up the person who utters it! Malevolent spirits shrink from it, and it neutralizes poison. You have been gifted knowledge of its secrets and virtues. Wherever you look, you will see its glory. So do nothing—go nowhere and stay nowhere—without mentioning it. Through it, one finds happiness, protection, salvation, and one's daily bread. All of that is folded into *bismillāh al-raḥmān al-raḥīm*. The Prophet[75] used to heal all of people's pains and ailments with it.

DIVINE NAMES BEGINNING WITH *B* (*BĀʾ*)

Celestial vision. According to a shaykh, if a person writes the letter *b* on Friday, after fasting the preceding Thursday, and carries it on their right upper arm,[76] God shall open their heart and remove any sluggishness from them. Blessings shall surround them. They shall see the mysteries of the letter *b* and the lights of the angels; their form shall manifest, from the celestial and sublunary realms. A beauteous, fragrant being shall appear—standing and in full form,

75 Alternative version: Jesus.

76 In some places, today, these things are bound to the arm with cloth.

which only the spiritual elite see—speaking the letter *b*. He shall shine an unwavering light; when the mysteries of *b* are uttered, his light shall surround his form, for it is one of the secretly treasured names.

The divine names containing *b* heal dry pain and ease difficulties, by the permission of God. Divine names with *b* include the Good (*al-birr*), the Maker (*al-barī*), the Eternal (*al-bāqī*), and the Resurrector (*al-bāʿith*); in it lies the secret of perpetuity. Thus, in *bismillāh al-raḥmān al-raḥīm*, *alif* heads *b*; it is spread across its essence, as is *l*. *B* also appears in the divine names "the Seeing" (*al-baṣīr*) and "the Inner" (*al-bāṭin*); each name has its own mysteries. The divine name "the Good" (*al-birr*) aids the righteous in doing good deeds (*aʿmāl al-bir*) and in doing good to their parents (*birr al-wālidayn*).

For any matter. The divine name *al-birr* can be recited two hundred thirty-three times daily for any matter after mixing the name of the target with the name. For example, say the target's name is ʿAmr (spelled *ʿ-m-r-w*). Beginning with the first letter of *al-birr* (spelled *a-l-b-r*), alternate the letters of *ʿamr* and *al-birr* as such:

a-ʿ-l-m-b-r-r-w

Then, move the letters around, until the first line repeats, as you see here. Know and be guided! By God, who speaks the truth and guides to the right way.

ا ع ل م ب ر ر و	*w-r-r-b-l-l-ʿ-a*
و ا ر ع ر ل ب م	*m-b-l-r-ʿ-r-a-w*
م و ب ا ل ر ب ع	*ʿ-b-r-l-a-b-w-m*
ع م ر و ر ب ل ا	*a-l-b-r-w-r-m-ʿ*
ا ع ل م ب ر ر و	*w-r-r-b-m-l-ʿ-a*

Remove the last line, which repeats. You will then have four lines left. Write this to attain anything you wish, place it in your pocket, and recite over it:

> O Lord of Lords, who cares for all with Your subtle governance, make the streams of your subtlety flow towards me faster, that I may immerse myself in that sweet ocean which the spirits delight in, by the power of Your mysteries! Grant me one of Your powerful names—those names which protect from all harm, either in the heavens or on earth—which protect from all that is scattered across the lands, digs its way up from the earth, falls from the sky, or rises up to it. You are subtle, aware, the guardian, the knower.

The divine name "the Maker" *al-bārī* is useful for healing swelling and illnesses. "The Eternal" and "the Resurrector" (*al-bāqī* and *al-bāʿith*) also have specific applications, which shall be discussed later, God willing.

DIVINE NAMES BEGINNING WITH *S* (*SĪN*)

This section discusses the second letter in *bismillāh*, *s*.

WE NOW RETURN to our discussion on *bismillāh*. When God created it in His World of Command, he sent down with it nine thousand eight hundred eighty angels. It was the first letter to meet *b* and holds the mystery of union with it, and is one of the manifest letters in God's Greatest Name. The Greatest Name has both manifest and hidden letters; the manifest letters uphold the heavens, and the hidden letters uphold the celestial realms, including the Divine Seat and the Throne. Therefore, *s* was placed in the first heaven, and in the third degree of the Divine Seat. Since *b* has been affixed to divine power—and it is a letter filled with mysteries—it travels from you to God, since you say "He is He" (*huwa huwa*), and He says "By Me, by Me" (*bī ,bī*).

A word search. Surah Yasin (Chapter 36 of the Qur'an) is replete with divine names expressing God's wisdom. Should you stumble upon them and write them, then wash them down with water [and drink the water] while in a state of ritual purity and facing the direction of prayer [Mecca], and repeat this for the number of days that is equal to the numerical value of the names, God shall make that you speak wisdom. These names are in the middle of the chapter and contain sixteen letters. Two of the letters have a dot on top, and two of the letters have a dot on the bottom. Altogether, they are five words; they begin with *s* and end with *m*.

The letter *s* appears in the divine names "the Peace" (*al-salām*), "the Hearing" (*al-samīʿ*), and "the Quick" (*al-sarīʿ*); the latter name is useful for those entreating a quick response to their prayers. Mayhaps, it shall hasten a response to their prayers.

Answered prayers. Whoever recites "the Quick" (*al-sarīʿ*) for a certain number of days[77] and asks God for something shall attain what they seek.

Fulfilling needs. If someone is desperately in need of something from God, they may write it on the palms of their hands, raise their hands in prayer, and beseech God through this name (multiplied by the number of days); they shall receive a response after invoking God for that number of days. The number is equivalent to the number of days multiplied by four thousand two hundred seventy-seven.

Seeing the celestial spirits. A person wishing to see the celestial spirits should beseech God to remove the veil from their eyes and grant them certain vision. They shall speak with the spirits and ask them whatever they wish; the spirits shall respond. In this lie arcane mysteries and momentous deeds. Keep at it; you shall attain what you seek.

Reviving the unconscious. "The Hearing" and "the Perceiving" (*al-samīʿ, al-baṣīr*) may be written at a suitable time and hung upon someone who has lost consciousness. The unconscious person shall come to at that very moment.

77 Alt. "for the number of days equivalent to its numerical value."

Know that some mystics in Barca[78] had once sought to do this. They went to see Ibrahim ibn Jaruh and found that he had fallen faint near the city gate. So they drew up a square and hung it on him. After they recited the name seven hundred times, he awoke and did not lose consciousness again, by the grace of God.[79]

Hearing and seeing jinn, and discovering secrets. One who inscribes these names on gold and carries this tablet on their person shall hear the language of jinn and see the jinn. The bearer of that tablet shall also be able to command the celestial spirits to carry out his will. Should the bearer of the table consistently recite these names, all of the secrets of creation shall be revealed to him. He shall know what people hide in their minds, and what people do openly. These mysteries have been witnessed.

Protection and salvation. The divine name "the Peace" (*al-salām*) is useful for petitioning for security. It is said that, on the Day of Judgment, when our master Muhammad is watching his followers cross the bridge, he will be invoking, "O *salām*, save them!"[80]

THE LETTER *M* (*MĪM*)

Al-Buni now proceeds to the letter *m*, being the third letter in the phrase *bismillāh al-raḥmān al-raḥīm*. It looks like this: م.

78 Barqah; an ancient city in Libya also known as Antaeopolis.

79 The astute reader will notice that, in this story, (a) they have written the names in a magic square, and (b) al-Buni only says they recited one name, as opposed to the two names mentioned in the instructions. No explanation is given, although the latter could simply be a copyist's error.

80 According to Islamic eschatology, the bridge (*ṣirāt*) is a bridge over hell which all people must cross on the Day of Judgment. Some people will cross it quickly, some people will cross it slowly, and some will fall over the edges. Also, according to Islamic eschatology, merely being a Muslim does not guarantee a person salvation; they will be accounted according to their intentions and deeds, and sent to either heaven or hell. However, the faithful are encouraged to have hope in the Prophet's prayers for them. Regarding the actual narration presented here, the text notes that there is an alternate version in which the Prophet says "*sallim, sallim*" ("save them, save them") instead.

THE LETTER *M* (*mīm*) is one of the letters which is an anagram; that is, its first and last letters are the same.[81] So too are the letters *w* (*wāw*) and *n* (*nūn*). The letter *m* alludes to meeting (*jamʿ*) because it is a circle, and alludes to rest (*sukūn*) because of the awe within it. It is one of the letters of the Tablet.

When God created it, He created it as a circle of light devoid of light. It is one of the letters of the Intellect, due to its encompassing nature. It upholds the Sun in the fourth celestial sphere. Through it, God erected His worldly and celestial kingdoms (*mulk* and *malakūt*), thereby manifesting divine knowledge through *m*. He aided deeds with the secret of the *mīm*-like *nūn*. The last letter of *bism*, in it lies the secret of the age of wisdom; as God says: "Until he matures, at forty years of age..." (Qur'an 46:15)—since the numerical value of *m* is forty.[82] God entrusted it with ninety angels who are guardians of the Tablet. It is a secret which God has placed in the name of His prophet Muhammad—may God's peace and blessings be upon him—for it begins his name. This is one of the secrets linking him to the celestial and earthly kingdoms (*malakūt* and *mulk*).

Prosperity. Gazes upon the figure of the letter *m* daily for forty days while reciting the following Qur'anic verses:

> O God! King of the Kingdom! You grant kingship to whom You will, and seize kingship from whom You will. You elevate whom You will, and abase whom You will. In Your hand is goodness; You have power over all things. You make the day pass into the night, and the night pass into the day. You bring forth the living from the dead, and the dead from the living. You provide for whomever You will without reckoning. (Qur'an 3:26–27)

God will open the doors of sustenance to you in this world and in the afterlife. By "figure," we mean the eight-by-eight form which is associated with Mercury and Wednesdays.

81 The letter *m* is called *mīm*, and the word *mīm* begins and ends with *m*.

82 The age of forty is traditionally taken as the age of full maturity, especially spiritual maturity, in the Islamic tradition, although, in the eyes of the religious law, adult responsibilities begin at puberty.

Enlightenment and protection. Its numerical sigil may be written on an unblemished piece of parchment while facing the direction of prayer and in a state of ritual purity. This should be done after fasting for forty days while remaining in a continual state of ritual purity and being mindful of God (*dhikr*). It should also be done when the Moon is in the mansion called the Most Fortunate (*saʿd al-suʿūd*, the twenty-fourth lunar mansion) and during the hour of the Sun. Then, it should be carried on one's person. Whoever bears this shall think no untoward thoughts. God shall allow the bearer to understanding the realities of faith and the sacred lights. He shall protect the bearer from any harm and gift them an aura of awe.

Fulfilling needs. God shall take care of anything you need if you entreat God through it on Friday while fasting and keeping up regular remembrance of God (*dhikr*).

Sustenance. If you are struggling to make a living, you will find much good in it if you carry it with yourself. God shall grant you provision in ways you never would have imagined.

Love and affection. It also may be used to unite people's hearts or to seek acceptance from someone—and more, through its blessings. There are lessons in this, for those who ponder it—for those whom God inspires understanding of its secrets in. Its form shall be discussed later, in the appropriate section.

Fulfilling needs. This can be done through combining the numerical values of the divine names, as I will show you later, along with their figures. I will explain how to attract people's hearts, gain people's acceptance, and attract various types of love and obedience. This is something you will not find in any book, so keep it to yourself, guard it preciously! For it is the philosopher's stone[83]—the greatest treasure and the most famous lodestone.

Know—O brother—that the one to whom the secrets of *m*—with its roundness, congruity, and all else it contains from the realms—are revealed shall witness the wonders of creation.

83 Lit. "red sulfur" (*al-kibrīt al-aḥmar*), which was a legendary powder said to be ground from the philosopher's stone and which was believed to transmute elements.

Memorization. Similarly, a person who wants God to make it easier for them to memorize things should write a corresponding numerical cipher on Thursday while ritually pure and facing the direction of prayer [Mecca], along with the name of the Prophet Muḥammad forty times, then wash it off with honey-water and drink it, then say: "O God! Through the blessings of what I have drunk, make it easy for me to memorize and understand." This should be done for forty days; God shall inspire the person inwardly and outwardly. This is for the one who would understand the secret of the letter *m*, so that they may witness the power of what lies in it—in each realm upheld by the secret of *m*. It is through this aspiration that God shall open the way.

Foreseeing the future. The letter-form of *m* is one of the hidden secrets. Someone who wishes to know how a certain matter will turn out in the future may write it on an unblemished piece of paper on Monday during the hour of the Moon and incense it with storax. They should also fast that day with the sincere intent of fasting only for the sake of God. Then, they should break their fast[84] upon a bit of bread, say their prayers, then go to bed—while in a state of ritual purity—and sleep on their right side with the paper under their head. While the paper is under their head, they should recite the chapter of the Qur'an which begins "Blessed be the one in whose hand is the kingdom."[85] After that, they should not speak to anyone and go to sleep. God shall inform them of how the matter will transpire. Note that this is only suitable for the pure-hearted—who also keep themselves bodily clean—who carry out ascetic practices.

Wisdom. It may also be written on a glass goblet, then washed off and drunk; God shall grant the one who does that wisdom.

Wise speech. God will grant ease of comprehension to the person who hangs it upon themself, and make them speak words of wisdom.

84 According to the Islamic tradition, at sunset, after abstaining from food and water during daylight hours.

85 Chapter 67 of the Qur'an.

Respect. A person who writes it along with "there is no god but God" eighty times and affixes it to the right upper arm, or else writes it on a garment that they wear, shall be treated kindly and respectfully.

COMMANDING THE FAITHFUL JINN

This section illustrates how verses of the Qur'an are employed to summon jinn. Although the verses here are not specifically about jinn, when written or spoken independently, they impart a sense of authority upon the summoner—situating the summoner in the position of the divine—and convey the theme of summoning, such as in "When He calls you forth with a single call, you shall come forth."

As elsewhere, this section prescribes fasting. In the Islamic tradition, fasting involves abstention from food, drink, and carnal pleasures from sunrise to sunset. Traditionally, if someone were fasting in preparation for summoning jinn, they also would only eat minimally at night and abstain from meat or animal products, and sometimes onion, garlic, and spices, although the author does not mention that here. It is held that this improves the summoner's spiritual senses and also makes the summoner more palatable to the jinn.

Although most Muslims do not speak Arabic as a native language, it would be expected that the Qur'anic excerpts be recited and written in Arabic, since the original Arabic text is believed to be the divine word and thus to have a special intrinsic power that a translation would lack.

SHOULD YOU WANT your faithful brethren from the jinn to do something for you, or to hasten to obey you, wash your clothes, and fast from Wednesday until the fourth Saturday that comes after that. Each day of the fast, bathe, and recite the following sections of the Qur'an in a clean place isolated from other people:

¶ Chapter 112 of the Qur'an ("Sincerity") one thousand times
¶ Chapter 36 of the Qur'an ("Ya Sin") one time
¶ Chapter 44 ("The Smoke") one time
¶ Chapter 32 of the Qur'an ("The Prostration") one time, and
¶ Chapter 67 of the Qur'an ("The Kingdom") one time.

Then, get seven slips of paper, and write on them the following verses of the Qur'an:

¶ On the first piece of paper, write: "He is the one who gives life and death, and alternates night and day" (23:80), "When He has decreed that something be, he says to it 'Be!' and it is" (40:68), and "God shall suffice them; He hears and knows" (2:137).
¶ On the second piece of paper, write: "Your Lord is the one who created the heavens and earth in six days, then mounted the Throne. He makes the night cover the day, which pursues it swiftly; the Sun, Moon, and stars obey His command. Are creation and the command not His? Blessed be God, the Lord of the worlds!" (7:54), "He encompasses whatsoever is with them and keeps a numbered count of all things" (72:28), and "God shall suffice them; He hears and knows" (2:137).
¶ On the third piece of paper, write: "And [he will be] a messenger to the Israelites, [saying,] 'Truly I have brought you a sign from your Lord. I will create for you out of clay the shape of a bird. Then I will breathe into it, and it will be a bird, by the leave of God. And I will heal the blind and the leper and give life to the dead, by the leave of God. Leave. And I will inform you about what you eat and what you store up in your houses. Truly in that is a sign for you, if you are believers'" (3:49), and "God shall suffice them; He hears and knows" (2:137).
¶ On the fourth piece of paper, write: "When He calls you forth with a single call, you shall come forth" (30:25), and "God shall suffice them; He hears and knows" (2:137).

¶ On the fifth piece of paper, write: "They shall proceed from their graves to their Lord" (Qur'an 36:51), and "God shall suffice them; He hears and knows" (2:137).

¶ On the sixth piece of paper, write: "The trumpet shall be blown, and all in the heavens and earth shall fall faint, except for those whom God wills. Then the trumpet shall sound again, and—behold!—they shall stand upright, looking about" (Qur'an 39:68), and "God shall suffice them; He hears and knows" (2:137).

¶ On the seventh piece of paper, write: "A day when they shall hasten forth from their graves, as if racing towards a goal" (Qur'an 70:43), and "God shall suffice them; He hears and knows" (Qur'an 2:137).

This should be done after praying four units of prayer, in which the following chapters of the Qur'an are recited:[86]

¶ In the first, recite Chapter 1 ("the Opening") and Chapter 36 ("Ya Sin").

¶ In the second, recite Chapter 1 and Chapter 44 ("The Smoke").

¶ In the third, recite Chapter 1 and Chapter 32 ("The Prostration").

¶ In the fourth, recite Chapter 1 and Chapter 67 ("The Kingdom").

Then, in the final prostration, say:

> Glory be to the one clad in might, who stands in might! Glory be to the one who graces all with splendor and generosity! Glory be

86 A "unit" (*rak'ah*) of prayer, in the Islamic tradition, refers to a set of movements and recitations repeated a fixed number of times during the five daily prayers. It is comprised of standing and reciting two chapters or sections of the Qur'an, bowing, standing, prostrating, sitting up, prostrating, and sitting up; between each of the latter, specific words of praise are uttered. Reciting each of these chapters of the Qur'an from memory is ideal, but no harm would be incurred from holding a book or inventively pasting them to a wall. Of course, since the summoner will have been reciting them daily while fasting, perhaps the summoner will have memorized them by now, if they were not already memorized.

> to the one who enumerated all things in His knowledge![87] Glory be to the only one who deserves glorification! Glory be to the one who, when He wills something, it is; and when He does not will something, it is not! Glory be to the one replete with gifts, bounties, and blessings! Glory be to the one replete with knowledge and wisdom! Glory be to the one replete with might and bounty! Glory be to the owner of the Throne, Tablet, Pen, and light!

Then raise your head and say:

> O God, I beseech You! By the confluence of might at Your Throne, by the utmost mercy from Your Book, by Your Greatest Name, by Your most generous countenance, and by Your perfect words. Subject to me a faithful jinn aide to assist me in whatever worldly matters I desire!

Seven beings will appear before you in human form; they will be chiefs and noblemen of the jinn.

Before reciting the prayers, you will have already hung the seven pieces of paper from your head, so they dangle down like pommels from a dervish's hat.[88] You will also need a candle. Take the first paper, which you wrote upon and recited [over] in your prayers, and read it aloud to them, then say: "Which of you matches this piece of paper?"

One of them will say, "It is mine."

Ask him, "What is your name?"

He will say, "My name is so-and-so, son of so-and-so."

Write his name atop the paper, then say to him: "Give me your seal."[89] Take the thread [with the paper] and candle, and imprint

87 This expression is an allusion to the last line of the chapter of the Qur'an called the Chapter of the Jinn (Chapter 72), which is also sometimes recited for the purpose of attracting jinn due to its sympathetic nature, and may have been included for this reason.

88 Al-Buni is envisioning a brimless hat, with the papers hung down from it with thread, as if they were pommels.

89 The implication here is that the jinn physically gives the summoner a seal to stamp in the candlewax, similar to how people stamped letters with their

the seal on the bottom of the paper, as if you were sealing a letter. Then return his seal, and do the same with each of the six others.

Then, once you have finished with the seventh, say:

> I adjure you by the names on these papers to appear and respond obediently to my call, when I call you.

Then say:

> Depart, may God bless you!

Keep the papers in a clean place until you find yourself facing some need—for instance, you need food or drink, to find out something, to find or hide a buried treasure, or something else. Call them, and they shall respond to you faster than lightning or the wind, by the permission of God.

Beware, my brother! Only do this have you have a staunch heart and a firm resolve. If you have a sound intellect, a lofty aspiration, a firm character, and a strong heart, and you are well-versed in knowledge, then go ahead. Otherwise, beware of summoning them, for you will harm yourself.[90] For they are great kings. And beware of looking at them, for it will bare all in your heart. If you suffice yourself with the seal discussed next, that will be enough for you.

A POWERFUL SEAL WITH THE LETTER *M* (*MĪM*)

Illness, and other matters. The seal (illustrated below) may be written upon a gazelle-skin parchment and hung upon a person suffering from a bodily ailment, such as fever or chills; they shall recover. It may also be used to make someone affectionate towards you, or to foretell the future, for God will show you wonders through it.

---

personal seals in the olden days.

90 One version says you will harm your soul, and another says you will harm yourself. In the context of jinn summoning, this may be taken literally, since jinn summoning is said to expose the practitioner to physical danger or death when done improperly.

SECRETS OF THE LETTER *M* (*MĪM*)

God will show you wonders through it, for the secrets of the numbers lie in the power of the intellect. The numbers point towards the letters (through reception), and the letters point towards the numbers (through ascent). The numbers point to the spiritual realm, whereas the letters point to the material realm, whose interior is spiritual.

Whoever understands the secret of *m* will have understood why the descent of divine revelation was likened to the clanging of a bell. The Prophet was once asked, "What is it like for you to receive revelation?" He said, "Sometimes it comes to me like the clanging of a bell, and sometimes an angel appears to me and speaks to me, and I retain what he says." The bell mentioned here is like a cowbell. Have you not seen that when cowbells are hung from the necks of horses and cattle and so forth, and the herd moves, the bells ring out and can be heard jangling from afar? The Prophet said, "This type of revelation weighs heaviest on me. Then it departs from me, and I retain what was said."

The letter *m* resembles a bell because both of them are ring-shaped, closed circles, and because they are very heavy matters. Have you not heard what the Prophet said about the angel Isrāfīl—how fearsome he is, how strong he is, and how he bears upon his back one of the enormously heavy pillars of the Throne? And how he stands before the preserved Tablet, despite its enormity and grandeur? Then, there is his trumpet.[91] He already put the trumpet to his lips, although it is five-hundred years wide. In a single stride, he can traverse the seven earths. The Prophet said: "He has already put (*iltaqama*) the horn to his mouth."

So, then, what of *m*? It ends the verb *iltaqama*,[92] for it resembles the trumpet, which inspires fear and dread, felling and reviving creatures. Meanwhile, Isrāfīl stands at the Throne, awaiting the

91 To be blown at the end of time; see previous note on the trumpet and Isrāfīl.

92 The final -*a* in the verb *iltaqama* is not written in Arabic; therefore, the final letter of *iltaqama* is *m*.

command to blow his trumpet. Just as a horn can only be blown by putting one's lips around it in a circle, the letter *m* can only be produced by closing up the lips; it cannot be vocalized any other way. Thus, it resembles the clanging of a bell through the force of its sound.

Understand here the difference between the clanging of a bell and the clanking of chains, which is how Moses described his experience of revelation. When a person hears the clanging of a bell, it moves their spirit; when a person hears the clanking of chains, it moves their body. The *m* encompasses both—the celestial and the terrestrial. Thus *m* has two aspects: one celestial and one terrestrial, each with their secrets. In its long form (*m-y-m*, i.e. *mīm*), it is hot and moist for it contains the letter y and is surrounded by the hot m on each side, making it unruly but selfcontained. Were the y not mediating between the two m's, they would have crushed all between them.[93] The letter *m* is hidden inside every lofty name, and the loftiest of them is *bism*.

Now I shall speak to you about three of the magnificent divine names: *Allāh, al-raḥmān*, and *al-raḥīm*. The name *Allāh* is the Greatest Name, which encompasses the other divine names. For that reason, God begins and ends His book with it. Through it, His servants worship Him; it points towards Him. By it, He is known—through the phrase "He is *Allāh*." The letter *m* points to the name of the Prophet, Muhammad.

Influence, victory, and love. Draw out the figure and square associated with the letter *m*. Then, recite the following invocation and verses over it. Carry it with you when you take audience with kings, judges, or officials. You will speak persuasively, and they will accept what you say. You will be like a lion whom others fall meek before—this is the level of respect that the bearer of this figure enjoys. If

93 The expression here refers to two mountains in Mecca called "al-Akhshabayn." It is related in the collections of Prophetic narrations known as *Bukhari* and *Muslim* that an angel offered to crush the Prophet's opponents between the mountains, but the Prophet declined that offer.

you carry it into battle, you shall vanquish your enemies; if anyone dares to come near you, God will make you victorious. People will honor, love, and respect whoever bears this. Anyone who lays eyes on the bearer shall immediately love them and want to be friends with them. It has other, great secrets.

This is what it looks like:

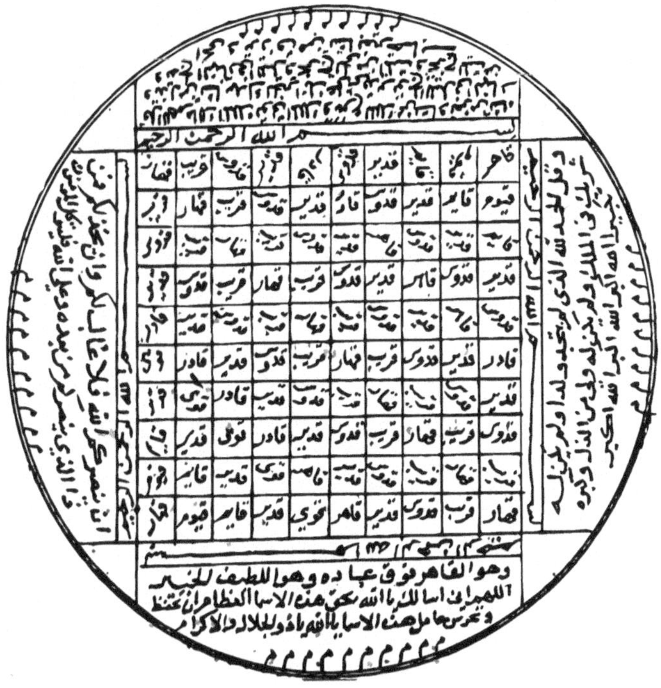

SEEING BEYOND

An imam once dictated this approach to seeing the higher realms. First a person must dedicate themself to ascetic practice; uproot any lust, anger, or despicable traits; and cease any wrongdoing. Then, they should sit in a secluded place, block off any sensory input, and open their inner ears and eyes, setting their heart in line with the celestial realm. Inwardly, they should endeavor to repeat *"Allāh, Allāh"* continuously—with the heart but not the tongue—until it is as if they no longer exist as an independent being and see nothing but God. At that point, God shall truly grant them the power of sight.

While awake, that person will see what they normally see during sleep.[94] They shall see angels, prophets, and handsome, beautiful forms; the kingdom of the heavens and the earth shall be made plain to them, and they shall see things that are truly indescribable. The Prophet said: "The earth folded itself up before me, and I saw all of its horizons."[95] And God said to the Prophet: "Remember the name of your Lord and devote yourself to Him with complete devotion" (Qur'an 73:8). "Devotion" (*tabtīl*) here means cutting one's self off from everything else and purifying the heart, imploring God wholly. In our day and age, this is the Sufi path.

Know that one of the special characteristics of God's lordship lies in His lofty, beauteous, magnificent names and descriptions—especially the name *Allāh*, for the name *Allāh* is so great that none other can be denoted by it.[96] There is no god but He; He has no father and no son; He is the sole divinity. For that reason, once, a saint asked a religious scholar, "Do you want me to teach you something that will benefit you, if you are able put it into practice?"[97]

The scholar said, "Yes."

So the saint told him, "Dedicate yourself to the continual recitation of *Allāh, Allāh, Allāh*. Say nothing but that. During the day, fast; at night, as much as you can, continue reciting this. Do not stop reciting it, night or day, and do not speak to anyone. Seclude yourself from other people for seven days. You will see wonders—that is, wonders of the earth. Then continue this for another seven days; you shall see wonders of the heavens (*samawāt*). Then continue this

94 In the Islamic tradition, it is held that, when asleep, a person might speak with the prophets, saints, or even the ordinary deceased; witness higher spiritual truths; foresee the future; or see and hear jinn. However, this is only for some dreams; other dreams are merely replays of what the person experiences and thinks about during the day.

95 Lit. "easts and wests," oftentimes understood to mean the varying places where sun rises and sets in different locales.

96 Many of the other divine attributes can be used for created beings and things. For instance, God is described as "the light" (*al-nūr*), but the same word is also used for conventional light. However, only God may be referred to as *Allāh*; it is not used for any other being or demiurge.

97 One source simply says that the saint was teaching "one of them," not specifically a scholar.

for another seven days; you shall see wonders of the highest celestial realm (*malakūt*). If you continue this for forty days, God shall show you how to perform miracles, and grant you control over everything in existence."[98]

ON THE NATURE OF GOD

It is narrated from the Prophet that whenever a faithful person says "O God!" (*yā Allāh*), God says, "I am here, My servant! I am God, so what do you need?" And God is the one who knows God best; none truly grasps His greatness except Him. He is the Lord of all and knows all. People debate whether God's essence can be known at all. Some people hold a thing can only be known if can be seen by the eyes or—if that is not possible—understood by analogy to something else. However, God can neither be seen by the eyes, nor is there anything like Him.[99] He is hidden from people's eyes, but knows what they see.[100]

An enlightened shaykh one spoke of how God pre-existed before the beginning of time, and will continue to exist after the end of time. He is singular, but not in number.[101] His attributes are unlike those of creation, and no one can ever truly describe His essence.[102]

98 The number forty figures strongly in the Islamic mystical tradition. Specific acts of worship are often prescribed for forty days. As mentioned previously, the age of maturity is considered to be the age of forty years. In the esoteric tradition, it is not unusual for fasts or other lengthy deeds to also be prescribed for forty days. This anecdote also illustrates the belief that a high level of piety enables a person to see the spiritual realms and perform miraculous acts.

99 Referring to Qur'an 42:11—"There is nothing like God."

100 Referring to Qur'an 6:103.

101 That is, it is not appropriate to say God is "one," because saying that there is "one" of something implies there might be a second or third or fourth of like kind. Rather, God is singular and unique.

102 That is, the way God's attributes are enacted in God is different from how they are enacted in creation. For example, one might say that a person is knowledgeable and God is Knowledgeable (*al-ʿalīm*); however, God's knowledge is of a different type than human knowledge. Or, one might call God "the Light" (*al-nūr*); however, God's light has different characteristics than worldly

Were that not the case, there would be likenesses of God in creation, and these would fall prey to death and destruction, which is impossible for God.

PRAYERS

Al-Mahasibi—may God be pleased with him—says that the angel Jibra'il brought God's Greatest name to the Prophet on a sheet of paper from Paradise. The paper was sealed with musk. On it was written: "O God! I beseech You by Your hidden name: the Pure, the Purifying, the Sacred, the Ever-living, the Everlasting. In the name of God, the Compassionate, the Merciful—Mighty and Generous."[103]

Once, an eminent pious man was asked to compose a few sentences that someone could use to beseech God for an important matter. In response, he wrote this short prayer:

> O God! I ask You, because You are God, in absolute truth! And because You are God, whatever condition or fortune I am in. And because You are God, the Sacred. You alone are the Unique, the Eternal. You have no opposite or like, no opponent or peer. And because You are God, whom none is like! "And He is Hearing, Seeing."[104]
>
> Bless our master Muhammad and the family of Muhammad, and bless whoever loves Muhammad.
>
> Take care of what I need—all of it—in a way that will be beneficial for my worldly life and my afterlife—so that I may be guard-

---

light, even though there is a similarity in function—for instance, light illuminates, beautifies, and guides the way.

103 At this point, in the modern printed edition, the text quotes someone as saying not to teach the Greatest Name to women or children. However, since this was not present in the primary manuscript consulted, it was not included here.

104 A Qur'anic description of God; for instance, in Qur'an 42:11.

> ed by Your shepherding, protected from pitfalls, looked after by Your care. O You who always returns good! O revered and forgiving! O source of blessings!
>
> O God, I ask you this as a servant to Your mighty lordship. I am demonstrating my belief that You know the unseen and know what we seek even before our hearts do. So carry this out beauteously, O best of those who are besought! And bless the beloved of the hearts [Muhammad].

This prayer is said to contain the Greatest Name of God, just as it is said that *bismillāh al-raḥmān* contains the Greatest Name of God, and that the distance between it and the Greatest Name is like the distance between the pupil and white of an eye.

God speaks the truth and guides to the right way. May God bless our master Muhammad, his family, and his companions.

Chapter 6

SECLUSION: THE MYSTICS' DISCOVERIES

While Islam does not have a formal monastic tradition, in the Islamic esoteric tradition—both occult and mystical—it is often prescribed for a person to go into seclusion for a period of time, sometimes in a windowless room or in nature. During this time, the person would be expected to focus on prayer, fasting, and—in the case of the occult tradition—workings. Here, the author does not outline regulations for seclusion—perhaps assuming that the reader is already aware of these. Instead, he tells instructive stories of how a mystic had a vision of a tablet and seal, to demonstrate the virtues of temporary seclusion, and then concludes with some practical applications.

KNOW—MAY GOD MAKE you and me obedient towards Him—that this is a tremendously important subject, and one which pertains to the divine names "the Mighty" (*al-ʿazīz*) and "the Merciful" (*al-raḥmān*).

One of the pious, righteous imams went into seclusion in a chamber in the Great Mosque of Aleppo. It was pitch black, like a grave. Light could only come in through the door; when the door was shut, it was like a grave. He used to pray with the congregation. At noontime, when he heard the final call for prayer, he would venture out, but with his back to the congregation. By the time the prayer had finished, he would be in a supra-sensory state in which he was facing Mecca, but not looking at anyone. For the rest of the time, he would pray and entreat God copiously to teach him God's Greatest Name.

One night, he was sitting, imploring God and reciting God's names, when a tablet of light materialized before him. On it were drawn various figures. He turned away from it, lest it distract him from God. However, it prodded him on the face, and a voice told him, "Take what will benefit you."

At that, he opened his eyes and began to scrutinize the tablet. It was bounded by four lines: on the top, bottom, right, and left. Inside it were two concentric circles, with a vowel-mark's distance between them.[1] A line divided the inner circle in half, and, in the upper half of the circle rested an upright triangle. "Nay, He is God!" (Qur'an 34:27) was written along the vertical axis of the triangle, ending in the center of the circle. The letter *j* occupied one corner of the triangle, and the letter *d* occupied the right-hand corner of the triangle. Nearby, at the edge of the triangle, was written the divine name "the Eternal" (*al-ṣamad*); it extended from the line of the triangle towards the circle. Then, the letter *dh* was written at the edge of the circle along the diameter line. Near the circle was the letter *alif* and the divine name "the One" (*al-wāḥid*), in front of the divine name "the Eternal" (*al-ṣamad*). In one corner of the triangle was written the divine name "the Vanquisher" (*al-qahhār*). Inside the triangle was written the letter *y*, and in the left corner of the triangle, the letter *h*. On the top, outside the triangle but inside the circle, the divine names "the Merciful" (*al-raḥīm*) and "the Compassionate" (*al-raḥīm*) were written; "the Compassionate" was followed by "the Forgiving" (*al-ghafūr*). Inside the triangle, on the axis, was the letter *ṭ*.

The lower part of the circle had four curves looping out of it. On one was written "manifested" (*mutajall*); on the next, "by the light" (*bil-nūr*); and, on the next—facing the letter *z*—"it has arrived" (*qad atāka*). There were two lines to the left and right inside the quarters of the circle. On one was written the letter *ḥ* in Indian script, and outside of it was written "Our servant" (*ʿabdan lanā*). Then, on

1 The length of the vowel *fatḥah*, which is a short line written over an Arabic letter to denote the short vowel *a*.

the other was written "the Chosen" (*al-mukhtār*)[2] In line with *al-mukhtār* was written "through guidance" (*bil-hudā*).

Towards the middle of the circle was the letter *w*, repeated ten times. On the top half of the outer circle was written: "*A-l-m*. There is no god but God, the Ever-living, the Everlasting!" (Qur'an 3:1–2).[3] The letters *a-l-m* were facing the *j* which was inside the triangle, and the *y* in "the Ever-living" (*al-ḥayy*) was facing the letter *w* which was beneath the circle. The *m* in "the Everlasting" (*al-qayyūm*) was facing the letters *a-l-m*, and, around the outside of the circle was written "God encompasses them" (Qur'an 85:20). On the other side, it was written outside of the circle: "Nay, it is a glorious Qur'an, on a preserved Tablet" (Qur'an 20:21-22).

The mystic who had that vision of the tablet relates:

> Although the tablet soon vanished, I engraved it in my memory. Then, after I had prayed the dawn prayers and was sitting reciting my liturgies (*wird*), sleep overtook me, and I dreamt of the Commander of the Faithful, ʿAli ibn Abi Talib,[4] may God bless his countenance. He asked me, "Where is the tablet that you saw—which was inscribed near me?"
>
> I handed it over to him. He spoke highly of it, and explained its secrets to me; however, I only understood one thing that he said. That was when he placed his finger atop the letter *j* in the corner of the triangle, in the upper half of the circle, and said, "From here, divine majesty (*jalāl*) emanates." From that, I understood that it represented a divine name, before which other divine names are subordinate. I also understood that it was one of the

2 "The Chosen One"; a proper name for men, and also a title of the Prophet.

3 Some of the chapter of the Qur'an begin with single letters, the meaning of which is unknown.

4 ʿAli ibn Abi Talib (599–661 AD), the fourth Muslim caliph and a central figure in Islamic spirituality; most Sufi lineages trace back to him. The expression "may God bless his countenance" is used exclusively for him.

names divesting the sacred divine essence of any sort of imperfection or limitation (*tanzīh*).[5]

I said, "O Commander of the Faithful, I have not understood what you said."

He replied, "Muhammad ibn Talhah will explain it to you, God willing."

Then I woke up, finished my liturgies, and went to see Muhammad ibn Talhah; we had sworn an oath of brotherhood towards each other. After I told him what had happened, he praised God and began to explain it to me. He also told me that he had thought that no one else would learn of it, so he sought God's forgiveness for that. Then he provided his explanation and titled it "A String of Pearls: God's Greatest Name."[6]

After that, I had a vision of the Prophet, may God's peace and blessings be upon him. He was sitting in his prayer-niche while the Commander of the Faithful was nearby, talking to the Prophet about the tablet. ʿAli commented, "The sacred name is symbolized nowhere better."

Then the Prophet said, "This is indeed the truth. This is what my brother Jibrāʾīl—peace be upon him—the Trustworthy Spirit[7]—told me."

When I awoke, I went to the shaykh and told him what had happened. He fell silent for a long while, then reached somewhere behind him and pulled out a paper upon which was written this exact expression: "The sacred name is symbolized nowhere better."

5 "The Trustworthy Spirit" is an appellation of the angel Jibrāʾīl.
6 *al-Durr al-Munazzam fi Ism Allah al-Aʿzam*. A work by the same name is attributed to the famous Islamic scholar al-Suyuti (c. 1445–1505 AD).
7 A common appellation of the angel Jibrāʾīl.

> When I saw that, I demanded, "Why didn't you say that before?"
>
> He said, "I assumed that no one else would be told of it." Then he sought God's forgiveness again and added it to his commentary, "A String of Pearls."

It is one of the secrets of God—a secret which can only be accessed by the truthful, the reverent, and the devoted (*murābiṭūn*). It is God's greatest name, a splendorous secret. If you know but a smidgen of it, humans and jinn shall obey you, and it will unlock to you treasures of knowledge and treasures of the earth. Hide it from the unworthy! Only touch it when ritually pure. This is it, as you can see; and God guides to what is right.[8]

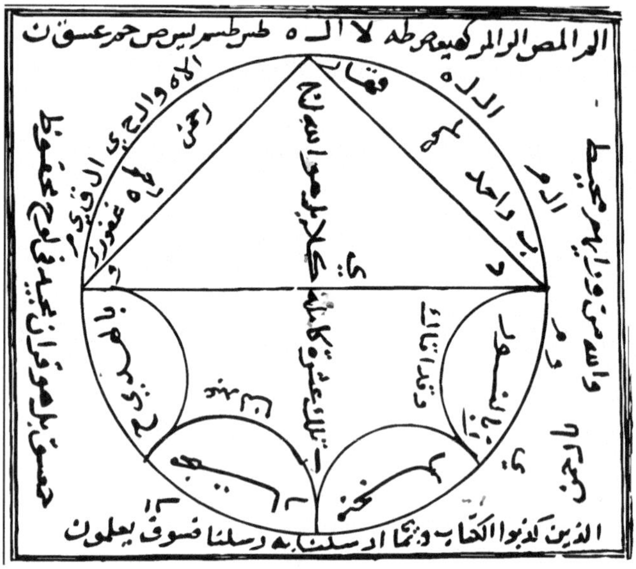

Know that the letters in the corners of the triangle correspond to the numerals one to nine.[9] The letter *y* corresponds to ten. They each stand for an abbreviated divine name, which forms the following

8 The diagram presented here largely matches the description given in the text, but with some variations. The diagram was based on a drawing in the Feyzullah Efendi manuscript.

9 That is, *a* = 1, *b* = 2, *j* = 3, *d* = 4, *h* = 5, *w* = 6, *z* = 7, *ḥ* = 8, *ṭ* = 9, and *y* = 10.

invocation: "O God, O Resurrector, O Glorious, O Perpetual, O Guide, O One, O Taintless, O Protector, O Pure" (*yā Allāh, yā bāʿith, yā jalīl, yā dā'im, yā hādī, yā wāḥid, yā zakī, yā ḥāfiẓ, yā ṭāhir*).[10] This can be followed by the prayer we mentioned at the end of the previous chapter, since it corresponds to this sublime seal. We will repeat the prayer here:

> O God! I ask You, because You are God, in absolute truth! And because You are God, whatever condition or fortune I am in. And because You are God, the Sacred. You alone are the Unique, the Eternal. You have no opposite or like, no opponent or peer. And because You are God, whom none is like! "And He is Hearing, Seeing."[11]
>
> Bless our master Muhammad and the family of Muhammad, and bless whoever loves Muhammad.
>
> Take care of what I need—all of it—in a way that will be beneficial for my worldly life and my afterlife—so that I may be guarded by Your shepherding, protected from pitfalls, looked after by Your care. O You who always returns good! O revered and forgiving! O source of blessings!
>
> O God, I ask you this as a servant to Your mighty lordship. I am demonstrating my belief that You know the unseen and know what we seek even before our hearts do. So carry this out beauteously, O best of those who are besought! And bless the beloved of the hearts [Muhammad].

This prayer corresponds to this sublime seal. Aspire to whatever you wish from it, and extract from it whatever you wish; you will find it effective for all matters, and it shall suffice you. It is the philoso-

10 From this, one can also deduce a method of empowering letters through associating them with divine names.

11 A Qur'anic description of God; for instance, in Qur'an 42:11.

pher's stone, the supreme cure. Those who understand its secrets shall attain whatever they desire, by the permission of God.

A MYSTICAL BUT PRACTICAL SEAL

He also said, may God be pleased with him:

> I was in seclusion, and I saw two concentric circles, in the middle of which was the name *Allāh*.[12] Other names of God branched off from it and repeated the same name, except for the name "the Beautiful" (*al-jamāl*). Once this luminous figure had been inscribed into my heart, it went away, and I emerged from my reverie. So I copied it onto a piece of paper and pondered upon it. I said to myself, "Maybe I can derive the ninety-nine other names from this name."
>
> I set to work on that, when all of a sudden I was overwhelmed, and a voice pronounced to me: "Give thanks for this explanation and blessing!"
>
> I sought God's forgiveness and praised him. Then I went back to thinking about it. These are nineteen names which I deduced from the Name of Majesty (*Allāh*); added to the Name of Majesty, they make twenty names.

There is no doubt that this is extremely handy for a person who understands how to make use of it; I will explain some applications of it here.

For any material or spiritual matter. Purify yourself, enter a secluded place, face the direction of prayer, and pray two units of prayer. Intend something good, and place your hope in God. Do this

12 The texts says this is in the form of *jalālah*, which is generally used to refer to the word *Allāh*. However, when analyzing a supranormal geometric figure, all assumptions are off!

at midnight or afterwards. Then, recite the twenty divine names while your heart is present; do not think about anything else. Recite them one thousand six hundred seventy-three times; or, if you prefer a shorter recitation, recite them one-hundred eighty times. Then, after invoking God, ask for what you need. God shall make it come easily to you, especially you are petitioning for greater ease in learning, for God shall clear the way to your goal along a path originating in His mighty name. He shall show you wonders, some of which can be described, and others which are inexpressible.

Protection. Some of these utterable wonders pertain to protection. If you prepare this seal and place it in your baggage, you will be kept safe, both at home and on the road, by the will of God. If you affix it to your upper arm and stride straight into the clutches of your enemies, God shall save you, and your enemies shall be sorely disappointed. Should you have to face a tyrant whose machinations you fear, the tyrant shall humble himself and yield to you. God shall cool his wrath and cut short his plots, before your very eyes. God shall make sure that you will get what you need, and will protect you from any evil, due to the glorious, wondrous secrets of this seal.

Curing diseases. If these names are written with an ink made of rosewater steeped with musk, saffron strands, and sweet camphor, and administered[13] to a person suffering a physical or psychological ailment, the patient shall be cured.

Respect. A person who bears these names shall enjoy physical, psychological, and spiritual strength, for these names beget an aura of awe and majesty; the effect of this shall be seen without any doubt.

Independence and popularity. If you recite these names seventy-seven times every day after the dawn prayer, and make it part of your liturgy (*wird*),[14] you shall witness its blessings—in your material life, in your spiritual life, and in yourself. Your aspirations will no longer be tied to other people. Instead, creation shall obey you

13 Via washing them down with liquid and giving them to the patient to drink.

14 Specific recitations of the names of God and other homilies practiced by Sufis, often prescribed by one's teacher, but which do not fall under the generic prescriptions of Islamic ritual law.

and be at your disposal. People shall love you dearly, and you shall love them.

Vengeance against tyrants. If a tyrant has oppressed or overpowered you, and you wish to take vengeance against him, recite this prayer and these names: "O God, O Quick, O Quick, O Resurrector, O Originator, O Just, O Empowerer, O Doer!"[15] Do this during the first hour of Saturday. Then invoke God's wrath against the one who has overstepped his bounds and harmed you. God shall take vengeance for you against him before a week has passed and bring victory to the downtrodden.

Reconciling the estranged. To reconcile two estranged people who utterly hate each other, write the twenty divine names along with their names. Then dissolve the names into water, and have them drink it; they shall make up and be bosom friends, by the permission of God.

Love and obedience. You can do the same to spark affection in someone's heart—if you want that person to love and obey you, to be at your beck and call. Write your name and their name, along with the twenty divine names, and give it to them to drink. That person shall love you ardently and never wish to part from you. Write the names on Sunday during the hour of the Sun or the hour of Mercury, and after you have perfumed yourself with a sweet-smelling incense, such as aloeswood, amber, benzoin, musk, or mastic. It shall be done, if God wills.

There are many other ways that this seal can be used, but we sufficed ourselves with only a brief mention of them, lest this section become tedious.

These are the twenty divine names we have been referring to:

> O God—O Hearing—O Knowing—O Quick—O Expander—O Just—O High—O Great—O Elevated—O Mighty—O Indulgent—O Resurrector—O Doer—O Raiser—O Revered—O Preventer—O Creator from Anew—O Benevolent—O Gatherer—O Originator.

15 *Yā Allāh, yā samīʿ, yā sarīʿ, yā bāʿith, yā badīʿ, yā ʿadl, yā muʿizz, yā faʿāl.*

Yā Allāh—yā samīʿ - yā ʿalīm—yā sarīʿ - yā wāsiʿ - yā ʿadl—yā ʿaliyy—yā ʿaẓīm—yā mutaʿāl—yā ʿazīz—yā ʿafuww—yā bāʿith—yā faʿāl—yā rafīʿ - yā maʿbūd—yā māniʿ - yā muʿīd—yā nāfiʿ - yā jāmiʿ—yā badīʿ.

This is the circular seal we have been speaking of, and God guides to what is right:

Say this prayer in conjunction with the circle:

In the name of God, the Compassionate, the Merciful. Lord, I ask you by Your name which opens the doors to Your realm of command and creation, so that truth may manifest its splendor and descend—exalted in command and existence, the depths of which are perceived by those whom You have aided. It is known to those who have witnessed it, but hidden from those You will to hide it from. Many things may resemble it, but none strike the

> mark of what You have decreed.[16] O Knowing, O Wise, O Opener, O God, O Lord!
>
> I ask you—O Hearing, O Knowing, O Quick, O Expander, O Just, O High, O Tremendous, O Elevated, O Mighty, O Indulgent, O Resurrector, O Creator from Anew, O Raiser, O Revered, O Preventer, O Point of Return, O Benevolent, O Gatherer, O Originator!

I ask You by the secret linking the realm of existence with the divine decree. And I ask You by what You have unrolled and pronounced in Your celestial realms, which has left its traces on the material world. And I ask You by what You have hidden from the intellects—the secrets of the depths of Your mercy, and what You have enshrouded and enfolded throughout creation. And I ask You by the secrets hidden within the various revelations—that You protect me from the alluring voice of Satan and his temptations—which turn good into evil, ocean into desert, and benefit into harm. I ask that You protect me from all calamities and mishaps. And I ask that You grant me Your all-encompassing grace and immense honor, in relation to the luminous realm of the gnostics. Grant me deep understanding and knowledge—O Kind, O Giving, O Lord of the Worlds!

HOW JESUS USED TO RAISE THE DEAD (THROUGH THE PERMISSION OF GOD)

This section can be considered a preview of the next chapter, which is on the same subject.

16 This comes across as an allusion to Qur'an 3:7, which says that some Qur'anic verses are of clear meaning (*muḥkam*), and others are ambiguous (*mutashābih*); only those with firm knowledge understand the true meaning.

THIS WAS DONE through God's greatest name—the most tremendous, the purest, the most untarnished, the most perfect, the most treasured, the most hidden name, which none of the other names could ever compare to.

I was told this by Asad ibn Musa. He was told this by al-Kalbi, who heard it from Abu Salih, who said:

> This is the secret, hidden name. A person may write it on a gazelle-skin parchment or unblemished piece of paper. This should be done on Sunday at sunrise, while fasting, wearing clean clothing, and having bathed. Then, it should be incensed with aloeswood and red sandalwood. After that, they should affix it to their forearm. Good things shall hasten to them. They shall witness so many blessings and amazing things that they shall have no doubt in it.

This is the name which Moses used to work miracles:

> I am God. There is no God but Me, so worship Me! (Qur'an 20:14)

Zubaydah also used to use this name to control the caliph Harun al-Rashid;[17] he always did whatever she said.

Acceptance by others. You can write this name, incense it, and hang it facing the sun, from sunrise to sunset; the sun must shine on it all day. It will make people accept you. This is the invocation that accompanies it:

> I beseech You, O God, O Mighty, O Upholder, O Maintainer, O Near, O Powerful, O Holy, O Powerful, O Ancient, O Vanquisher![18] You are the one who strengthened Your friends through Your

17 The women of the court, including wives and slave-girls, were known for pulling the strings of the caliphs during the Abbasid caliphate. Zubaydah also appears in *The Arabian Nights*.

18 *Yā qāhir, yā qayyūm, yā qā'im, yā qarīb, yā qadīr, yā quddūs, yā qādir, yā qadīm, yā qahhār*. All of these names start with *q*, considered to be a powerful letter which could beget strength.

prophets.[19] You adorned Your prophets with Your trials. You subdued the vile by expanding Your powerful reign.

I ask You by Your might, a bulwark against threats; by Your vast generosity which overcomes all things; and by Your right over Creation, mighty or low. Make me powerful among Your creatures. Make me needless of them and only in need of You.[20] Honor me with Your flowing, hidden wellspring of life so I may take refuge in it and turn to You. Make me one of Your beloved friends, now and forever, who are drawn towards You. Make me beloved at the door to truth, firmly witnessing things, so I may turn towards You. Spread love for me among the hearts of the faithful, so I may partake in the secret of Your generosity when some need arises, and Your response stands as proof.

O Kind, O Giving! You whisper intimate secrets. You teach wisdom and reverence. You inspire higher, secret truths in the hearts of those whom You love, wherein You also manifest Your glory. You hear the tiniest, most hidden things. You see all with Your unsleeping eye. Nothing is hidden from you, not even the silent creeping of a black ant upon a rock beneath layers of dust on a dark night.

19 A "friend of God" (*walī*) is essentially a saint or a highly pious person, such as the mystic in the story at the outset of this chapter. Here, "saint" was avoided due to its formal religious connotations.

20 This phrase is, to some degree, dependent on the dual meaning of *ghanī*, meaning both "wealthy" and "independent" or "self-sufficient." A common theme in the Islamic tradition is asking for God to provide for or enrich a person such that they would no longer have to abase themselves by asking for assistance from other people and would only have to depend on God. One of the names of God is *al-ghanī* ("the Wealthy" or "the Self-sufficient"), and the human being is considered to have an existential poverty before God—either because the human being requires God to provide their daily bread, or—according to some Islamic philosophers—because God is continually emanating and bestowing existence on the universe, and therefore all beings are perpetually in need of renewal to continue to exist.

O God! I ask you by the subtleties you granted to hearing and sight—some in one but not the other—and the truths between them—that You bestow upon me the secrets of what the eye sees, and vision of the lights settling upon the eyes and ears. Bestow upon me Your luminosity, and allow me to continually contemplate the will of Your sacred presence. Aid me in understanding my lower self through careful self-evaluation. You gather all good and repel all harm, O Lord of the Worlds![21]

O God, I ask You—O Vanquisher, O Near, O Holy, O Upstanding, O Everlasting[22]—I ask You by Your singular essence and eternal attributes—O Everlasting who never sleeps, O King who is never overthrown—bless our master Muhammad and his family, and fulfill my needs: both what I am asking for, and what I am not asking for but which would merit Your satisfaction. By Your Mercy, O Most Merciful of the Merciful!

21 Here, it is worth observing that the Arabic language lacks clear-cut duality between good and bad, or good and evil, that some other languages enjoy. While there are expressions for good and bad, or good and evil (for instance, *khayr* and *sharr*), they do not immediately always come across as opposites or pairs. Here, *khayr* ("good") is being treated as the opposite of *ḍayr* ("harm," "inquity," "offense").

22 *Yā qahhār, yā qarīb, yā quddūs, yā qā'im, yā qayyūm, yā qarīb*—again, all names beginning with *q*.

Chapter 7

THE NAMES THAT JESUS USED TO RAISE THE DEAD

KNOW—MAY GOD MAKE you and me obedient towards Him, and make us understand the secrets of His names—that these names are of supreme, sublime importance. Al-Khwarizmi—God bless his soul—said: "I sought God's Greatest Name for forty years, and finally found it with a man in China. He had compiled many things about this name, and written them in the Himyarite script so that the unworthy would not be able to read them."[1]

Al-Khurasani—God bless his soul—says:

> Fast for seven days. Then, on the seventh day, write these names on a gazelle-skin parchment with rosewater and saffron. Then invoke the angels of the current quarter of the year[2] along with the names of the winds—the names which Abraham told us of. Follow that with any request. It is better if it can be cast into flowing water or hung in sunlight. Be sure to mention the names of the angels of the season, those angels' aides, the winds, and the planets that they rule, and your request shall be taken care of, by the permission of God.

1 The Himyarite language is an ancient Semitic language spoken in Yemen, now extinct, which Arab scholars considered to be incomprehensible.

2 The *thāqūfah*, mentioned in the next chapter.

Al-Khwarizmi also related about the shaykh mentioned previously:

When I met that shaykh, I asked him about God's Greatest Name.

He said, "All of God's names are glorious."

"Yes," I said, "but I have already learnt of many of these names."

He asked me about the angels of the seasonal quarters (*thāqūfāt*) as known to Balʿam ibn Baʿūra,[3] and as known to Joseph, so I told him what I knew of each.

Assuming that I had not come across any of the hidden names, the shaykh then said, "Come near me, for, by God, no one better than you has approached me about this."

I assented and approached the shaykh, and we began communing about the noble divine names. After asking me about the names that were on the staff of Moses, he dictated to me the Greatest Name.

Then he said to me, "My son, know that these are God's most glorious names. They have been written in foreign tongues, and some in Hebrew, so that no one can read them. These are the glorious, blessed, excellent names that Ziyad ibn ʿAbd Allah—may God be pleased with him—spoke about, when he said that he heard a scholar saying, 'The virtue of these names compared to all the other names is like the virtue of the Night of Power over all other nights, or like the virtue of Friday over other days.'"[4]

3 Balʿam ibn Baʿura is said to have been an ascetic man who, due to his prayers and piety, had been gifted knowledge of God's Greatest Name, through which any prayer would be answered. However, he was tempted either by women or by wealth to misuse this name, thereby committing great wrongs. There are various stories of how this happened—for instance, being bribed to pray against Moses and his people—but the message is the same. He is said to be referred to in Qur'an 7:176, although the Qur'an does not give details.

4 The Night of Power (*laylat al-qadr*) is considered to be the most sacred night

> I discovered them written in the Himyarite script in a place called Qazvin.[5] A person who truly understands their significance will hide them from the unworthy. Fear God! They are invaluable to someone who has suffered a fright or grief, who has heart palpitations, or continuously needs to rush to the washroom. Ziyad ibn ʿAbd Allah instructed, "Fast three days, and write this verse upon a pure white gazelle-skin parchment with saffron ink. If a person suffering from excess wind, an eye problem, melancholy, or something similar carries this on their person, they shall soon be cured."

Another version of this narration says:

> Write these names on Saturday, when fasting and ritually pure, and when the Moon is in its domicile.[6] Carry them; you shall attain your goal, God willing.

Through these names, Jesus used to raise the dead and cure the blind and the lepers. These names are written in the heavens. Scholars concur in their views about them. The Commander of the Faithful, ʿAli ibn Abi Talib—may God bless his noble countenance—said:

> Whoever recites these names continuously shall witness supernatural acts and attain their goals. Beware of taking them lightly! Hold them in the highest esteem. Recite them night and day; you shall ascend to the level of the saints.

---

of the year. It falls in one of the last ten odd-numbered nights of the month of Ramadan and is considered to be the time when God finalizes what shall be fated for the next year. Muslims generally spend that night in prayer. The Qur'an says that this night is more valuable than "one thousand months" (97:3). In the Islamic tradition, Friday is considered to be the most blessed day of the week and is day of the main congregational prayer.

5 A city in Iran.

6 That is, in Cancer.

This is the circle with all the names; know and be guided!

This is a sigil to be used with the circle:

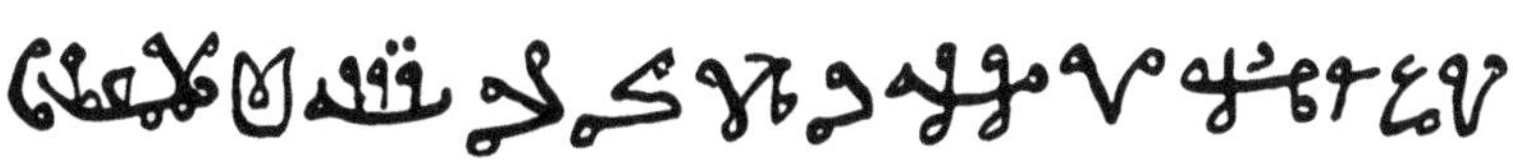

It is related from Abu Hudhayl, may God be pleased with him:

> When Jesus—may the peace and blessings of God be upon him—wanted to raise the dead, he used to pray two units of prayer. Then, he would invoke God through the names "O Ancient, O Everlasting, O Singular, O One, O Eternal."[7]

Seeking specific needs. Maqatil ibn Sulayman—may God be pleased with him, said, "For forty years, I was on a quest to find the names that Jesus had used to raise the dead. Then, I found a scholar who

7 *Yā qadīm, yā dā'im, yā aḥad, yā wāḥid, yā ṣamad.*

knew them." He mentioned the same names as in the previous narration, and then continued, "A person who recites them one hundred times after the dawn prayer and then makes any request shall have their request fulfilled."

Destroying tyrants. To destroy a tyrant, pray the dawn prayer. Then, while still seated, before speaking to anyone, pray:

> In the name of God, the Compassionate, the Merciful. All power and strength are vested in God, the Exalted, the Mighty. O Ancient, O Abiding, O Singular, O Unique, O One, O Eternal, O Ever-living, O Everlasting, O Generous, O Merciful, O Supporter of those who have no support, O You who is relied upon, O You who has neither sire nor son, nor any peer—Alone, Glorious, and Noble![8]

Repeat this one hundred times, then ask God for anything you need. It shall be done swiftly, especially if you are invoking God's wrath against an oppressor.

How to use these names. If you want to use these names, draw a circle like the disc of the Sun and write in the names inside it. Incense it with aloeswood, amber, or something similar, then carry it on your person. You shall attain what you seek, and God knows best.

The prayer associated with the circle. This is the prayer to be recited when using the circle:

> O God, I ask You through what Jibrā'īl besought when he prostrated before Your mighty Throne. By the right of Your name: *Allāh! Allāh! Allāh!* Subject to me Your powerful angels, the servants of Your Throne, those present before Your sovereignty: Kasafā'īl, Dardā'īl, Samḥiyā'īl, Samʿiyā'īl, Rūqiyā'īl, Nūriyā'īl, Samkiyā'īl, Ṭahṭahā'īl, Jibrā'īl, Darʿiyā'īl, Samsamā'īl, Ṭaṭā'īl,

8 *Bismillāh al-raḥmān al-raḥīm. Lā ḥawla wa lā quwwata illā billāh al-ʿaliy al-ʿaẓīm. Yā qadīm, yā dā'im, yā fard, yā witr, yā aḥad, yā ṣamad, yā ḥayy, yā qayyūm, yā karīm, yā raḥīm, yā sanad man lā sanad lah, yā man ilayhi al-mustanad, yā man lam yalid wa lam yūlad wa lam yakun lahu kufwan aḥad, yā dhā al-jalāl wa al-ikrām.*

Ḥarmiyā'īl, Ṭayṭiyā'īl, Isrāfīl, 'Azrā'īl, Mīkā'īl, Karmā'ih, Karshā'ih, Sarfiyā'īl, 'Arqiyā'īl, Thaṭbiyā'īl, and 'Īniyā'īl.

Answer, O honorable angels and unblighted spirits who confess to God's oneness, by the right of the name God over you! God, the Unique, Mighty, the Light, the Holy—whose Name I have celebrated above all other names, be they mighty, glorious, powerful, or sublime. Subject to me these honorable angels, so they will do what I need. (Insert what you need here.)

Be careful to only seek something that God would be pleased with, and beware of chasing after the unlawful. For Bal'am ibn Ba'ura knew the Greatest Name, but after he used it to curse Moses, God set Moses against him, as mentioned in the Qur'an: "Recite to them the account of the one whom We gave Our signs to, but he cast them off" (7:175).

For the sake of God, do not take these names lightly! Do not use them to disobey God, lest they work against you. Protect them; guard them from the unworthy. They are a secret which God gifts to His near and dear ones. Many of the learned and righteous immersed themselves in them, and thereby attained their wishes and goals. We have only presented a brief summary about this here; God guides whom He wills to the straight path.

SPECIAL INVOCATIONS

Overcoming an enemy. Know—may God make you and me obedient to Him—that if you draw this square while pure in body and clothing, God shall handle your material and personal concerns, assist you in obeying Him, and grant you victory over your enemies; any despot who lays eyes on you shall be terrified of you.

Humiliating tyrants and fortifying the heart. Write this and carry it on your head.[9] All pompous tyrants shall fall meek before you; so

9 Presumably under a hat, turban, or other head-covering.

too will Satan. God shall invigorate you, inwardly and outwardly, and strengthen your heart for spiritual and material endeavors.

Quarrels and altercations. If you carry this and get into a fight, you will win. Whoever bears this shall enjoy divine aid, through the blessings of God and the blessings of this bounteous square.

Victory on the battlefield. If you carry this into war, God will aid you against your enemies, and you shall come to no harm, through the permission of God.

Kings who require obedience. If a king carries this on his person, his commanders, soldiers, aristocrats, and dignitaries shall obey him. He will enjoy divine aid.

Here is the square:

314	260	116	117	124	138	411	282	103
312	453	226	463	258	248	321	214	271
211	245	228	218	250	240	212	262	212
309	299	219	25	441	214	256	246	274
309	299	219	25	441	214	256	246	274
308	221	260	244	233	316	255	229	275
224	344	252	330	225	257	247	212	243
1270	216	244	232	297	215	229	222	147
281	222	372	266	279	289	572	17	169

Chapter 8

THE FOUR SEASONS

KNOW, MY BROTHER—MAY God make you and me obedient towards Him—that this chapter is the core of this book. It contains great secrets, for in it are the names of the angels who rule over the four quarters (*thāqūfāt*) of the year, along with the names of the winds and the associated planets. Guard this knowledge, for all else revolves around it.

Known that the year is divided into twelve months and four quarters, each which has three months. There are four quarters which fall in each of the four seasons:

¶ The first quarter, which is in the spring, begins on the twenty-fourth of March and continues until June twenty-fourth.

¶ The second quarter, which is in the summer, begins on the twenty-fourth of June and continues until September twenty-fourth. During this time, the Sun passes through seven lunar mansions: the Nose-tip, the Twinkling Eyes, the Mane, the Weather-change, the Howling Dogs, and the Sky-raiser.[1]

¶ The third quarter, which is in the autumn, begins on the twenty-fourth of September and continues until the twenty-fourth of December. During this time, the Sun passes through seven lunar mansions: the Shrouded, the Claw, the Crown, the Heart, the Stinging Tail, the Ostriches, the Wasteland, and [a bit of] the Slaughterer's Joy.

¶ The fourth quarter, which is in the winter, begins on the twenty-fourth of December and continues until the twenty-fourth of March. During this time, the Sun transverses seven lunar man-

1 For a list of the lunar mansions, see the Appendix.

sions: the Slaughterer's Joy, the Voracious Auspice, [the Most Fortunate], the Tent Poles, the First and Second Spouts, and the Belly of the Fish.[2]

Each quarter is called a *thāqūfah*, for this is what the prophet Abraham, the friend of God, called them.

The angels of the four directions and the four seasons

The angel of the east is Danyā'īl. The angel of the west is Dardā'īl. The angel of the north is Anyā'īl.[3] The angel of the south is Ṣarfyā'īl.

The angel of the east rules over summer. The angel of the west rules over winter. The angel of the north rules over spring. And the angel of the south rules over autumn.

The angelic assistants who rule over the four cardinal directions

Since manuscripts vary, an alternate set of names has been provided in the footnotes. Most of the differences occur due to the presence or absence of dots over letters, an easy mistake for a copyist unfamiliar with these names. To compound the matter, in some sources, the names for the north and south are swapped.

The angelic assistants of the east are Darjamiyā'īl, Jartiyā'īl, and Samʿā'īl.

The angelic assistants of the west are Jibranqīl, Qaṣmā'īl, and Sharaghyā'īl.

The angelic assistants of the north are Qamyā'īl, Marḥyā'īl, and Ḥarmakyā'īl.

The angelic assistants of the south are Farʿaq'īl, Ṭākhīl, and Alalūl.[4]

2 An alternate version of the text has some of the quarters begin on the twenty-first rather than the twenty-fourth of the months, which seems more apt.

3 انيائيل, not to be confused with عنيائيل (ʿAnyā'īl), the angel who is said to rule Friday and the planet Venus.

4 An alternate version says that the angelic assistants of the east are

The names to use when addressing the wind, Sun, and Moon during each the four quarters

Most of these names are of obscure provenance. Note that some of these names are slightly different from the names used in the evocations in the next section.

	FIRST QUARTER (*spring*)	SECOND QUARTER (*summer*)	THIRD QUARTER (*autumn*)	FOURTH QUARTER (*winter*)
West wind	Marbaʿā	Mabrdūd	Māsūr	Maghmūr
South wind	Māsūr	Samrā	Yaʿfūr[5]	Idʿārūm
East wind	ʿAqīdūn	Kābadyākh	ʿAbrīrah	Alranḥ[6]
North wind	Ṭafīr	ʿAbūrā	Kāfūr[7]	Ḥamrīdūn[8]
Sun	Yāqūt[9]	Yājrūn	Shamyās	Ijār
Moon	Sīlī	Abāḥūn	Thiqāl[10]	Jārʿī

Evocations for each seasonal quarter of the year

These evocations are a curious admixture of conventional Islamic prayers with non-Arabic names originating from outside the standard Islamic corpus; generally, anything addressed as a "spirit" (*rūḥāniyah*) does not fall under the rubric of orthodoxy. They illustrate the multi-layered, multivalent nature of the *Sun of Knowledge*, in that they combine material from dis-

Darḥamiyāʾīl, Ḥarqiyāʾīl, and Samʿāʾīl; the angelic assistants of the west are Ḥibrīqīl, Qaṣmāʾīl, and Shawaʿiyāʾīl; the angelic assistants of the north are Farghawʾil, Ṭākhīl, and Alalūl; and the angelic assistants of the south are Qamyāʾīl, Marhyāʾīl, and Ḥarmakiyāʾīl.

5 "Earth-colored gazelle."

6 This name was penned unclearly.

7 "Camphor."

8 This name was penned unclearly.

9 "Ruby"—appropriate given the astrological correspondence between rubies and the Sun.

10 "Weighty," perhaps referring to the brilliant Harvest Moon.

parate currents into a coherent whole. The evoker prays to God and then asserts the authority of the divine to wield power over the ruler of the hour and the day—an approach shared with ancient texts—followed by a prayer to wield power over the ruler of the seasonal quarter, and an appeal to a jinn king. Most of them conclude with the formula "now! quickly! this moment!" (*al-waḥā, al-ʿajal, al-sāʿah*) which frequently ends Arabic adjurations. The addresses to the spirits and jinn kings are followed by "may God bless you," which is always considered good form.

While the inclusion of Qur'anic verses and divine names is specifically Islamic, the overall framework of the evocations is not dissimilar to that in the Greek Magical Papyri (which do also sometimes appeal to the Abrahamic God)—for instance, through the appeal both to and through divinity, building up the presence of divinity through a series of epithets, the command to the spirits, multiple names of the Sun, the nod to the daemon of the day and hour, and the insistence that the work be done quickly. (One gets the sense in ancient texts that divinities, daemons, and demiurges sometimes acted a bit slow for the conjurer's taste.) Perhaps, these evocations also simply cover all bases—something also popular with the ancients.

Because many of the names are non-Arabic, they would have been unfamiliar to copyists and difficult to discern in handwriting; as result, different versions of the *Sun of Knowledge* have varying readings of these names. Possible rectifications to the text have been presented in square brackets. There are also different vowellings of the names, since the Arabic script lacks short vowels. The names given here are largely based on what is found in the Fayzullah Efendi manuscript. An alternate set of names has been provided in the notes.

The astute reader will notice some subtle differences between the structure of the for evocations; for instance, one of them presumes that the evoker is calling the spirits into a scrying mirror. Rather than treating each approach as being suitable only for that specific season, the structure of the text for one season could presumably be applied to another.

THE FOLLOWING four seasonal evocations include the names of the angels, the angelic assistants, the Sun, the Moon, the wind, the heaven, the earth, and everything else you need. Savor this honey and do not ask about the bees, for it has come to you flowing and pure.

SPRING. To call upon the ruler of the seasonal quarter during spring, say:

In the name of God, the Compassionate, the Merciful.

I adjure you, O angel Anāʾīl, and your angelic assistants Farʿūthīl, Ṭākhīl, and Alalūl. I adjure the four winds ʿAqdūn, Māsūr, Manʿā, and Ṭabīʿtīn. I adjure the Sun and Moon, Nāḥūt and Saqīsmāl [or Yāqūt and Sīlī]. I adjure Barnār, Miyālakh, Qarkhalaf, and Baṣā; and her sister Sīlnūn [or Wasīlnūn].[11]

11 An alternate version of this paragraph reads: I adjure you, O angel Anāʾīl, and your angelic assistants Farghawʾil, Ṭākhīl, and Alalūl. I adjure the winds ʿAqdadūn, Māshūl, Māsūrā, Samʿā, and Ṭabʿatīn. I adjure the Sun and Moon, Yāḥafat and Saʿsamiyāh. I adjure Yūnār, Miyārakh, Jarjagafah, Baṣād, and her sister Basīlīṣ. (Note that Farghawʾil ends with -il, not -īl).

The name Sīlnūn (and the name of the Moon "Sīlī" in the previous section) seem reminiscent of the Greek "Selene," although it is hard to prove an etymological link. Still, it is easy to forget that civilizations are not separated by impenetrable walls; while Arabic civilization reached prominence after the time of Islam, for millennia beforehand, the peoples of the Near East and Mediterranean mingled and migrated around, and parts of the Middle East and North Africa were under ancient Greek and Roman rule. Therefore, it is only natural that there shared words between Greek, Latin, Arabic, and other regional languages dating back to ancient times, not only after the advent of Islam.

In the name of God, the Originator, Lord of the last and first—boundless, endless—who owns all in and between the heavens and the earth, and all beneath the ground. God—the great, the source of unending blessings, crusher of enemies, merciful, compassionate, powerful and never overpowered, vanquisher and never vanquished, firm in justice on the Day of Resurrection. There is no god but God, the Mighty, the Wise, the Compassionate, the Merciful. There is no god but God—the King, the Sacred, the Peace, the Bestower of security, the Overseer, the Mighty, the Compeller, the Dominant. Exalted be God above the partners they ascribe to Him! He is God—the creator, the maker, the fashioner. To Him belong the most beautiful names. Everything in the heavens and on the earth glorifies God; He is the mighty, the wise (Qur'an 59:23–24).

O God, O Mighty! I ask You to bestow upon me Your mercy—here and now—and to fulfill my need! (Insert your need.) You wield power over all things, and all strength and power lie in God, the Mighty, the Great. I ask You, O God, by Your perfect name—O Living, O Eternal; all but You perishes. O God! O God! O God! I believe in You, that there is no god but You. There is no lord but You! By Your Greatest Name, which outstrips all Your other names!

Grant me control over the ruler of this day, the ruler of this hour, the ruler of this seasonal quarter, and the rulers of the four cardinal directions, so that they will fulfill my need, by Your will. O God, You decree justly but are subject to no one's decree.

I adjure you, O legion of kings and spirits![12] Fulfill my need, by the right of the Mighty and Dominant, the Living, the Eternal, the Everlasting, the Ever-abiding, the Undying! Who be unlike any other thing, whose name is never forgotten, whose light never perishes, whose Throne never vanishes, and whose Seat

12 *Mulūk* and *rūḥāniyyah*. "Kings" presumably refers to the jinn kings.

never quakes! And who sent the Book to His Prophet Muhammad—may God's peace and blessings be upon him.

O God! O God! O God! I ask you—and there be no god but You, ruler of this world and the hereafter—fulfill my need, and grant me control over the spirit of this quarter and this season; You have power over all things. Hasten, O Abyaḍ, may God bless you![13]

SUMMER. To call upon the ruler of the seasonal quarter during summer, say:

In the name of God, the Compassionate, the Merciful.

I adjure you, O angel Danyāʾīl, and your angelic assistants Darjamāʾīl, Jibriyāʾīl, and Samʿiyāʾīl. I adjure the four winds Kaydaḥ, Masmiyūn, Marmūn, and ʿĀdūd. I adjure the Sun and Moon, Bāḥūn and Bāḥūn [Yājrūn and Abāḥūn], and ʿAjramīsh, Barkhalāsh, Saylsūn, Barhawān, Yaljān, and Balthādarūḥ.[14]

In the name of God, and by God, and all strength and power lie in God, the Mighty, the Great. O God! I beseech You, O Lord, for You are the living who never dies, the vanquisher who is never vanquished, the creator who was never created, the seeing and hearing who never doubts, the strong who never bullies, the eternal who never dwindles, the near who is never far, the witness who is never absent, the divinity who never harms, the powerful who never oppresses, the perpetual who never eats, the guardian who never sleeps, the reliable who never falters,

13 An address to the jinn king al-Abyaḍ, who corresponds with the Moon and Monday.

14 An alternate version reads: I adjure you, O angel Danyāʾīl, and your angelic assistants Darḥamiyāʾīl, Ḥarqiyāʾīl, and Samʿaiyāʾīl. I adjure the winds Kaydaḥ, Mashaymūn, Mashamiyūn, Marmūd, and ʿĀdūd. (Possibly, five winds are mentioned here because the copyist was not sure how to render Mashaymūn, and took two guesses.)

> the just who never tyrannizes, the self-sufficient who never faces need, the treasure that never runs out, the protector who never overbears, the strong that never weakens, the good who never connives, the guardian who is never absent, the singular with no peer, the unique with no duplicate, who gives with no strings attached, quick and never confounded, generous and never miserly, mighty and never abased, guardian who never forgets, perpetual who never disappears, the good who never wrongs, the responsive who never tires, the eternal who never ages, the one with no like, who faces no argument when He acts.

This is what one version says; according to another version, say instead:

> O God! I ask you, O Lord, for You are the living who never dies, the creator who was never created, the guardian who never sleeps, the truthful who never wavers, the just who never wrongs, the hidden who is never seen, the defender who never falls, the good who never connives, the guardian who never tires, who answers quickly without being confounded, the generous who is never miserly, the mighty who is never humbled, the protector who never neglects, the eternal who never perishes, the good who is never forgotten, the unique whom nothing resembles. There is no god but You, the Lord of the Worlds!

Then continue:

> By Your might, I beseech You, fulfill my need, and grant me control over all the spirits (*rūḥāniyyah*), by Your glory and the light of Your beauteous face! That is easy for You.
>
> I adjure you, O legion of spirits! For the sake of God, the mighty, and His hidden, treasured name, be my assistants in this task. By the One who possesses the highest word, answer me in what I call you to do! Hear and respond to my call; carry out this task!

Quickly, O Madhhab![15] Do what I have commanded you to do! Now! Quickly! This moment! God bless you all.

AUTUMN. To call upon the ruler of the seasonal quarter during autumn, who is also the ruler of the south, say:

In the name of God, the Compassionate, the Merciful.

I adjure you, O angel Isrāfīl [or Ṣarfyāʾīl], and your angelic assistants Qamyāʾīl, Farkhāʾīl, Marhiyāʾīl, Marʿīyāʾīl, and Ḥarmakiyāʾīl. I adjure the four winds ʿAnyāʾīl, Yaʿfūn, Maysūr, and Kāfūn. I adjure the Sun and the Moon, Samyās and Taʿāʾīl, and Huwayqīm, Mahūlāj, al-Nūkh, Mithāl, Sabā, and Badrūkh.[16] Descend into my mirror, and carry out all that I desire and all that I request.

O God, I beseech You, O light, light of lights, knower of secrets. You are God, the king, the strong. There is no god but You, and none worthy of worship but You. O God! O God! O God! By the right of these great names—*Allāh, Allāh, Allāh*—the high, the magnificent—*Allāh, Allāh, Allāh*—the forbearing, the generous—*Allāh, Allāh, Allāh*—the living, the eternal—*Allāh, Allāh, Allāh*—the singular, the everlasting, who neither sires nor was sired and has no peer. I beseech you by Your might, and by the way You settled Yourself upon Your Throne.

Fulfill my need! Grant me control over the ruler of this day, the ruler of this hour, the ruler of this seasonal quarter, and the rulers of the four cardinal directions; You can do all that You will! Fulfill my need, for You decree justly and are subject to no one else's decree. Let them come to my aid in what I seek from them.

15 The jinn king associated with Sunday and the Sun.

16 An alternate version reads: I adjure you, O angel Ṣarfyāʾīl, and your angelic assistants Qamyāʾīl, Marḥiyāʾīl, and Ḥarmakiyāʾīl. I adjure the four winds Qandīd, Yafʿūn, Maysūr, and Kāfūn. I adjure the Sun and the Moon, Sabās and Taʿābal, and Huwayfīm, Mahūlāḥ, al-Nūḥ, Mithāl, Sabā, and Badrūḥ.

(Insert your need here.)

O God! O God! You are the one whom there is no god but You! Hidden and unseen; Your light is not perceived by the eyes. I believe in You and put my trust in You. You are God, whom all creatures humble themselves before. You are the light of lights, the powerful, high above Your Throne, of indescribable majesty. O light of lights! You have illuminated Your heavens and earth. O God! O God! O God! You are too lofty to have a partner or peer. O light of lights! All light praises Your light. O king! All other kings perish. O eternal, who never changes or perishes. O God! O God! O God! You are merciful and compassionate, so bestow upon me a mercy that would extinguish Your wrath. Grant me felicity with You and allow me to enter Your heaven, where the best of Your creation reside. O God! O God! O God! O most merciful of the merciful!

Fulfill my need, and grant me control over the spirits, that they may be my aides in (insert your need). O God! O God! O God! O Lord of the worlds! Quickly, O Shamhūrash, may God bless you![17]

WINTER. To call upon the ruler of the seasonal quarter during winter, who is also the ruler of the west, say:

In the name of God, the Compassionate, the Merciful.

I adjure you, O angel Dardāʾīl, and your angelic assistants Jabrīqīl, Qaḍāʾīl, Qaṣmāʾīl, and Ṣarfiyāʾīl. I adjure the four winds Majdūd, Darʿādūm, Maʿmūr, and Jarīdūm. I adjure the Sun and Moon, Jād and Khayārīm, and Jālīnad, Yabīn, Thalāthūn,

17 Shamhūrash (also popularly known as Shamharūsh) is the jinn king associated with Thursday and Jupiter. He is known for having been particularly benevolent, fair, and religiously minded, although it is commonly held that he is now deceased and that his son has taken over in his stead. There is a shrine to Shamhūrash in the Atlas Mountains of Morocco.

Yaltiyārukh, Madhiyā'īl, and Samīdraysam.[18] Fulfill my need, by the right of what I speak of to you.

O God! I beseech You by Your might, O light of lights, knower of secrets! You are the dominant, mighty, powerful king. Praise, glory, honor, and grace are Yours. I believe in You. There is no god but You! I ask You, O God, Lord, Merciful, Compassionate, King, Encompassing, Knower, Powerful, Wise, Forgiver, Seeing, Expansive, Maker, Hearer, Sufficient, King, Appreciative, Divinity, Singular, Forgiving, Forbearing, Contractor, Expander, Living, Eternal, Exalted, Great, Guardian, Needless, Praiseworthy, Giver, Upholder, Quick, Watchful, Reckoner, Witness, Clement, Savior, Protector, Wright, Strong, Subtle, Powerful, Aware, Giver of life and death, the best ally and the best aid! O Protector, Near, Watchful, Answerer, Strong, Glorious, Loving! He who does as He wills, Great, Elevated, Kind, Creator, Truthful, Inheritor, Resurrector, Generous! O Truth, O Apparent, O Light, O Guide, O Opener! O Appreciative, Forgiver, Acceptor, Witness, of plenteous blessings, Sustainer, of firm power, Originator, Possessor, Empowered, Eternal, Glorious, Generous, the First, the Last, the Manifest, the Hidden, the Sacred, the Peace, Bestower of security, the Guardian, Mighty, Dominant, Powerful, Creator, Maker, Fashioner, the Origin and the Return, Singular, Eternal, who neither sires nor is sired and has no peer.

O God! O God! O God! There be no god but You! I ask you, O Lord, by the right of these names before you, and Your might. Grant me control over the spirits and rulers of this day, this hour, this seasonal quarter, and the four cardinal directions. You can do all that you will!

I adjure you, O noble spirits, be my aides in fulfilling my need.

18 An alternate version reads: I adjure you, O angel Dardā'īl, and your angelic assistants Jabrīqīl, Qaṣmā'il, and Sawaghiyā'īl. I adjure the earthly winds Majrad, Darʿādūm, Maʿmūr, and Jarīdūm. I adjure the Sun and Moon, Jād and Jayādīm, and Jālyatad, Siyyīn, Lātūn, Nīshāraḥ, Madhhabāyin, and Samīdarīs.

Answer, O Jīlhūth,[19] and rend the veils between me and you, by the one who told the heavens and the earth: "'Come willingly or unwillingly!' They said, 'We come willingly'" (Qur'an 41:11). Hurry, quickly, now, this moment, God bless you!

Thus be the four adjurations of the seasonal quarters, along with the associated names.[20]

Employing the divine names "the Merciful" and "the Compassionate"

Targeted recitations of the divine names to produce a certain effect, spiritual or material, are common throughout the Islamic tradition. Sufi teachers often prescribe them to their students. In fact, aspirants are often advised to accept prescribed recitations only from a teacher, due to the belief that extensive recita-

19 Other sources present this name as Khīlṣūb and Jalhūn. Unlike the previous names of the jinn kings, which are commonly known, these names are not commonly used. Based on the precedent of the preceding three seasonal evocations, one could consider substituting here the name of a suitable jinn king.

20 Some versions of the text include a square here to be used in conjunction with the above adjurations. However, the versions of the square differ from each other and none appear to be correct. Therefore, it has been omitted from the main text. One version of the square is as follows:

5	79	19	25	33	83	52	67	1
77	93	74	7	51	42	29	36	66
12	28	62	97	10	38	86	82	53
89	2	91	52	78	18	40	44	25
94	53	9	81	26	61	45	16	35
37	1	47	63	88	75	3	60	98
64	34	30	49	12	5	81	99	73
64	34	30	49	12	15	81	99	73
21	48	22	14	68	56	95	8	90
55	87	74	31	166	100	68	22	17

tion of an attribute of God instills that attribute inside a person, and, if it is not done wisely, a person can become unbalanced.[21]

THE FOLLOWING are some particularly useful invocations involving the divine names "the Merciful" (*al-raḥmān*) and "the Compassionate" (*al-raḥīm*).

In times of fear. The fearful and distressed may engrave these names on a silver ring on Friday, after noon, then wear it. They shall come to no harm.

Kind treatment. Whoever recites these two names frequently shall be treated kindly in all situations.

The divine names *al-raḥmān* and *al-raḥīm* are both derived from the word-root *r-ḥ-m* ("mercy," "womb," "family ties"). It is related that God said: "I am the Merciful, and *raḥm* are your kin. Whoever maintains their family ties maintains a link with Me, and whoever severs their family ties severs their link with Me."[22] If you look carefully, you will discover the names *al-raḥmān* and *al-raḥīm* intertwined in the letters *a-l-m*, *a-l-r*, and the seven *ḥawāmīm*. And God knows best.[23]

Curing cruel-heartedness. Write name *al-raḥmān* eight times on a clean dish when the Moon is exalted, then wash the ink off with rainwater and give it to someone with a hard heart to drink. The person's heart shall soften, by the permission of God.

21 The translator is of the view that she experienced this in her youth through a misguided, extensive repetition of the divine name "the Last" (*al-ākhir*), aimed at developing spiritual vision; she now suffers from chronic tardiness. God knows best!

22 Attributed to the Prophet Muhammad in the book of prophetic narrations called *Ṣaḥīh Muslim*.

23 *A—l—m* and *a—l—r* are two of the sets of disconnected letters of uncertain meaning which begin some chapters of the Qur'an. Seven chapters of the Qur'an that begin with the disconnected letters *ḥ* and *m*.

Fever. Write this four-by-four square, then wash off the ink with water and give it to someone who has a burning fever to drink. Their fever shall be cured, by the permission of God.

ن	م	ح	ر
7	201	49	41
202	10	38	48
39	47	203	9

Protection from misfortune. Write *al-raḥīm* while the Moon is exalted and carry it on your person; God shall protect you from all calamities and misfortunes. It may also be engraved upon a silver ring; the person who wears the ring shall be protected from all disasters, calamities, and misfortunes. Use this square:

م	ي	ح	ر
65	58	63	72
59	68	69	62
70	61	60	67

The other divine names

Wrapping today's pharaohs around your finger. Reciting "the King" (*al-malik*) frequently will place pharaoh-like rulers under your command; they shall rush to protect you and do what you need.

Protection from snakes and the snakelike. Reciting "the Peace" (*al-salām*) frequently protects you from calamities. Reciting it so copiously that you fall into a trance will enable you to touch a snake or scorpion without incurring any harm.

This is the square associated with it. A king who carries it on the battlefield shall be protected from any mishaps.

م	ا	ل	س
61	99	2	31
3	43	58	28
27	56	41	4

Protection from the plague. Regularly reciting "the Bestower of security" (*al-mu'min*) one hundred thirty-two times protects a person from the plague.

Protection from devilish beings. Engrave "the Guardian" (*al-muhaymin*) five times on a ring when the Moon is in exaltation and wear it. You will be protected from all devilish beings—humans and jinn.[24]

Protection. Reciting "the Mighty" (*al-ʿazīz*) frequently will shield you from the enemies of God.

Respect. Reciting "the Compeller" (*al-jabbār*) frequently will make people treat you with awe and respect.

The *gift of the gab.* Reciting "the Immense" (or "the Proud," *al-mutakabbir*) frequently will make you speak persuasively.

Siring children. Engrave "the Creator" (*al-khāliq*) on a silver ring when one of the fire signs of the zodiac is rising. Then wear it and lie with your wife; she shall conceive, by God's will.

Arcane knowledge. God shall reveal wonderful secrets and an un-

24 *Shayāṭīn al-jinn wa al-ins.* The Qur'an speaks of *shayṭāṭīn* ("mini-satans") who are both human and jinn.

derstanding of the subtleties of cause and effect to a person who recites the name "the Maker" (*al-bāri'*) frequently.

Calling down spirits. God shall cause spirits to descend in human form to a person who frequently recites "the Fashioner" (*al-muṣawwir*).

Protection in battle. Reciting "the Forgiver" (lit. "the Coverer," *al-ghaffār*) frequently shall shield you in battle from the roving eyes of your enemies.

Overpowering lusts and appetites. Reciting "the Victorious" (*al-qahhār*) frequently grants you power over your lusts and appetites.

Answered prayers. God answers the prayers of a person who recites "the Giving" (*al-wahhāb*) frequently.

Sustenance and prosperity. God shall open the door to sustenance to you if you frequently recite "the Sustainer" (*al-razzāq*) and grant you provision from whence you could never have imagined.

Inward and outward good. God shall open the doors to goodly things—outer and inner—to whoever frequently recites "the Opener" (*al-fattāḥ*).

Speaking wisdom. God shall make whoever frequently recites "the Knowing" (*al-ʿalīm*) utter words of wisdom.

Awe and respect. Reciting "the Restrainer" (*al-qābiḍ*) frequently bestows upon you an aura of awe in respect, in all the realms.[25]

Expanding one's consciousness. Reciting "the Expander" (*al-bāsiṭ*) frequently expands one's innermost consciousness.

Eliminating oppressors. Should you recite "the Abaser" (*al-khāfiḍ*) frequently and beseech God to remove an oppressor, that oppressor shall be annihilated, at that very moment—as long as your recitation fulfills the necessary conditions.

Status. Reciting "the Raiser" (*al-rāfiʿ*) frequently will increase your status and skills.

Honor. God honors whoever frequently recites "the Honorer" (*al-muʿizz*), in this world and in the afterlife.

Casting down the high and mighty. God shall humble the high and mighty before you if you recite "the Abaser" (*al-mudhill*) frequently.

25 That is, in both the material and immaterial realms.

Answered prayers. God shall respond to your prayers—whatever you ask—if you recite "the Hearing" (*al-samiʿ*) frequently.

Sharpening the intellect. Write "the Seeing" (*al-baṣīr*) one hundred times on a glass cup, then wash the ink off with rainwater and drink it first thing in the morning. God shall sharpen your intellect and increase your capacity to understand.

Swaying judges. The divine name "the Judge" (*al-ḥakam*) is useful for speaking persuasively before judges.

Acting justly. God shall inspire you how to act justly in all situations if you recite the name "the Just" (*al-ʿadl*).

Recovery from illness. God alleviates the afflictions of the severely ill who frequently recite the divine name "the Subtle" (*al-laṭīf*).

Curing thirst. Write "the Aware" (*al-khabīr*) on a gemstone during the first hour of Friday, and place it in your mouth. Thirst shall not ail you. Or, place it in a jug of water and drink from it; your thirst shall be easily sated and you will no longer long for water after that.

Protection during difficult times. Reciting "the Forbearing" (*al-ḥalīm*) frequently protects you from chaos and tumult during difficult times.

Stature. God magnifies a person who recites "the Great" (*al-ʿaẓīm*) frequently in the eyes of the people.

Protection. God protects a person who recites "the Forgiving" (*al-ghafūr*) from whatever they fear.

Status. God increases the rank of whoever recites "the Thankful" (*al-shakūr*).

Protection from evil. Reciting "the Protector" (*al-ḥafīẓ*) frequently will protect you from the machinations of the evil, wherever you come and go.

Curbing the pangs of hunger. Reciting "the Nourisher" (*al-muqīt*)[26] shall still the pangs of hunger.

Fulfilling needs. If you frequently recite "the Reckoner" (*al-ḥasīb*), you shall have whatever you need.

Abundance. Whoever frequently recites "the Glorious" (*al-jalīl*)

26 Another version says that "the Giver of Death" (*al-mumīt*) should be recited; however, this version makes more sense in this context.

shall enjoy abundance and prosperity in all circumstances.

Answered prayers. Whoever frequently recites "the Generous" (*al-karīm*) finds their prayers answered.

Finding a way out of difficulty. Whoever frequently recites "the Responder" (*al-mujīb*) shall always find a way out of any difficulty they fall into.

Foreseeing the future. God grants whoever frequently recites "the Watcher" (*al-raqīb*) knowledge of the future.

Flowing wisdom. God causes springs of wisdom to flow from the heart to the tongue of whoever frequently recites "the Wise" (*al-ḥakīm*).[27]

Affection. Reciting "the Loving" (*al-wadūd*) frequently renders a person beloved to the masses. Everyone who lays eyes on them will love them![28]

Expanding your kingdom. A king who wishes to expand his kingdom should frequently recite "the Expander" (*al-wāsiʿ*).[29]

Authority. God shall always let someone who frequently recites "the Witness" (*al-shahīd*) have the last word in a matter.

Divine presence. God acquaints whoever frequently recites "the Watcher" (*al-raqīb*) to His watchful presence during spiritual retreats.[30]

Pest control. Engrave the five-by-five square corresponding to the name "the Truth" (*al-ḥaqq*) on a piece of marble when Scorpio is rising. Put it at your door. All snakes, scorpions, and annoying bugs shall beat a hasty retreat, by the permission of God.

Spiritual valor. Reciting "the Strong" (*al-qawī*) frequently shall strengthen your soul and make others love you.

27 Another version says "the Expander" (*al-wāsiʿ*) should be recited; however, this version makes more sense in this context.

28 Another version says "the Wise" (*al-ḥakīm*) should be recited; however, this version makes more sense in this context.

29 Similarly, another version says that "the Loving" (*al-wadūd*) should be recited here. Probably, these three names were jumbled during copying. The address to kings is a reminder that, up until the modern era, experts on the occult sciences were considered part and parcel of a healthy court.

30 Some versions say that "the Resurrector" (or "the Sender," *al-bāʿith*) should be recited here instead.

Curing weakness. Reciting "the Firm" (*al-matīn*) strengthens the weak.

Friendship and alliance with God. God shall bring near Himself whoever frequently recites "the Protector" (or "the Friend," *al-walī*), and be their guardian and friend.[31]

Treating illness. Frequently recite "the Praised" (*al-ḥamīd*). Then, write it the number of times equivalent to its numerical value on a seal, and wash off the ink with water. Administer it to a patient to drink. God will cure the patient.

Protection. Reciting "the Enumerator" (*al-muḥṣī*) frequently protects you from calamities.

Starting new things. Recite "the Originator" (*al-mubdi'*) when starting something new.

Missing people. If a traveler or servant is missing, write "the Creator from anew" (*al-muʿīd*) in a four-by-four square when one of the cardinal zodiacal signs is rising.[32] Hang it in the wind, and recite the name all night with the aim of bringing the missing person back. The missing person shall return from whence they departed, by the permission of God.

Enlivening the heart. God enlivens the heart of whoever frequently recites the name "the Giver of life" (*al-muḥyī*) with the light of true gnosis.

Curtailing evil desires. God curtails the evil desires of whoever frequently recites "the Giver of death" (*al-mumīt*).

Protection from accidents. Write "the Living" (*al-ḥayy*) one hundred twenty times above your door while Venus is exalted. Everyone living in that house shall be protected from accidents, as long as they remain there.

Inner gnosis. Recite "the Upholding" (or "the Ever-abiding," *al-*

31 The word *walī* comes from the root meaning "to be adjacent to something" and carries the connotations of overseeing, governance, alliance, and friendship. For instance, a person who takes God as their *walī* puts all their matters in the hands of God because they have sincere and complete trust in God. God, in turn, would look after their best interests with affection and sincerity. The word can also be used for an alliance between equals.

32 Aries, Cancer, Libra, or Capricorn.

qayyūm) frequently; inside yourself, you shall discover wisdom and unique truths.

Faith. God bestows faith and piety upon a person who recites "the Finder" (*al-wājid*) frequently.

True exaltation. God exalts whoever frequently recites "the Glorious" (*al-mājid*) and turns them away from worldly matters.

Perspicacity. Reciting "the One" (*al-wāḥid*) frequently makes you fear copious wealth.

Scholarship. Reciting "the Unique" (*al-aḥad*) frequently distinguishes you as a scholar.

Perpetuity. Reciting "the Singular" (*al-fard*) frequently keeps you from being replaced and keeps them from feeling the pangs of hunger, ever.

Spiritual power. Reciting "the Eternal" (*al-ṣamad*) frequently grants you spiritual power and the capacity for gnosis.

Divine assistance. God shall facilitate any situation for you if frequently recites "the Supreme" (*al-muqtadir*).[33]

Effecting material change. God grants control over the realm of cause and effect to the person who frequently recites "the Hastener" (*al-muqaddim*).

Hiding secrets. Reciting "the Delayer" (*al-muʾakhkhir*) frequently hides your secrets and keeps your business behind locked doors.

Goodness. Reciting "the First" (*al-awwal*) frequently drives a person towards wellsprings of good.

Secrets. Knowledge of the divine name "the Last" (*al-ākhir*) is a guarded secret.

Understanding. God grants knowledge of the right way and hidden matters to a person who frequently recites "the Manifest" (*al-ẓāhir*).

Petitioning others' assistance. If you frequently recite "the Hidden" (*al-bāṭin*), people will help you whenever you ask.

Respect in the human world. Reciting "the Guardian" (*al-wālī*) frequently will grant you respect.

33 Another version says that reciting *al-muqtadir* frequently grants the reciter control over spirits.

Respect in the higher realms. God will grant a magnificent spiritual light and everlasting respect to whoever frequently recites "the Exalted" (*al-mutaʿāl*).

Favor. Whoever recites "the Good" (*al-barr*) frequently will always be treated well.

Repentance. Reciting "the Accepter of repentance" (*al-tawwāb*) frequently makes others treat you kindly. You may also write it in a four-by-four square and beseech God to forgive You; He shall do so.

Curing drunkards. Write "the Avenger" (*al-muntaqim*) in a dish and wash the ink off with rainwater, then give it to a wine-bibber to drink. They shall develop a deep hatred of wine.

Protection from kings. Reciting "the Pardoner" (*al-ʿafw*) the number of times equivalent to its numerical value protects you from a king or other person whom you fear.

Divine mercy. God is kind and merciful to whoever frequently recites "the Kind" (*al-raʾūf*) and keeps the eyes of overweening tyrants off of them.

Kingship. Whoever seeks kingship may recite "the Absolute Sovereign" (*mālik al-mulk*) frequently; God shall grant them what they seek.

Divine gifts. God shall give you anything you ask for if you frequently recite "Possessor of glory and strength" (*dhū al-jalāli wa al-ikrām*).

A balanced character. Frequently reciting "the Fair" (*al-muqsiṭ*) will render you balanced and wise in all circumstances.

Finding lost objects or servants. Reciting "the Gatherer" (*al-jāmiʿ*) frequently will help you find lost objects or missing servants.

Profit and wealth. Reciting "the Enricher" (*al-mughnī*) frequently increases your wealth and sustenance. Writing it and affixing it to your person increases your profit in trade.

Independence. Reciting "the Needless" (*al-ghanī*) renders you needless of other creatures.

Impenetrable defenses. Write it on the city walls in one hundred sixty places while the imam of the mosque is giving the Friday sermon. God shall protect the city from all foes. Some sages did this along the walls of the fortress at Mardin, and no enemy was able to capture it, by the will of God.[34]

Deposing oppressors. Recite "the Afflicter" (*al-ḍār*) frequently; whenever you ask God to topple an oppressor, you will see wonders in the ocean of cause and effect.

Healing the ill. The divine name "the Beneficial" (*al-nāfiʿ*) contains healing for the ill and succor for the poor. If you frequently recite it, God shall cure you. If you be truthful and recite this name so intensely that you slip into the higher realms, you will be able to cure the ill just by laying hands on them. If you engrave its four-by-four square on a silver ring while the Moon is exalted, any ill person who wears the ring will be cured by God. Do you not see that this name resembles the divine name "the Giver of health" (*al-muʿāfī*) and "the Healer" (*al-shāfī*)? This is the square; understand and be guided.

ع	ف	ا	ن
2	49	71	79
52	3	78	68
77	69	51	4

Illuminating the heart. God will illuminate the heart of whoever frequently recites "the Light" (*al-nūr*). Reciting "the Light" *al-nūr* along with "the Beneficial" (*al-nāfiʿ*) shall heal any ailment or pain caused by the cold.

It may be written in a four-by-four square and the ink washed down with water. This water will assist the ailing person; it is best to pour the water on them. And God knows best what is right. This is the square:

34 Mardin is a city in southeast Turkey, known for its strategic location.

فع	نا	ر	نو
مجيد	199	52	مطلع
49	148	58	202
عاصم	59	147	50

Illuminating the heart. God will illuminate your heart and guide you to the secrets of His gnosis if you frequently recite "the Guide" (*al-hādī*).

Should you face a severe challenge pertaining to your worldly or inner life, perform ritual ablutions, and pray two units of prayer, reciting the Throne Verse (Qur'an 2:255) in the first unit and Chapter 112 of the Qur'an ("Sincerity") in the second. Then, keep reciting this name until your breath runs out; you shall be guided to what you seek.

Learning new things. Whoever recites "the Originator" (*al-badīʿ*) frequently shall always learn new things about God and the religion.

Inheritance. If you want to inherit from one of your relatives, recite "the Inheritor" (*al-wārith*) frequently; God shall make it so.

Good results. All things will go well for whoever recites "the Eternal" (*al-bāqī*) frequently.

Firmness. God shall grant firmness in the face of adversity, important matters, wild beasts, and the vagaries of time to whoever frequently recites "the Patient" (*al-ṣabūr*).

Chapter 9

THE RING OF SOLOMON

Solomon figures prominently in the Qur'an as well as the Islamic esoteric tradition. According to the Qur'an, God gave the prophet Solomon an enormous kingdom and control over the jinn and the winds. It is said that his ring enabled him to control the jinn; therefore, the design of his ring has been of great interest past and present in esoteric literature.

These sections contain several non-Arabic names and words, as is common in Arabic esoteric literature. Some are Hebrew, and some are likely Syriac or pseudo-Syriac. Names ending in *-ūsh* are typically understood to be proper names of jinn.

This material lies towards the end of Chapter 17 of the *Sun of Knowledge* but was included here because it was referenced in the earlier chapters, and because it ties together many themes of the book, including the virtues of *bismillāh al-raḥmān al-raḥīm*, channeling the force of divinity to command spirits, and the evocation of jinn.

Any would-be modern-day Solomons are advised that, at least from an Islamic theological perspective, the boisterous jinn known as the *ʿifrīt* is real, not a fantasy creature, and unlikely to take kindly to being ordered about. Therefore, for those who actually wish to give this a try, caution, or at least tact, is advised.

KNOW THAT THIS ring bestows power and might. Those who wear it must abstain from sins, be pure in body and clothing, speak little, obey God, and be certain in God, for it is a ring of obedience.

An account of the inscriptions on the ring

Wahab ibn Munabbih said:

> The ring of Solomon had four layers; each layer had an inscription. The right side said: "I am God who never perishes." The left side said: "I am God, the Living, the Eternal." The third side said: "I am God, the Mighty; none is truly mighty but Me and whoever wears My ring." The fourth side had the Throne Verse (Qur'an 2:255) written on it, surrounded by the expression "Muhammad is the messenger of God."

Another account of the inscriptions on the ring

It is said that these names were inscribed on the ring of Solomon:

> There is no god but God, alone, with no partner. I am God. I have exerted My might through My kingdom and sovereignty. *Īl, īl, īl.* I am God. I have exerted My might and power. *Yāh, yāh, yāh.* I am God, he Living, the Eternal, who never sleeps. *Īh, īh, īh.* I am God, the Aware, the Powerful. Obey Me in all! *Anūkh, anūkh, anūkh.* I am God, the Merciful, the Compassionate. *Dhāʿūj, rayʿūj, dāʿūj.*
>
> "There is no god but God" is My fortress; whoever enters it is safe from My wrath.[1] I take refuge with the names on this ring, and with the Mighty and Dominant. I seek protection from my enemies through the only source of power and strength, through the Mighty and Sovereign. I hand over my concerns to the Living who never dies; I cast those who would harm me towards the source of all power and strength—God, the Exalted, the Sublime.
>
> God suffices us and is the best protector. "Say:[2] O God! King of

1 This sentence is a narration attributed to the Prophet Muhammad. It is said that the angel Gabriel told it to him in the words of God.

2 Many verses of the Qur'an begin with "say," addressed to the Prophet Muhammad.

the Kingdom! You grant kingship to whom You will, and seize kingship from whom You will. You elevate whom You will, and abase whom You will. In Your hand is goodness; You have power over all things. You make the day pass into the night, and the night pass into the day. You bring forth the living from the dead, and the dead from the living. You provide for whomever You will without reckoning." (Qur'an 3:26–27)

Still another account of the names on the ring

It is related that these names were upon the ring of Solomon. This ring held enormous blessings, especially for matters of kingship and authority. The names were:

Īl, īl, īl. I am God. I have exerted My might through my might and power. *Yāh, yāh, yāh.* I am God, the Living, the Eternal who never sleeps. *Āh, āh, āh.* I am God, the Unique, the Eternal, the Powerful. Nothing escapes Me. *Anūkh, Anūkh, Anūkh.* I am God, the Mighty. None is mighty but Me. I have no likeness and no peer. *Dāʿūj, tayʿūj, dayʿūj.* "There is no god but God" is My fortress; whoever enters it is safe from My wrath. I take refuge in the Mighty, Powerful Sovereign. I take refuge in the Mighty and Powerful. I put my trust in the Living who never dies. I cast those who would harm me, plot against me, betray me, or call to falsehood towards the only source of power and strength—God, the High, the Sublime. I take refuge in God and put my trust in God. By God; by the hidden, treasured, noble, glorious divine names: *āh, āh, āh. ʿĀdā yūm ṭālūm qayyūm daymūm.* And I seek protection by the right of *ḥā-mīm-ʿayn-sīn-qāf, kāf-hāʾ-yāʾ-ʿayn - ṣīn*, and the *ḥawāmīm*—and all of the glorious verses between them—and through the might of God, who created through it Muhammad.[3]

3 The first two sets of letters start Chapter 42 and Chapter 19 of the Qur'an, respectively. The *ḥawāmīm* are the chapters of the Qur'an which begin with the disconnected letters *ḥ* and *m*.

Employing these names

It is related that these names were inscribed in a shining light which outshone everything else. When Solomon sat at court, the jinn used to quaver before him, in fear and awe of these names, which were:

> There is no god but God. To God alone belongs the command. There is no vanquisher but God. *Nūr, nūr, nūr* ("light").
>
> Exalted be He whose light overpowers all other lights. Only God—the High, the Sublime—holds power and strength. *Kāf—hā᾿—yā—ʿayn—ṣād. Jahlās, Wāḥsalī, Wal, Jasmā, Kasṭasṭī, Ahaṭ, Maṭīhaṭhaṭ, Ahaṭ, Ahaṭ, Haf.*
>
> Respond! There is no god but God, who shone and illuminates all! *Ṭūb, Ṭūb.* Glorious! Glorious! *Hayṭūṭ, Hayṭūṭ.* Holy, the lord of the Angels and Spirit, who settled Himself on His Throne and embraced His kingdom.[4] To Him belong the beautiful names. No one can hinder what He decrees or gifts. He does what He wills in His kingdom and decrees for His creation whatever He wishes. He has power over all things.

Write this on a gazelle-skin or sheepskin parchment, with ink of musk and saffron, and incense it. There are seventy-one uses for this, including taking audience with kings and rulers; freeing prisoners; clearing the way; easing breathing, fevers, and boils; sparking love between men and women, or brothers and sisters; and buying and selling. There are many ways this can be used. If you recognize its worth it, you will guard it. Beware of using it sinfully, for in it lies the Greatest Name of God!

It is narrated from Kaʿb al-Ahbar that upon Solomon's carpet were names which astounded and burned the jinn. The jinn obeyed

4 "Glorious, holy be the lord of the angels and Spirit" is phrase appearing in Islamic prayers (albeit not usually separated by other names). The "Spirit" can be taken to mean the Angel Gabriel or, especially in the Shi'i tradition, a separate, powerful created being.

him because of them, and he punished the jinn through them. In the middle of his carpet were four encrypted Hebrew names; the jinn and malevolent spirits used to obey him because of those and would never disobey him, not even for the blink of an eye. The attendants to the carpet were responsible for them. Attached to them were four ʿ*ifrīts*,[5] who were Solomon's most important jinn-viziers. Solomon had three hundred human viziers, the most important and last of whom was Asif ibn Barkhiya, and three hundred jinn viziers, the most important and last of whom were these four: Ṭamriyāt, Sanʿīq, Hadliyāj, and Shūghāl.

These names instill a wondrous spirit of obedience among jinn and malevolent spirits (*shayāṭīn*). Learn them, but do not divulge them to anyone else! Beware of commanding his aides to obey you directly; rather, say:

> O legion of aides and viziers! You have been commanded to do as I say, and carry out my will, by the right of the prophet of God, Solomon.
>
> "One of the jinn, an ʿ*ifrīt*, said, 'I will bring it to you before you rise from your place. I am strong and trustworthy.'" (Qur'an 27:39)
>
> "It is from Solomon, and it says: '*Bismillāh al-raḥmān al-raḥīm.* Do not exalt yourselves against me. Instead, come unto me in submission.'"[6] (Qur'an 27:30–31)

Write each name in the corresponding day during an auspicious hour while you are ritually pure, wearing clean clothing, and in a clean place. Incense it with a worthy incense, place it beneath the

5 A particularly boisterous and powerful sort of jinn; naturalized into English as "afreet."

6 The first verse refers to when Solomon asked a member of his court to instantly bring him the throne belonging to the Queen of Sheba. The second verse refers to a letter which Solomon sent to the Queen of Sheba and which she is reading here. Both verses tend to be used heavily in jinn evocations.

stars at night,[7] and [recite] Chapters 36 and 67 of the Qur'an ("Ya Sin" and "The Kingdom"). Then use it for whatever you desire.

The following four days correspond to each of the four names:

¶ The first name, that of the ʿ*ifrīt* Damriyāṭ, is to be inscribed on Sunday, during the first hour after sunrise. This hour is ruled by al-Madhhab, the great.[8] His name has nine letters and is Hashṭashlahkūsh.

¶ The second name, that of the ʿ*ifrīt* Shūghāl, is to be inscribed on Tuesday, during the first hour after sunrise. This hour is ruled by al-Aḥmar, the father of jinn-stalkers.[9] His name has nine letters and is Kashkashlīʿūsh.

¶ The third name, that of the ʿ*ifrīt* Hadliyāj, is to be inscribed on Wednesday, during the first hour after sunrise. This hour is ruled by al-Burqān and the planet Mercury.[10] His name has nine letters and is Bakhlahlashṭūsh.

¶ The fourth name, that if the ʿ*ifrīt* Ṣanʿīq, is to be inscribed on Saturday, during the first hour after sunrise. This hour is ruled by Maymūn Abā Nūkh.[11] His name consists of nine letters and is Shaṭlaṭṭashkūsh.

Each name has nine letters because nine is the last of the single digits and hence is powerful. Here is a diagram of the ring:

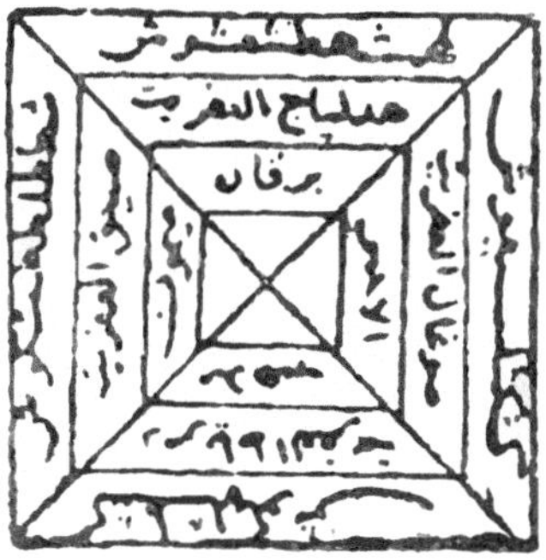

7 "Starring" things, or placing them beneath the stars, occurs frequently in the Arabic esoteric tradition.
8 The jinn king associated with the Sun.
9 The jinn king associated with Mars.
10 Al-Burqān is the jinn king associated with Mercury.
11 The jinn king associated with Saturn.

This conjuration is said to have been used with it:

> O God! O Strong; none is strong except God! O Creator of the night and day! O One who does whatever He wills and wants! O One from whom nothing is hidden! O He who fears no consequences and seeks no reward! Powerful through His power, Merciful through His mercy!
>
> I ask you, O spirits, by His name—the Merciful, the Compassionate. I ask you by the Trustworthy Spirit Jibrāʾīl. I ask you by the enormous, exalted angel Mīkāʾīl. I ask you by the angel entrusted with the Trumpet, Isrāfīl. I ask you by the angel who strikes fear into the hearts of all, ʿAzrāʾīl.[12] All of whom bear the Throne!
>
> Do as you are commanded! Do what I need! Carry out my will, by the right of the prophet of God Solomon! And by the right of [the verses]: "One of the jinn, an *ʿifrīt*, said, 'I will bring it to you before you rise from your place. I am strong and trustworthy.'" "It is from Solomon, and it says: '*Bismillāh al-raḥmān al-raḥīm.* Do not exalt yourselves against me, but come unto me in submission.'"[13] (Qur'an 27:39, 27:30–31)
>
> O God, I beseech You through these honorable spirits to grant me control over these four *ʿifrīts*. Through Your power and glory! *Lahshaṭash, Mashash, Faṭūsh, Kahyūsh, Kashkash, Layūsh, Nashkhashlūt, Jaḥaj, Jaḥaj*! Respond and do as you are told!

12 ʿAzrāʾīl is the Angel of Death.

13 The first verse refers to when Solomon asked a member of his court to instantly bring him the throne belonging to the Queen of Sheba. The second verse refers to a letter which Solomon sent to the Queen of Sheba and which she is reading. Both verses tend to be used heavily in jinn evocations.

Chapter 10

A MISCELLANY OF TRIED-AND-TRUE TALISMANS

This chapter furnishes a cornucopia of interesting, practical talismans which address most of the vagaries of life. Although some features of the text hint that much of it was added after the time of al-Buni, it has been included here because reflects how the Arabic occult tradition works in practice, especially how verses of the Qur'an are employed to trigger material results. The stories at the end—even if spurious—also shed light on the traditional student-teacher relationship.

Although these talismans are centered on the Qur'an, their style and approach resemble that found in other Mediterranean traditions. Additionally, some of these talismans employ non-Arabic names originating in Hebrew, Syriac, pseudo-Syriac, or other languages; in my view, some may trace back to ancient Greek manuscripts.

Most of the talismans in this chapter contain seals, squares, sigils, or drawings linked to Qur'anic verses. While the instructions often just say to inscribe the verses, often, the operator is meant to inscribe the pictures associated with the verses, rather than the actual verses. Some of the talismans also do not contain complete instructions. Perhaps the operator was expected to know what to do, perhaps the instructions were lost, or perhaps the instructions were intentionally obfuscated.

Arabic-speaking cultures have historically been heavily patrilineal, and, before modern surnames, individuals were identified by the name of their father or eldest son. For instance, the author, Ahmad ibn ʿAli al-Buni, is literally "Ahmad, the son of ʿAli, from Bunah." However, as this chapter amply shows, the occult tradition diverges from this by identifying targets via their mothers. This could simply be for the sake of being more certain about parentage, or to intentionally set the work apart from the norms of everyday life. However, it could also have eschatological roots, since some narrations attributed to the Prophet Muhammad say that, on the Day of Judgment, people will be summoned by their names and the names of their mothers. It could also simply be regional, since a similar form of identification occurs in the Greek Magical Papyri.

Regardless of the native language of the operator, the Qur'anic verses would always have been recited or inscribed in Arabic, never in translation; for those who have an interest in such matters, the Arabic text of the Qur'anic verses is readily available online and in print. This material comes from Chapter 19 of Part 2 of the Egyptian lithographed edition of the *Sun of Knowledge*.[1]

KNOW—MAY GOD HELP you and me to be obedient towards Him and understand His names—that all Qur'anic verses have their own letters and numbers, and each number has a magic square. Combining a verse's letter, number, and square unveils wonders.

Each verse matches a specific image, known only to those vested with secrets. When a spiritual master gazes upon one of these images, it responds. Combining these things yields material results. Do you not see that the sages could properly combine these verses with other things planted the seeds of cause and effect? Lesser spiritual aspirants stumbled because they lacked an understanding of the

1 Some unrelated vignettes at the beginning of the chapter, such as one on a wizardly mastery of arithmetic, have been omitted. Some talismans whose descriptions were particularly incomplete have also been omitted.

four natures and how they are compounded. They built their buildings on water, and their buildings washed away; they placed a heavy weight upon a frail sheaf, and it shattered. The ignorant must be stronger than what he is ignorant of!

GETTING SOMEONE TO SPILL SECRETS IN THEIR SLEEP

Obtain information from a sleeping person with this verse:

> God brings forth what you were hiding. We said, "Strike him with a part of it." Thus, God gives life to the dead and shows you His signs, that you may understand. (Qur'an 2:72–73)

Use it with this square:

162	165	167	154
167	155	161	166
156	170	162	160
164	159	127	169

To do that, write the verse on your hand.[2] Then, place it on the chest of the sleeping person. Ask him whatever you want; he will tell you, by the permission of God. This can only be done by people with a strong sense of spiritual insight.

2 The text says *fakk* ("jaw"); however, this seems to be a misprint for *kaff* ("palm of the hand").

DESTROYING OPPRESSORS

Write the following verse on the bone of an owl which has been hunted with a weapon: "This is how your Lord seized the towns which were doing wrong. His seizing is painful, severe" (Qur'an 11:102). Draw this:

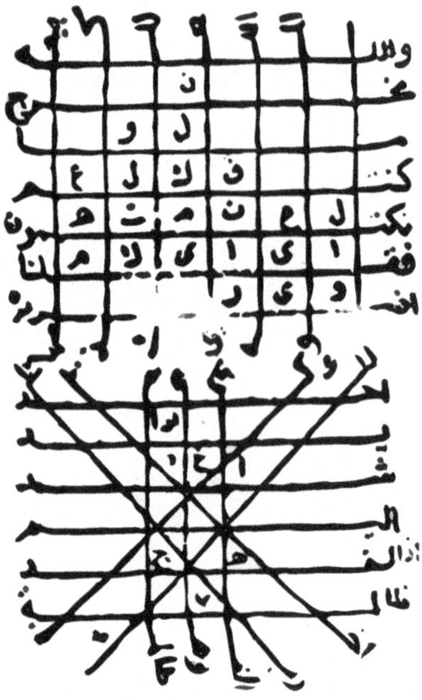

Deposit this in the oppressor's home; he will perish.

Know that when God wills a matter, He sometimes postpones enacting it directly and instead waits for someone to carry out the proper acts. This is because God's creatures[3] are His instrument for carrying out His will in His realm. There is no god but He.

CALMING WINDS

A divine name in this verse calms the winds and lessens gloom: "Sight comprehends Him not, but He comprehends all sight. He is the subtle, the aware" (Qur'an 6:103).

3 Lit. "God's servants." This expression is used to refer to human beings, other sentient creatures, and sometimes other animate or inanimate beings as well.

ENFORCED CELIBACY

The chapter of the Qur'an called "The Hypocrites" (Qur'an 63) may be used to stop someone from having intercourse.

VICTORY AND DIVINE AID

The beginning of the Qur'anic chapter entitled "The Victory" (Qur'an 48) is suitable for this; it overflows with fruits and blessings. Reciting it turns the meek into the mighty, the weak into the strong, the vanquished into victors, and difficulty into ease. God shall assist those who recite it in ways they fathom not.

These are some ways to use it:

¶ *Power, prestige, and victory.* Write it on a pure piece of parchment with ink of saffron, rose-water, and musk, then bind it to your upper arm. You will enjoy power and prestige before the people, and victory over your enemies. Thus, this is particularly suitable for emirs, soldiers, and commanders. And God knows best.

¶ *Victory and battle.* Write it on a battle-standard. Whoever carries it into battle will be strengthened and vanquish their enemies.

¶ *Love, honor, and protection.* Write it on a wooden cup, then wash off the ink and wash your face with the liquid. You shall be loved, honored, and protected, wherever you may be, by the permission of God.

¶ *Protection.* It is related from Al-Masʿudi that God will protect whoever recites Chapter 48 of the Qur'an every night in the month of Ramadan, beginning on the first night, during their supererogatory prayers.[4]

¶ *Overcoming difficulties.* Ibn Qutaybah says that a man from Mecca told him: "I was overwhelmed by difficulty and complained to one of the righteous. He told me to write the following Qur'anic excerpts on a piece of paper:

All of these verses include a word from the root *f-t-ḥ*, which connotates things such as "victory," "opening," "keys," and

4 *Ṣalāt al-taṭawwuʿ*.

"judgment." The word derived from *f–t–ḥ* is rendered in SMALL CAPITALS in each verse.

We have granted you a manifest VICTORY. (48:1)
If you were seeking a JUDGMENT and VICTORY, it has come to you. (8:19)
Mayhaps, God shall bring VICTORY, or a command from Him (5:52)
To Him belong the KEYS of the unseen; none knows them but Him. (6:59)
Our Lord! DECIDE between us and our people in truth; You are the best JUDGE. (7:89)
Had the people of the towns believed and been reverent, We would have OPENED up to them blessings from the heavens and the earth. (7:96)
When they OPENED their baggage, they found that their merchandise had been returned to them. (12:65)
They sought VICTORY, but every stubborn tyrant fails. (26:117–118)
Were we to OPEN a gate to the heaven for them, so they could ascend… (14:15)
He said, "My Lord, my people have disbelieved. So JUDGE between me and them, and deliver me and the faithful!" (15:14)
Whatever mercy God OPENS to humankind, none can withhold. (35:2)
Until they arrive, and its gates shall be OPENED to them. Its guardians shall tell them, "Peace be upon you; you have done well!" (39:73)
To reward them with a near VICTORY, and abundant spoils. (48:18–19)
We OPENED the gates of the heavens to pour down water. (54:11)
Help from God, and VICTORY near. (61:13)
And the sky is OPENED, as if it were gates. (78:19)
When God's help and VICTORY come, and you see people entering God's way in throngs, hymn the praise of your Lord and seek forgiveness from Him; He has always been forgiving. (110:1–3)

Then, he told me to hang it on my upper right arm. I did that, and God made things easy for me in a way I could never have imagined."

KIND RECEPTION

Engrave this verse upon a ring: "You will soon remember what I have said to you. I entrust my affair to God. Truly God sees His servants" (Qur'an 40:44). Wear this ring, and you will be treated kindly in all matters. If you must face a tyrant, recite this verse when standing before him; God shall look after you with His strength and power. This is the image:

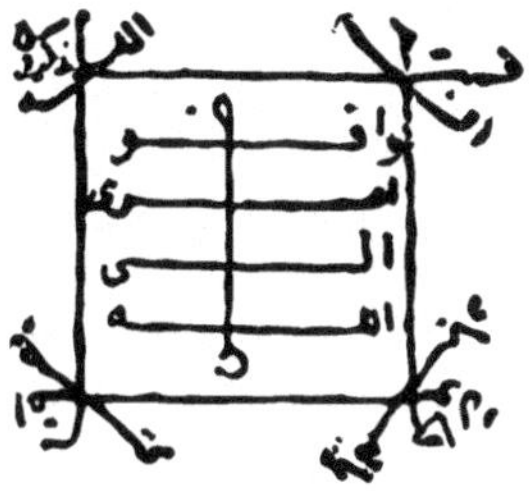

WEALTH AND TREASURES

According to a scholar, whoever seeks great wealth and treasures should inscribe these verses on a leaf of gold or silver, or a piece of parchment:

> O God! King of the Kingdom! You grant kingship to whom You will, and seize kingship from whom You will. You elevate whom You will, and abase whom You will. In Your hand is goodness; You have power over all things. You make the day pass into the night, and the night pass into the day. You bring forth the living from the dead, and the dead from the living. You provide for whomever You will without reckoning. (Qur'an 3:26–27)

This should be done on an auspicious day: during the first hour of Thursday.[5]

5 The hour and day of Jupiter, suitable for matters of fame, fortune, kingship, and religion.

UNENDING WEALTH AND TREASURES

If you seek enormous wealth and treasures, fast for forty days.[6] During this time, break your fast only on lawful food, and eat no meat or animal products. If possible, only break your fast on foodstuffs that other people have no interest in; this is better.[7] Every day, at sunrise, recite the chapter of the Qur'an called "The Daybreak" (Qur'an 93) one thousand times. After that, implore: "O God! Ease my situation, as You did for many of Your servants. Enrich me with Your wealth, so I need no one but You!" At sunset, repeat the same recitation the same number of times. On the first day, place the inscribed leaf or parchment in a clean bag with forty dirhams; whenever you want to spend anything, recite the chapter of the Qur'an the number of times corresponding to the value which you which to spend. The amount of money in the bag shall never lessen. This is specifically for spiritual aspirants.

The door to wealth has been opened to anyone who wants it! God speaks the truth and guides to the right way.

KINGSHIP AND SULTANATE

Know—may God grant you and me obedience towards Him—that kingship and sultanate are vested in these Qur'anic verses:

> O God! King of the Kingdom! You grant kingship to whom You will, and seize kingship from whom You will. You elevate whom You will, and abase whom You will. In Your hand is goodness; You have power over all things. You make the day pass into the night, and the night pass into the day. You bring forth the living from the dead, and the dead from the living. You provide for whomever You will without reckoning. (3:26–27)

If your ambition is to become a vizier or emir, employ these Qur'anic verses:

6 From sunrise to sunset, abstaining from food or drink.
7 Plain barley is sometimes recommended.

> Aaron, my brother. Through him, increase my strength. (20:30–31)
> We gave Moses the book and made his brother his vizier. (25:35)

If you seek love or obedience, employ these Qur'anic verses:

> I cast upon you [the infant Moses] love from Me, that you might be formed under My eye. (20:39)
> Had you spent all on the heavens and in the earth, you could not have united their hearts, but God united them; He is mighty, wise. (8:63)
> He [the human being] is fierce in his love for good things. (100:8)
> They love them like they should love God, but the faithful are more ardent in their love for God. (2:165)

If you desire victory, employ these Qur'anic verses:

> Aid only comes from God. (3:126)
> God shall grant you a mighty assistance. (48:3)
> Enter by the gate, for once you have entered it, you will be victors. And trust in God, if you are believers.[8] (5:23)

Understand that, for it is not possible to explain more. Consider what you have understood from these verses in light of what you have not yet understood.

WISDOM

For forty days, recite Chapter 93 of the Qur'an ("The Daybreak") after your devotions. Then implore: "O God! Enrich me, O needless one, O enricher! Enrich me with what you have allowed, so that I may be free from what you have disallowed. Enrich me in a way that I will never fear poverty again. Guide me, for I am lost. Teach me, for I know not." God shall send you someone to teach you wisdom, either when you are asleep or when you are awake.

8 Addressed to the people of Moses.

PROTECTION FROM JINN AND MEN

Inscribe the image linked to this verse:

> Muhammad is but a messenger; messengers have come and gone before him. If he dies or is slain, will you turn back on your heels? Whosoever turns back on his heels will not harm God in the least, and God will reward the thankful. (Qur'an 3:144)

Then, around the edges, write the names Muḥammad, Jibrīl, Mīkāʾīl, Isrāfīl, and ʿAzrāʾīl.[9] Whoever carries it will be protected from the evils of jinn and men, including the night-stalkers and day-strikers.[10]

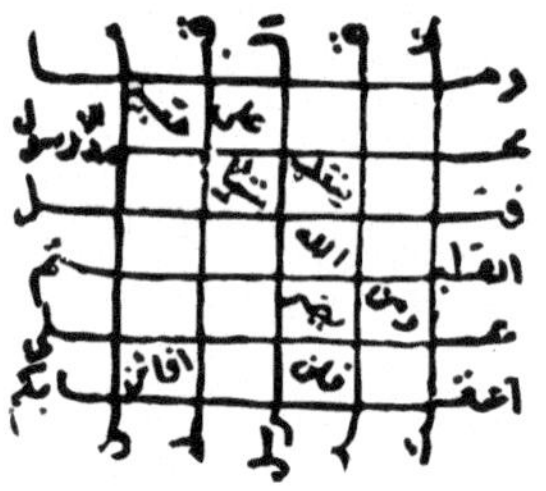

ATTENTIVE EARS

Write Chapter 47 of the Qur'an ("Muhammad") on a glass cup, then wash the writing off with water from the spring of Zamzam and drink it.[11] You shall be granted status before the people. They shall listen to what you say, and you will remember everything you hear, by the permission of God.

BLEEDING

With these verses, you can make someone bleed, wherever you may be:

9 Jibrīl being Gabriel and Mīkāʾīl being Michael. There are several spellings for "Gabriel" in Arabic, and multiple spellings are often employed in a single book; this is the one that is used here.

10 *Ṭāriq al-layl wa al-nahār*.

11 Zamzam is a sacred spring in Mecca; pilgrims often take the water home with them.

> When a single blast is blown on the trumpet, and the earth and mountains are borne away and ground up in a single blow. On that day, the event shall befall. The sky shall be rent asunder, for on that day, the sky shall be frail. (Qur'an 69:13–16)

Write these verses, along with the names of the target and the target's mother, on a sheet of lead while the Moon is in Scorpio. Write them with Roman cinnabar. Then, wrap it in linen or silk, tie it with red thread, and bury it near a stream which is flowing eastwards; use the thread to secure it near the stream. Be sure not to let it come out of the cloth and thread, because that will kill the target, and you will be held accountable before God on the Day of Resurrection. Do not leave it there for more than seven days, or else that will also kill the target.

When you are ready to untie it, remove the tablet and then wash the ink off with water. Then, write the Throne Verse (2:255), Chapters 112–14, and Chapter 1 of the Qur'an on a clean dish, wash the ink down with water, and give it to the target to drink. Their bleeding shall cease, by the permission of God.[12] God grants success. Draw this figure along with it:

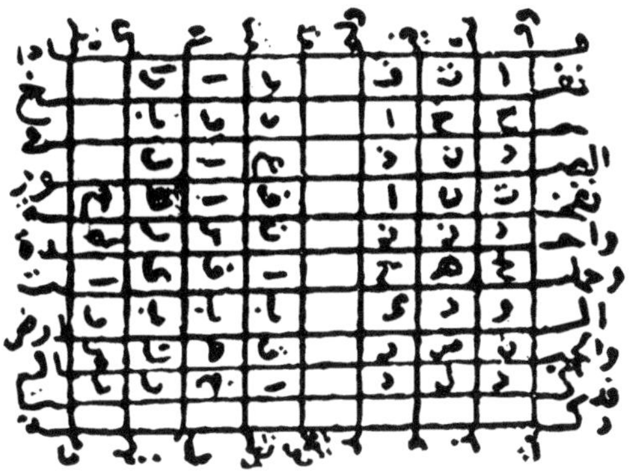

12 These parts of the Qur'an are typically used for healing and protection. While both European and Arabic texts tend to be discreet about the underlying goal of herbs or spells aimed at causing bleeding, the most ostensible purpose is abortion, especially if the operator feels motivated to heal the target at the end of the working.

SEPARATING WOMEN FROM THEIR HUSBANDS

This verse is effective in getting women divorced:

> Mayhaps, if he divorces you, his Lord will give him better wives in your stead: submitting, believing, devout, penitent, worshipful, and willing to migrate for their faith—previously married or virgins. (Qur'an 66:5)

Draw the following diagram associated of this verse on a blue bowl with ink made from tar, along with the targets' names. Wash it down with water, and sprinkle it around their house. They shall divorce and vacate the house. This is what you draw:

SILENCING ENEMIES

With these verses, you may bind someone's tongue, silence your enemy, or cut short a dispute:

> That is because they believed, then disbelieved. A seal was set on their hearts, so they understood not. When you see them, their appearances impress you. When they speak, you listen to what they have to say. But they are like leaning timbers. They think that every cry is against them. They are the enemy, so beware them. God curse them! How they are deluded! (Qur'an 63:3–4)

Engrave the following diagram on a sheet of iron when Libra is rising and Mars is in the first decan of Scorpio. Carry it with you when you face your opponent. Your enemy's tongue shall fall silent, and you shall be victorious over him. This is what you engrave:

STRENGTH, KNOWLEDGE, AND WISDOM

> Our Lord! We trust in You and turn to You; to You is our return. Our Lord! Do not make us a trial for the faithless. Forgive us, O Lord! You are mighty, wise. (Qur'an 60:4–5)

Engrave the square associated with this verse on an iron ring and place it in someone's house. God shall grant him victory and might, even if he is meek and humble. God shall teach him things that were never known before. God shall enrich him and assist him, for the verse speaks of trust in God, God's might, and God's wisdom.[13] God guides whom He wills to the right way. This is what you engrave:

13 This is referring to three of the divine names: *al-wakīl* (the Guardian), *al-ʿazīz* (the Mighty), and *al-ḥakīm* (the Wise).

TRADE AND PROFIT

This verse is suitable for increasing prosperity, profits, and trade:

> "I [Noah] said, 'Seek forgiveness from your Lord! He is forgiving. He will send you abundant rains, support you with wealth and sons, and give you gardens and rivers" (Qur'an 71:10–12).

Inscribe it on a shining silver ring and wear it on your finger. God will grant you unceasing prosperity. It truly is a miraculous thing that defies description. It overflows with blessings, goodness, and abundance, through the grace of God. This is what you inscribe:

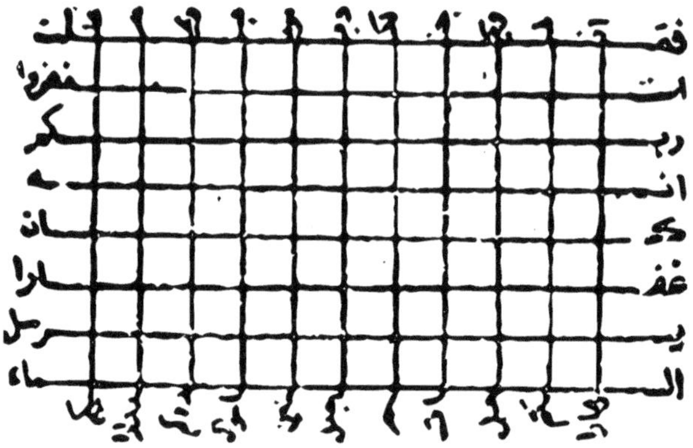

PENITENCE

> Your Lord knows that you stand vigil almost two-thirds of the night, or a half, or a third, as do a group of those with you; and God measures the night and day. He knows you will not keep count, so He has relented unto you (Qur'an 73:20).

This verse can make someone more worshipful and penitent. To do that, get two copper basins. On Friday, when people are at the noon-time prayers, inscribe the verse on them, then say: "So God has accepted the repentance of <name>." Then wash it down with clear water. Recite over it one hundred times, then drink it. God shall guide whoever does this to righteous, worshipful, devout works, by His power and strength.[14]

VICTORY

Write the following verses of the Qur'an on a blue cloth on Saturday during the hour of Mercury while the Moon is fortunately placed:

> When God's help and victory come, and you see people entering God's way in throngs, hymn the praise of your Lord and seek forgiveness from Him; He has always been forgiving (110:1–3).

Then, put it on your head. Whenever you get into a fight or quarrel, you shall win, by the permission of God.

To vanquish your enemies, write it when the Sun is exalted and Mars is in opposition to it. Whoever carries that cloth will be safe from injury, by the permission of God. This is what you write:

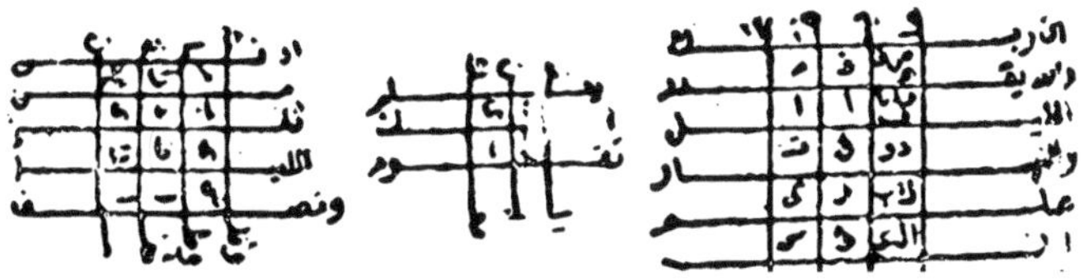

VICTORY, ESPECIALLY IN COURT

This verse may be used to triumph over adversaries, especially in court cases and disputes:

> We placed kindness and mercy in the hearts of those who follow him [Jesus]. However, they invented monasticism. We did not ordain it for them; rather, they ordained it for themselves, seeking God's pleasure. But they did not fully observe it. We rewarded the faithful, although many were insincere. (Qur'an 57:27)

14 The diagram for this paragraph seems as if it has been mixed in with the next set.

Should you wish to do that, write these verses on a gazelle-skin parchment with myrtle-water on Friday after people have dispersed from the Friday prayers.[15] Incense it with aloeswood and ambergris on a silver leaf and place it on your head. Then, take any enemy of your choosing to court, or face anyone before a judge. You will win, by the permission of God. This is the figure that you use; know and be guided.

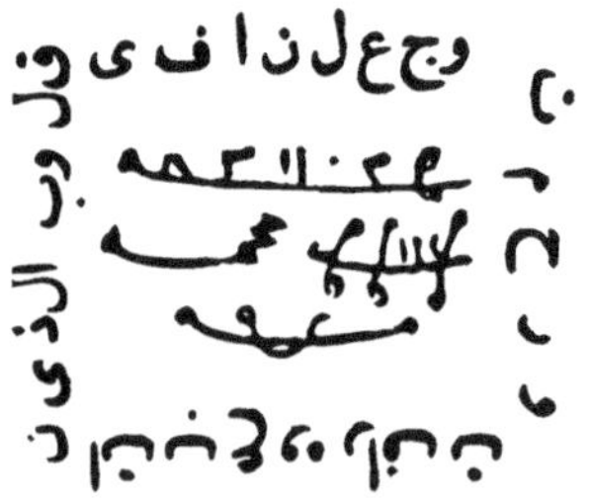

BINDING THE TONGUES OF SULTANS, VIZIERS, JUDGES, AND OFFICIALS

Know—may God bless you and me with obedience towards Him—that if you need to bind the tongue of a sultan, vizier, judge, or official to stop him from causing trouble, even if it kills him, write the following names on a gazelle-skin parchment with ink of musk, saffron, and rosewater. Then incense it with a sweet-smelling incense like aloeswood,[16] ambergris, or musk; it is best if this is done on Sunday during the hour of the Sun. Then put it in the front of your turban.

If you have any doubt over whether this has worked and want to test it, hang it on the neck of a sheep on its way to slaughter; it shall not be slaughtered as long as the parchment is hung on it. Or, bring it to the public baths; the baths shall cool as soon as you enter, by the permission of God.

15 This timing could relate to the blessings of Friday in the Islamic tradition. It could also, however, indicate a specific planetary hour, since Friday is the day of Venus, and the congregational prayers start at traditionally start at astronomical noon, and last about an hour.

16 The text lists aloeswood and *nidd*, which can refer of a blend of incenses, including aloeswood, ambergris, musk, and frankincense.

This is the talisman that you draw:

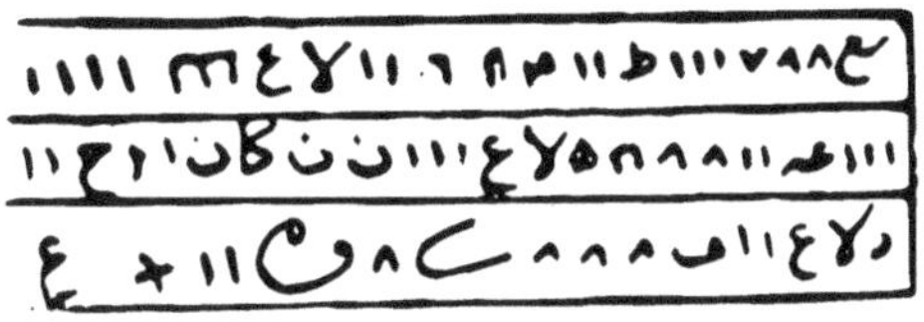

SUBDUING ENEMIES

To silence or dominate your enemies, the following Qur'anic verses may be used:

Approach and fear not! You are secure. (28:31)
Fear not! You have the upper hand. (20:68)
The messengers fear not before Me. (27:10)
Two men whom God had blessed and who feared God said, "Enter among them by the gate, for once you have entered it, you will be victors. And trust in God, if you are believers." (5:23)

[Then say:]

Come, O <target>, son of <target's mother>, like the preacher climbs the pulpit, and the sultan faces his army. I have bound the tongue of whoever disputes with him. None shall speak ill of whoever carries this writ. They shall speak good of him, or say nothing. *Deaf, deaf, deaf. Dumb, dumb, dumb. Blind, blind, blind; they do not see.*[17] I have made the bearer of this writ victorious and given him the upper hand against everyone, just like God aided His prophet Muhammad with the angels—Jibrīl on his right side, Mīkā'īl on his left side, and Isrāfīl behind his back—and the names of God have surrounded him. Crestfallen, their heads hang humbled before the Living, the Eternal. Sodden, lus-

17 This is an allusion to Qur'an 2:17-18, which says about those who prefer error to guidance: "They do not see; deaf, dumb, and blind, they shall not return."

terless, and perplexed (*māhat, bāhat, tāhat*)[18]—until the shadows have been obliterated.

Come—saved, victorious, aided, by the One, the Unique, the Singular, the Eternal, who neither sires nor was sired, who has no like!

THE JEDI HAND TRICK[19]

Know, my brother, that this is a wondrous talisman—a strange secret which the learned have hidden out of fear that it might fall into the clutches of the ignorant, who might use it to commit brazen acts with married women. By God! You—in whose hands this book has fallen—only use it for lawful endeavors. You will be accountable for whatever you do on the Day of Resurrection.

To use it, write it on your right palm with ink of musk, saffron, and rosewater, then incense it with a pleasant scent. Write it during the first hour of Wednesday, and then recite the adjuration which begins "in the name of God, the Holy, the Pure."[20] Then hide your hand inside your cloak, and approach the person you seek. When you are close enough for them to see what you have written on your hand, remove your hand and hold it in front of their face so they can see the writing. Then, turn away, and do not turn back towards them. The one you seek will follow you wherever you will. This is what you write:

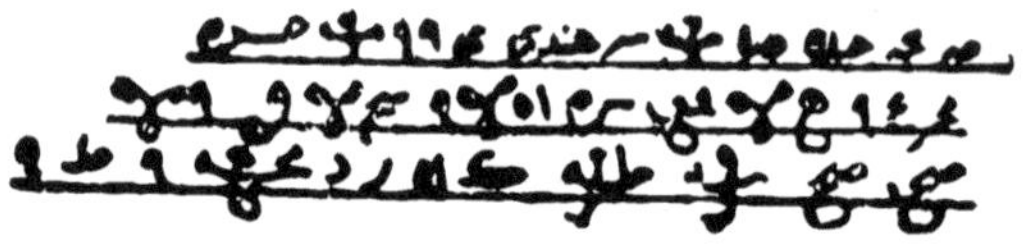

18 It seems these words were chosen for the sake of rhyming.

19 While, admittedly, this header is not in the book, it is not wholly far from the mark, given that some of the inspiration for *Star Wars* was taken from North African Sufism.

20 *Al-qasam al-kabīr*, beginning with *bismillāh al-quddūs al-ṭāhir*.

SPLEEN PAIN

If you come across someone suffering from spleen disease, write this blessed talisman on a piece of paper and place it above their spleen, atop their shirt. Then get a new spoon and place in it a little bit of ash. Put some burning embers atop that, then put the spoon on top of the talisman. If the patient feels it inside his abdomen, then the diagnosis rests proportionately on what the patient can handle. If the patient does not feel pain anymore, even when he uses the toilet, then he has been cured, by the permission of God. This is the talisman that you use:

A KEEN MEMORY

If you want to remember everything you hear and never forget, first these letters on a glass cup, then wash the writing down with clear water. Do this for three days. You will be amazed at how well you understand things. When drinking it, say, "We made Solomon understand it" (Qur'an 21:79).

This is what the talisman looks like:[21]

سفيحكم للحلمعحكم الله ملتحفف طلسم طلسم
ح ح د د ي احسه رب ع ولح فاطط لله لله اح فظ ع ل كـعـه افعله

RELOCATING YOUR NEIGHBOR

If you have an enemy or foul neighbor whom you want to move away, write this talisman on his roof. Alternatively, write it on a lead tablet or piece of wood, and bury it at his door. He shall move away. By God, only do this to those who deserve it. The talisman is the one that has already been mentioned.

SILENCING FLAPPING TONGUES

To bind someone's tongue, or stop people from gossiping altogether, write this talisman and place it at the front of your turban. You will be utterly astounded.

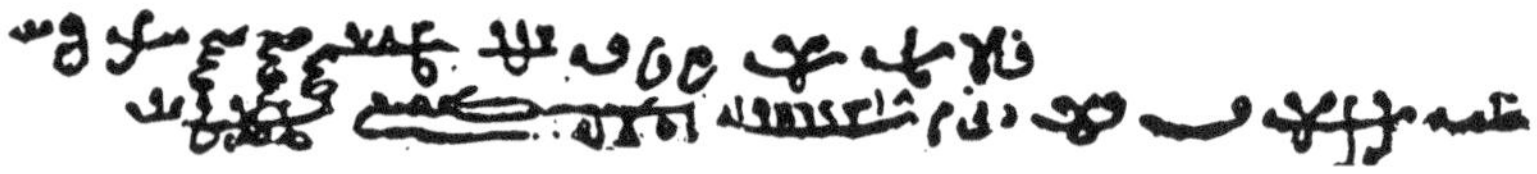

اصمت لسان كل ناطق الا بخير دومره مه | هـ ٧ ـ ٩ فلمه اعنقه يا
عنقود واربط الالسنة بحق الودود عجلا عجلا سحلطمعيليلعي
سلسلسلعملكحيل هيا العجل الساعة

Silence the tongue of all who speak anything other than good... O ʿUnqūd,[22] bind the tongues, by the right of the Loving (*al-*

21 These letters mostly do not have any intrinsic meaning. Presumably they have been encoded into the sigil beneath it. Often, this type of sigil is constructed by writing out letters, connecting them with a line, and obfuscating them so the original letters are not clear.

22 See the note on ʿUnqūd in the following section on "Reconciling people, especially spouses."

wadūd), quickly, quickly. Saḥlaṭlaʿīlīʿī, Salsalsalʿmlakhḥīl. Hurry, now, this moment![23]

QUIETING OBSESSIVE WHISPERS (WASWĀS).[24]

If someone is suffering from obsessive Satanic whispers internally, or during their ritual ablutions and ritual prayers, and wants them to go away, write these names on a piece of paper and have them bear it. They shall be shielded from obsessive Satanic whispers.

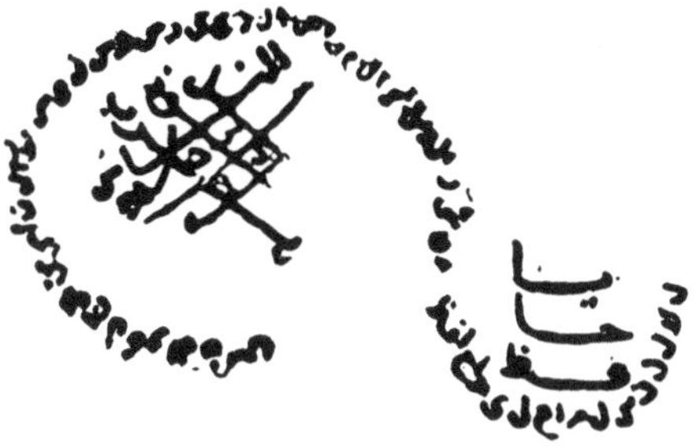

PROTECTION FROM THEFT

Should you fear that a thief, burglar, or bandit is angling for your money, belongings, or merchandise, write these names on a piece of paper and place the paper inside your cash-box, with your merchandise, or wherever else you want. God shall protect your property from what you fear, by His will. This is what you write:

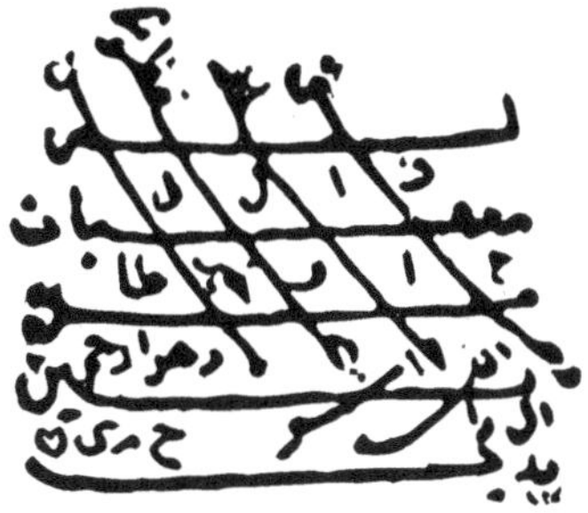

23 Some of the letters have an understandable meaning, and some are arcane.

24 *Waswās* refers to an obsessive concern over detail, especially in matters of ritual worship and cleanliness, to the point where it becomes debilitating. It can also be used for Satanic whisperings in general. The two are sometimes identified with each other.

OUTWITTING ENEMIES

Should you fear someone will betray you or otherwise wishes you ill, and should you wish protection, pray two units of prayer after the sunset prayer. In the first unit, recite Chapter 1 and Chapter 109 of the Qur'an. In the second, recite Chapter 1 and Chapter 113 of the Qur'an.[25] Implore: "O God, O Sufficer, protect me from the evil of <target> son of <target's mother>," then say what you want. Write these names and place them in your turban. God shall protect you from whatever you fear.

IMPEDING URINE

Should you wish to stop someone from urinating, Qur'an 108:1-3 may be used. Write these verses during an inauspicious hour on a white eggshell after writing the name of the target and the target's mother on a red or blue paper. Burn incense of ammonium chloride, myrrh, and pepper. Bury it by fire. The target will be unable to urinate, by the will of God. Do not leave it there for more than seven days or it will kill the target, and you will be held responsible on the Day of Resurrection.

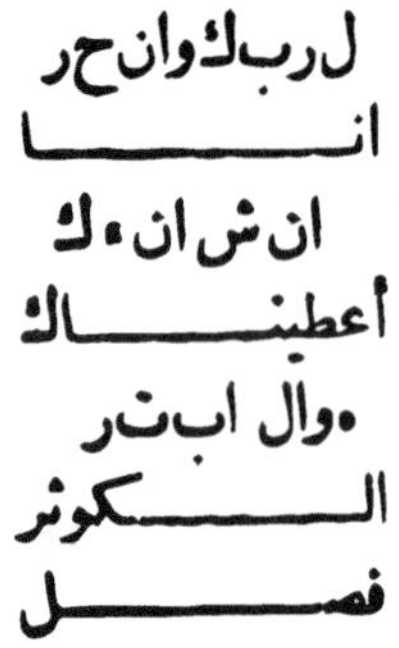

RECONCILING PEOPLE, ESPECIALLY SPOUSES

This talisman may be drawn and affixed to your target, or it can be placed beneath their pillow. The twain shall make up even if the sword stands between them!

25 Chapter 109 being "The Faithless" and Chapter 113 being "The Dawn." Both chapters are commonly recited for protection from humans or non-humans.

Write it on Friday while the preacher is giving his sermon. Incense it with aloeswood, mastic, guggul, and calamus root. This is what you write:

توكلوا يا خدام هذه الاسماء بالقاء المحبة والمودة بين فلان
ابن فلانة بحق هذه الاسماء عليكم

> Hasten, O servants of these names, to cast love and affection between <target> son of <target's mother>, by the right of these names upon you![26]

Also draw the following seal, then say:

> O Uniter of Hearts! Unite the hearts of <first target>, son of <first target's mother> and <second target>, daughter of <second target's mother>.
> By the right of what God told the heavens and earth! "'Come willingly or unwillingly!' They said, 'We come willingly'" (Qur'an 41:11).
> "I cast upon you love from Me, that you might be formed under My eye" (Qur'an 20:39).
> Hasten, O ʿUnqūd,[27] and cast love and affection between the

26 While the text has omitted it, one would presume that one would include the names of both disputants here. The timing could be aiming for Venus day and Venus hour, depending on the time of year.

27 ʿUnqūd is the name of a jinn commonly involved in love and binding rituals. Of interest may be a related incident, chronicled by the famous historian Ibn Kathir (c. 1300–1373) in his *al-Kamil fi al-Ta'rikh*. He relates that in Mosul and neighboring parts of Iraq, in the year 600 in the Islamic lunar calendar (1203–1204 AD), a disease struck people which caused pain of the throat; many people died. It transpired that a female jinn, called Umm ʿUnqūd, had lost her son ʿUnqūd, and it was believed that those who did not mourn his death were afflicted. Thus, mass mourning for ʿUnqūd broke out, with women and "common men" beating their chests to offer sympathy. Ibn Kathir, *al-Kamil fi al-Ta'rikh* (Beirut: Dar Beirut, 1966), I, 42. This account is also a reminder that, in the pre-modern era, historians also considered it appropriate to chronicle the metaphysical—although he does, on the same page, berate the idiocy of men who participated in a similar event, when mass mourning broke out for a jinn named Sayyidūk. In any case, while jinn are held to be born and die, mul-

hearts of these two disputants, by the right of these names! "Facing each other on thrones" (Qur'an 37:44).[28]

Hasten, O servants of this day and this hour, and attract the hearts of these disputants to each other, to beget love. Bring affection to them after separation, by the right of these names! By the right of Ayyūsh, Ayyūsh, Badūḥ! Love, affection, love, O Badūh![29] Bring love after hatred! Unite the separated—Ehyeh Asher Adonai Tsabot El Shaddai! "It is a great oath, if you but knew" (56:76). Hurry, now, quickly, this moment!

PUTTING AN END TO A TYRANT AND HIS REGIME

Place this talisman under the wall of a tyrant and recite the following imprecation against him. The wall shall crumble and destroy the one inside, scattering his forces. Fear God, and only do this to someone who is aggravating the masses through his hand and tongue. Be careful not to do it against the undeserving, lest you be held accountable on the Day of Resurrection! "And whoever pardons and reconciles shall have their reward from God; God loves not the oppressors" (Qur'an 42:40).

This is what you write:

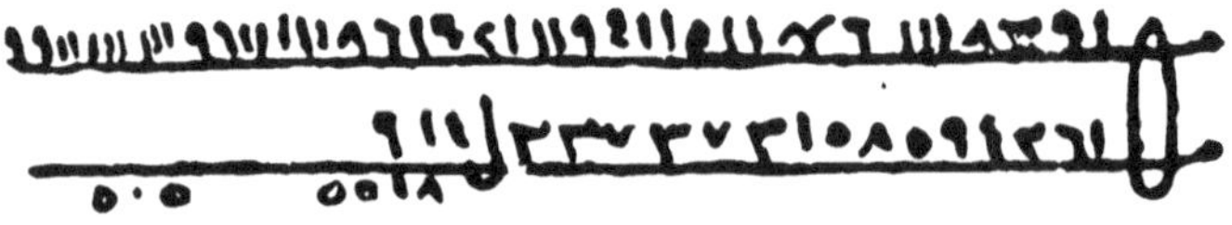

[Then say:]

tiple jinn often share the same name, so there is no reason to think that this ʿUnqūd is the same one being addressed here.

28 A reference to people in heaven.

29 *Ḥubb, wadūd, ḥubb yā Badūḥ!* Badūh is a numerically constructed name of God and also sometimes understood to be the name of a jinn. The name is associated with matters of love and affection.

> Hasten, O Quick, O Glistening,[30] O Khandash, O follower of al-Aḥmar![31] Remove <target> from this place by the right of these names. Do as you have been told, by the might of Karyārūs, ʿAkbū, Alkiyārūsh, with Alkiyūsh Halkamūhīsh Ṣārash Ṣalṣāwush.
>
> The angels trembled out of fear of Him and the creation obeyed Him. Ṭūr Hayā Hayālūrāthā! It shook in dread, the earth quaked, hearts quavered, and they undertook obedience towards Him. Respond, O Aḥmar—you and your tribe, followers, and minions! By the light of Shaʿtūfiyā, Raqbā, Rasmūmal, Wamār, ʿAbṭūr, Hārhār, Kaṭ, Salīmūr, Hashkūr, Hālūr, Hafṭūr, Hayṭūr. Do this now, quickly, this moment!

Fear God, for this destroys towns, lands, and civilizations.

ENDING LOVERS' QUARRELS

To reconcile two people who do not follow the law of God, draw the same picture on a raw sherd during the day and hour of Mars, and incense it with incense of fern leaves, grape leaves, and frankincense. Dissolve the sherd in wine vinegar mixed with a little tar and hot oil. Then sprinkle it at your target's door, and recite the incantation we previously mentioned. "And whoever pardons and reconciles shall have their reward from God; God loves not the oppressors" (42:40).

ARCHERY

To make sure your arrows always hit the target, write these names on a gazelle-skin parchment with ink of saffron and the liver of a hoopoe. Use a quill made from a feather of a vulture or eagle, and write it during an auspicious hour when the Moon is in an air sign. Incense it with frankincense. This is what you write:

30 *Yā sarīʿ, yā barīq.*
31 Al-Aḥmar is the jinn king associated with Tuesday and Mars.

HALTING TRAVELERS

Know—may God grant you and me obedience towards him—that the letter *sh* is found in Arabic, Syriac, and Coptic. It is a fiery, dry letter of the third degree. It can specifically be used to stop someone from sailing out to sea, or to halt a traveller on land. The letter *q*—written like this—stops others:

Inscribe it like this on a sheet of lead during an inauspicious hour and burn incense of sparrow and bat-head:

These are the verses:

> Wait concerning him, for a time. (23:35)
> Stop them; they are to be questioned. (37:24)

Then bury it by the road; you will be amazed.

EVERLASTING LOVE

To make someone to love you forever, until death do you part, write these names on seven white pieces of paper, along with your name, your mother's name, your beloved's name, and the name of your beloved's mother. Each day, burn one of them. Write it with a pen made of sweet basil and ink which has some musk in it. You will be amazed at the type of love and affection it instills.

Here are the instructions for each day.

Sunday. I have cast affection towards X into the heart of Y, by these names:[32]

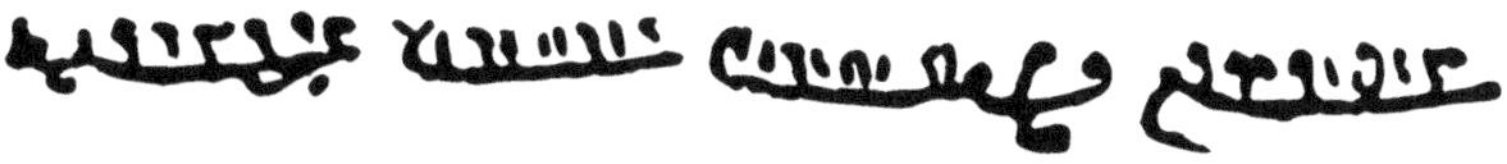

Monday. I have inflamed the heart of Y with the love of X. *Qāf*. I have cast between them love and affection, by these names: *Ḥāna maḥall fah haṭ ṣai saḥāʿah tah manah fadḥī.*

Tuesday. I have inflamed the heart of Y and instilled him/her with love towards X. His/her heart burns, just like fire courses through these names! Hasten, O servants of these names, and do as you are told! Now, quickly, this moment—by these names!

Wednesday. Hasten, O servants of these names, and Qalfaṭriyāt! Cast love and affection into the heart of Y! Spur on the spirit of love towards Y, and do not depart, day or night. Do not disobey your command, in word or deed. By these names, I have forbidden you from that!

Thursday. Hasten, O servants of these names, by the right of the king set over you! Obey what you have been commanded! ʿAṣlaḥlaʿyāʾīl, Haṭīl, Haṭīl, Kāl, Abḥah, ʿĪl, Ḥalḥal, Hahahalīl, Kān.

Friday. Hasten, O servants of these names! Attract the hearts of these two people. Cast affection and love between them, by the right of these names:

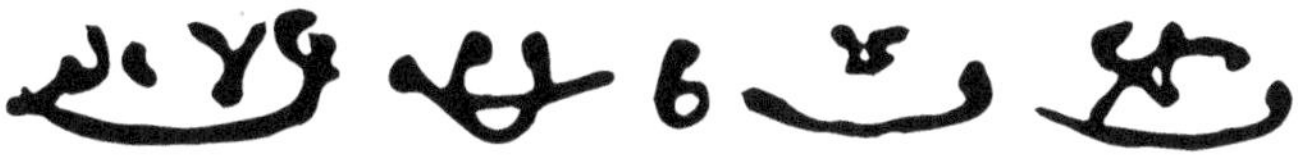

Saturday. Hasten, O servants of these blessed names! Spur on the spirit of love and affection so that it instills love between X and

32 The numbers 0212311 x x 511626546236 are also presented here; presumably, the numerical sigil is constructed from these numbers, which would then represent the names.

Y. Bind them with eternal love! By the right of these names over you and your obeidence towards them:

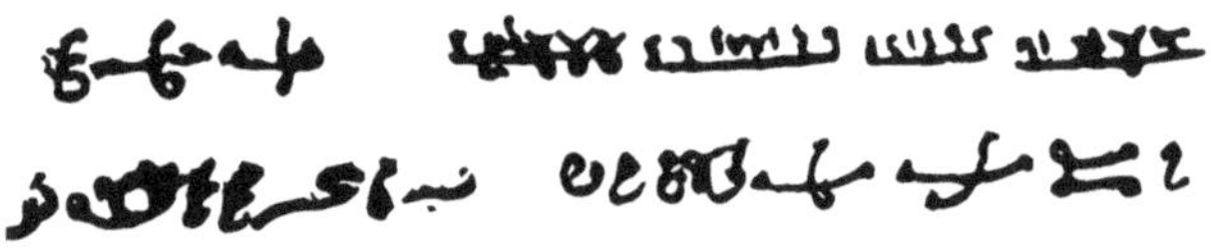

EVERLASTING LOVE, A SIMPLER APPROACH

Inscribe the following verses on a pure piece of parchment along with the name of the target, and carry it with you:

> He it is who brought you into being from a single soul, and gave you a dwelling-place and a repository. We have elaborated upon Our signs for those who understand." (6:98)

You beloved will never be able to leave you, so long as you carry that parchment. This is what you write:

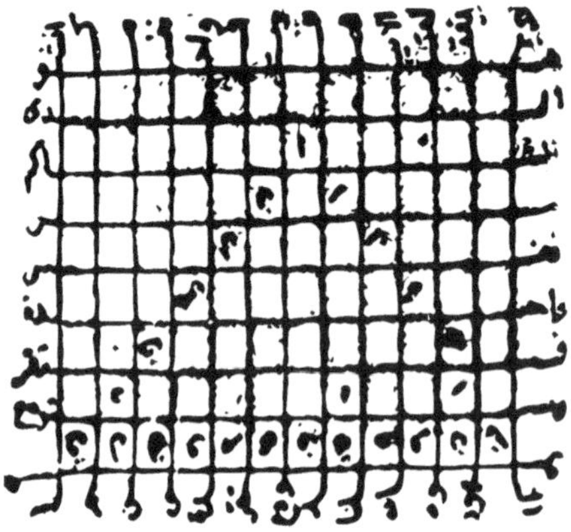

BRINGING BACK A SERVANT WHO HAS FLED, EVEN IF THEY HAVE BEEN CAPTURED AND ARE IN CHAINS!

Draw the following diagram, then procure a beetle—a male beetle if the servant is male, and a female beetle if the servant is female. Stick a pin in the center of the circle, and then tie the beetle to the pin and allow it to walk around the circle. The beetle will frantically rush to and fro, trying to escape, but stumbling back onto the talisman. This mimics how the servant flees—running away, and then stumbling back, even if in chains. God will bring back the servant through the blessings of this talisman, which is associated with the verse: "He is the one who brought you into being..." (6:98).

INSOMNIA AND COLIC

To help someone who is ill, in pain, or otherwise suffering go to sleep, write these names, and place them beneath his turban or pillow. He will fall asleep immediately and not wake up until you remove the names from his head. These names also help infants who cry incessantly go to sleep. They are:

> They tarried in their cave for three hundred years, plus nine.[33] (Qur'an 18:25)
> You would have though them awake, though they were asleep. We turned them to the right and left. (Qur'an 18:18)
> How many generations before them did we destroy? You sense nothing from them, not even a murmur. (Qur'an 19:98)

33 An allusion to the Sleepers of Ephesus, who slept in their cave for a miraculously long time, then awoke.

FETCHING SOMEONE

To bring a missing person or someone you love to you, write the following sigil on a sheet of copper with a pen made of sweet basil and ink of saffron and rosewater. Write it during the beginning of the hour of Venus. If the person is far away, put the copper leaf in a blazing fire. If the person is nearby, put the copper leaf in a calmer fire. Recite the evocation for the current seasonal quarter,[34] and adjure the spirits who serve that quarter; this will make your working stronger, firmer, and quicker. You can bring a person to you through this working, even if they are a three-month's journey away. Recite these names:

> Hurry, now, this moment, quickly, now, obeying God and His messenger and His names! I may be a created being, but you must obey God and His names. By the right of the one who told the heavens and earth: "'Come willingly or unwillingly!' They said, 'We come willingly'" (Qur'an 41:11).
>
> Now, quickly, this moment! Bring <target>, son/daughter of <target's mother>!

HOW THE AUTHOR DISCOVERED THE NAMES WRITTEN UPON THE STAFF OF MOSES

Know, my brother—may God help you and me understand the secrets of His names—that I was once sitting before my shaykh, ʿAbd al-Samad al-Anadlusi, may God bless him, when a man came and greeted the shaykh. The shaykh warmly returned his greetings, and then the man came close to the shaykh and whispered something to him. The shaykh remained silent, however, and the man badgered him to say something.

Once the man had worn himself out, the shaykh lifted his head and said, "O so-and-so! If that is what you want, fast for three weeks,

34 See Chapter 8.

and do not eat anything that has a soul or comes from a soul.[35] Then I will take care of what you need."

The man assented, and three weeks passed. Then he came back to the shaykh and said, "My master, I have done what you told me to do."

"Go and continue fasting for forty days," the shaykh replied. "Then come back to me, and I will take care of what you need."

The man left, finished his forty-day fast, and then returned to the shaykh. "My master, I have now fasted for forty days."

"Now," the shaykh said, "you merit this." He went inside; when he came out, he had a piece of paper. He opened it up and looked long at it. He kissed it, his head trembling, and gave it to the man, then advised him long and hard about it.

The man indicated that he had heard and would obey, then kissed the shaykh's hand.

I asked, "Master, what was on the paper you gave to that man?"

"Ahmad," he replied, "on it is a secret of God. No one knows it, apart from a few whom God willed goodness for through it."

"Master," I asked, "can you tell me about it?

He did not reply, so I decided to wait and ask him later. A few days later, I asked him again, but he would not tell me. For a year, I kept asking him, but he never replied.

Finally, after a year, the shaykh said, on his own accord, "Ahmad, were you asking me about something?"

"My master," I ventured, "I wish to know about those blessed names, and how to employ them."

"Ahmad," he said to me, "if you want to know that, fast for forty days, and do not eat anything that has a soul or comes from a soul. If you do that, I will tell you about it."

I assented, and applied myself towards fasting. When I had finished, the shaykh said to me, "Now you merit this."

Then he disappeared into seclusion and was unseen for a long time. When he returned, he was carrying a piece of paper. Kissing it, he asked, "Ahmad, do you know what this is?"

35 That is, no meat or animal products.

"I do not know," I said.

The shaykh said, "Know that these are the names that were written on the staff of Moses and the staff of Shuʿayb; they were written on Joseph's garments. They were on the sword of Daniel, and were with Abraham when he was cast into the fire. Jesus had them, and he taught them to his disciplies, the last of whom was Simon. Through them, he would beseech God to cure the ill. Beasts and other creatures would fear anyone who bore those names. God protected whoever bore them from the evils of jinn and men. Others' tongues were kept from them. They were affixed on iron, such that were the bearer to march into battle, none could touch him. Enemy armies fell.

"If someone suffered from head pain, an eye-sore, or any other sort of pain, these names could be written on a piece of parchment made from the skin of a bird or a gazelle; then, the parchment would be affixed to the ailing person. After that, the first chapter of the Qur'an, the Throne Verse (2:255), and the last three chapters of the Qur'an would be written in a glass goblet with ink of musk, saffron, and rosewater, and the patient would drink it, whereupon, by the grace of God, they would be cured of all that afflicted them.

"The names could also be written in a similar manner and worn by someone who was about to face a sultan, vizier, judge, or official. During the meeting, the person would say, inside himself: 'O God! I ask you by the right of these names to bind the tongue of'— and here, he would mention the name of the sultan and the sultan's mother. Then he would continue reciting, inside himself: 'Crestfallen! Crestfallen! Crestfallen! Faces will be humbled before the Ever-living, Ever-lasting. Whoever bears wrongdoing will have failed!'[36] Then he would blow three times. They would agree to take audience with him, while he would be secure from their plots, and they would do whatever he needed. Everyone would respect the bearer of these names. Anyone who laid eyes on him would awe and revere him."

They have other special merits and uses too, but we have said enough. We would not want to bore the reader! Nor would we want

36 The last two sentences are Qur'an 20:111.

the names to fall into the hands of the unworthy, who would not understand their value.

These are the names:

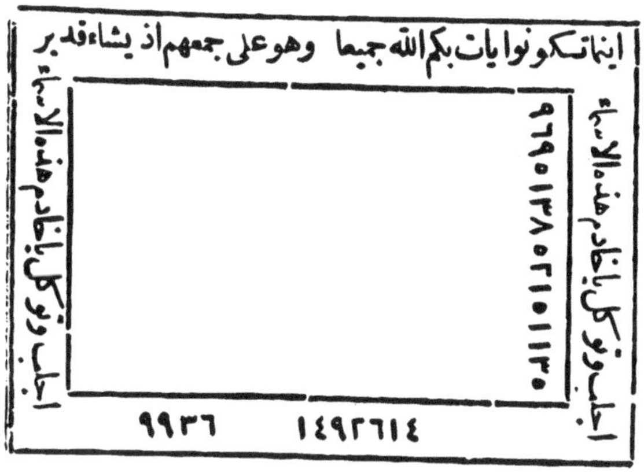

THE NAMES UPON THE STAFF OF MOSES

I recall that upon it were the names from the staff of Moses. It could be used to work wonders—if the names were written when the Sun or Jupiter was exalted. The names were written upon a gazelle-skin parchment with ink including myrtle-water, river mint-water, maidenhair-water, white willow-water, mullein-water, and saffron. The parchment was incensed over a sweet-smelling incense. Then it was rolled up and put into the hollow of a staff, with the names on it, and sealed shut.

Whenever I found myself somewhere ominous, or there were bandits, brigands, or beasts of prey about, I would strike the staff upon the ground three times and proclaim:

> O God! I ask You through the blessings of these magnificent names which were upon the staff of Moses, the son of ʿImrān, through which he parted the sea—"and it parted, as if each side were a mountain!" (Qur'an 26:63) Bar them from my way!

Then I would specify which men or beasts I wished to avert from me; all the while, saying: "Stop them; they are to be questioned" (Qur'an 37:24). By the grace of God, they would stop in their tracks.

This is the figure:

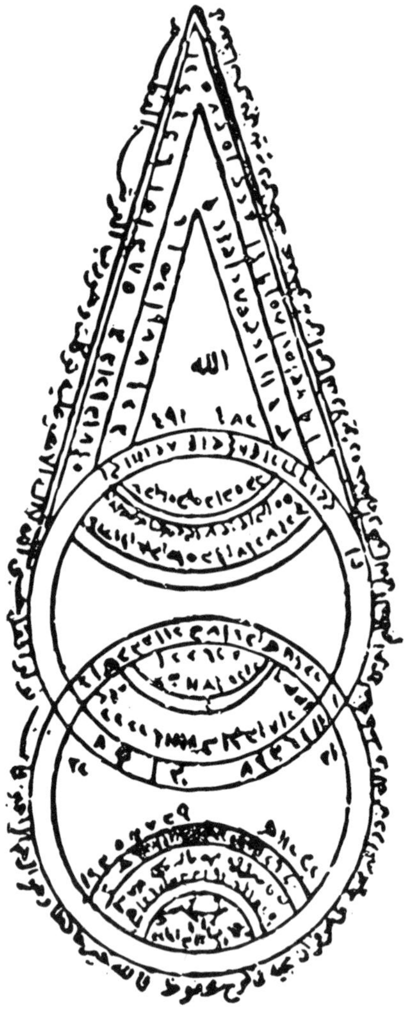

A WONDROUS DISCOVERY

When my shaykh, Abu ʿAbd Allah al-Sibti, passed away, and the body-washer stripped him of his clothes, I found a folded paper in his clothing. I pocketed it. Then, after he was laid to rest, I unfolded that paper and discovered that written upon it were three divine names, a prayer for the Mahdi three times,[37] the homily "all

37 Lit. "three *ʿajlahs*." The Mahdi is prophesized to arrive near the end of time

strength and power lie in God, the Exalted, the Mighty," and blessings upon the Prophet, his family, and his companions.

I had sought this from him his entire life, but he had refused to give it to me. Finally, I had decided, "Ahmad, do not busy yourself with this. Maybe it will come to you easily."

I was sitting there, pondering things the shaykh had said and asking God to bless his soul, and realized, "These are the breaths of the righteous men who are with God."

Suddenly, it was as if he was there, speaking to me. He seemed to be saying, "After my death, this shall come to you, with no effort on your part, and no questions asked." So I studied it well.

And lo! It said: "Know, my brother, that sublime names have fallen into your hands. Guard them from the riff-raff, for they fell to earth with Adam. Adam used to gaze upon them every day and say, 'Exalted be Thee! How magnificent Your stature is, and how enormous Your rule!'"

He then mentioned some special ways to use these names. If you knew them, you could use them to walk on water, and your feet would never slip. If you wanted, you could even fly through the air, from place to place, through the blessings of these names. Through the blessings of these names, the men of the unseen[38] appear and disappear, hidden from people's eyes. Were you to recite them and say, "O servants of these names! Take me to Mecca," they would take you to Mecca at that very moment. Thus you could come and go as you pleased.

There are many ways to use these names. Were I not fearful of disclosing this secret—lest it fall into the wrong hands—I would

---

and bring peace and justice to the world after a time of suffering and chaos. A pious formula used to pray for the quick advent of the Mahdi is *ʿajjal Allāhu farajahu* ("may Allah hasten his glad advent"); this expression is more commonly used by Twelver Shiʿis, although there is a fair amount of crossover between Sufi and Shiʿi practice. The expression "three *ʿajlah*s" could also refer to something else.

38 *Rijāl al-ghayb*. Some Sufis hold that there are certain spiritually perfected men who have specific functions in the unseen world and who can be contacted in the unseen world for learning, blessings, intercession, or other matters.

have spoken of wondrous wonders. This is the blessed talisman, beneath the staff of Moses. Guard it! Keep it out of the wrong hands!

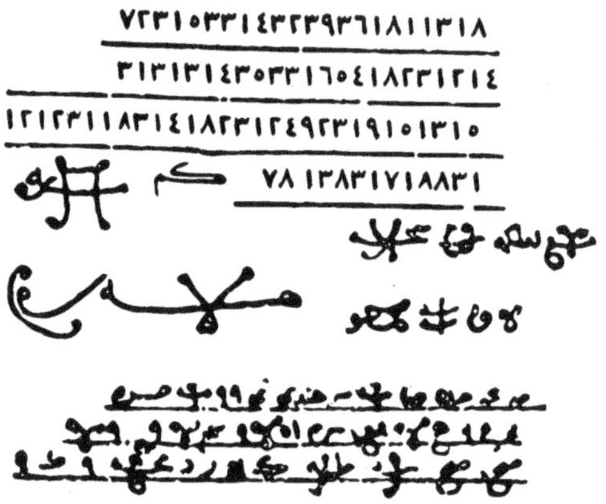

This is a description of these eminent names. Say:

> In the name of God, the Compassionate, the Merciful.
> O God, I beseech you, in whose hands are the springs of life! By the fragrance of Your luminous names. By the radiance illuminating Your throne, and by Your secret names preserved in Your Tablet!
> By what You revealed to Adam, the father of mankind, when You told him of the lights[39] sent to your pure, beloved one: "And God taught Adam the names—all of them" (Qur'an 2:31).
> By Your glory and the perfected, radiant, illuminated, beauty of Your kind, sacred, brilliant, sublime countenance! By the lights of Your secrets which You entrusted in the heart of the Sun and Moon! And by the right of these glorious names:

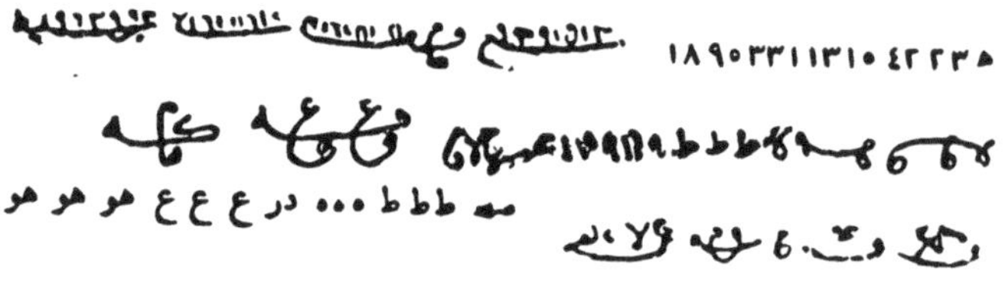

39 Some Sufis and Shiʿis believe that the Prophet Muhammad and his family were pre-created as lights that were deposited in Adam's loins and passed on from generation to generation until they were birthed in material form.

> *Hū! Hū! Hū! Hū! Yāh! Yāh! Yāh!* "Our Lord! We trust in You and turn to You; to You is our return" (Qur'an 60:4). "O Lord! Do not let our hearts falter after you have guided us, and bestow upon us a mercy from Your presence; You are the Bestower" (Qur'an 3:8).

All strength and power lie in God, the Exalted, the Mighty.

THE NAMES WRITTEN UPON JOSEPH'S GARMENTS

These are the names that were written upon Joseph's garments. They beget respect, acceptance, and love, and allow you to gain audience with officials, kings, viziers, and nobles.

A PRAYER FOR ALL THINGS

I recall something else that was very precious. Once, I had gone to the mosque to pray, and had found one of our brethren-in-faith who used to attend sessions with me and had studied under the same shaykh, Abu ʿAbd Allah al-Shaykh ʿAbd al-Haqq al-Sibti. I walked towards him to greet him, but realized that he kept looking up towards the heavens, then down at his palms. Then, when I came closer, I overheard him imploring:

> O God! You answer our prayers, fulfill our needs, and deliver us from difficulty—from aloft the seven heavens! O treasury of miracles! You respond to those who beg, hear our voices, forgive our slips ameliorate our errors, and bestow blessings. Your knowledge encompasses all things. Bless Muhammad and his family, and fulfill my need!

He mentioned something specific that he needed, then continued:

> By the right of these names: *Hā, hā, hī, hī, hū, hū, yāh, yāh, āh, āh*! Exalted, holy be the Lord of the angels and the Spirit![40]
> I beseech You, O Lord, by the names on this paper, and the blessings of these prayers—fulfill my need!

He had not yet even finished his prayer when it was answered.

> Then he saw me. He turned to me, came close to me, greeted to me, and said apologetically, "I pray to God for whatever I need, and my Lord fulfills my need generously."
> "My brother," I said, "I heard you praying. However, I also saw you looking at that paper."
> "I will tell you what happened," he said. "We used to serve our shaykh, the one whom you studied with for a long time. One day, he asked me, 'Is there anything you need?'
> "I said, 'Yes.'
> "He asked, 'What do you need?'
> "I said, 'I long for a prayer that I could recite to beseech God to take care of the things that weigh on my mind, and which He would answer.'
> "'All right,' he said. 'You have a right over us due to your long term of service.' Then he entrusted me with a paper; on it were written these names."

40 Islamic scholars generally take the "Spirit" (*rūḥ*) to refer to either the angel Jibrāʾīl or a created, enormous being at God's command.

These are the names, reproduced correctly:

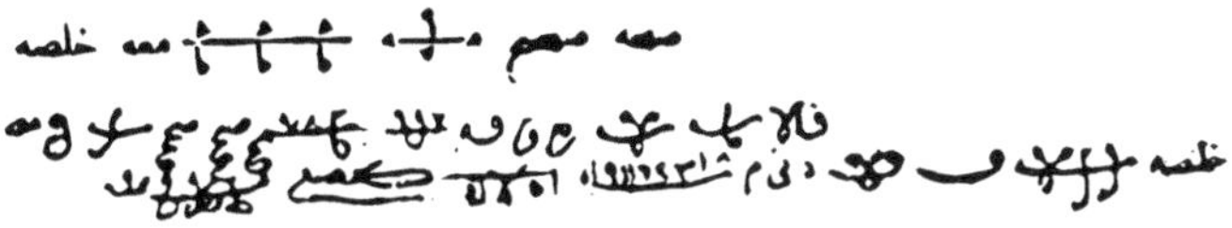

> *And We responded to him and saved him from grief, and thus do We save the faithful.*[41]

My brothers! Look after this prayer. Do not forget it in your times of need, for it elicits a quick response. Only use it to pray for righteous things, for if you use it to pray for unrighteous things, your prayers shall not be answerd.

And God—the Exalted—knows best.

Praised be God, and God knows best. God speaks
the truth and guides to the right path. May
God's peace and blessings be upon
our master Muhammad,
his family, and his
companions.

FINIS

41 Qur'an 21:88.

Appendix

ARABIC LETTERS AND THEIR NUMERICAL VALUES

VALUE	ARABIC LETTER	TRANSLITERATION
1	ا	*a (alif)*
2	ب	*b*
3	ج	*j*
4	د	*d*
5	ه	*h*
6	و	*w*
7	ز	*z*
8	ح	*ḥ*
9	ط	*ṭ*
10	ي	*y*
20	ك	*k*
30	ل	*l*
40	م	*m*
50	ن	*n*
60	ش	*sh*
70	ع	*ʿ (ʿayn)*
80	ف	*f*
90	ص	*ṣ*

VALUE	ARABIC LETTER	TRANSLITERATION
100	ق	*q*
200	ر	*r*
300	ش	*sh*
400	ت	*t*
500	ث	*th*
600	خ	*kh*
700	ذ	*dh*
800	ض	*ḍ*
900	ظ	*ẓ*
1000	غ	*gh*

ARABIC-STYLE DIGITS

0	٠
1	١
2	٢
3	٣
4	٤
5	٥
6	٦
7	٧
8	٨
9	٩

	NAME	MEANING	ZODIACAL DEGREES	ARABIC LETTER
1	al-sharaṭayn	the Two Signs	0° Aries– 12° 51′ Aries	ا
	al-natḥ	the Butting of the Ram		
2	al-baṭīn	the Belly	12° 51′ Aries– 25° 43′ Aries	ب
3	al-thurayā	the Pleaides, the Abundant Little Ones	25° 43′ Aries– 8° 34′ Taurus	ج
4	*al-dabarān*	the Follower, Aldebaran	8° 34′ Taurus– 21° 26′ Taurus	د
5	*al-haqʿah*	the Hair Whorl	21° 26′ Taurus– 4° 17′ Gemini	ه
6	*al-hanʿah*	the Leaning Stars	4° 17′ Gemini– 17° 9′ Gemini	و
7	*al-dhirāʿ*	the Forearm of Leo	17° 9′ Gemini– 0° Cancer	ز
8	*al-nathrah*	the Nose-tip of Leo	0° Cancer– 12° 51′ Cancer	ح
9	*al-ṭarfah*	the Twinkling Eyes of Leo	12° 51′ Cancer– 25° 43′ Cancer	ط
10	*al-jabhah*	the Forehead of Leo	25° 43′ Cancer– 8° 34′ Leo	ي
11	*al-zubrah*	the Mane of Leo	8° 34′ Leo– 21° 26′ Leo	ك

	NAME	MEANING	ZODIACAL DEGREES	ARABIC LETTER
12	*al-ṣarfah*	the Weather-Change	21° 26′ Leo–4° 17′ Virgo	ل
13	*al-ʿawwā*	the Howling Dogs	4° 17′ Virgo–17° 9′ Virgo	م
14	*al-simmāk*	the Sky-Raiser	17° 9′ Virgo–0° Libra	ن
15	*al-ghafr*	the Shrouded	0° Libra–12° 51′ Libra	س
16	*al-zubanā*	the Claw of Scorpio	12° 51′ Libra–25° 43′ Libra	ع
17	*al-iklīl*	the Crown of Scorpio	25° 43′ Libra–8° 34′ Scorpio	ف
18	*al-qalb*	the Heart of Scorpio	8° 34′ Scorpio–21° 26′ Scorpio	ص
19	*al-shawlah*	The Stinging Tail of Scorpio	21° 26′ Scorpio–4° 17′ Sagittarius	ق
20	*al-naʿāʾim*	The Ostriches	4° 17′ Sagittarius–17° 9′ Sagittarius	ر
21	*al-baldah*	The Wasteland	17° 9′ Sagittarius–0° Capricorn	ش
22	*saʿd al-dhābiḥ*	The Slaughterer's Joy	0° Capricorn–12° 51′ Capricorn	ت
23	*saʿd al-bulʿ*	The Voracious Auspice	12° 51′ Capricorn–25° 43′ Capricorn	ث

	NAME	MEANING	ZODIACAL DEGREES	ARABIC LETTER
24	*saʿd al-suʿūd*	The Most Fortunate	25° 43′ Capricorn–8° 34′ Aquarius	خ
25	*saʿd al-akhbiyah*	The Auspice of Tent-Poles	8° 34′ Aquarius–21° 26′ Aquarius	ذ
26	*al-fargh al-muqaddim (al-fargh al-awwal)*	The First Spout	21° 26′ Aquarius–4° 17′ Pisces	ض
27	*al-fargh al-muʾakhkhar (al-fargh al-thānī)*	The Second Spout		ظ
28	*al-rishā*	The Rope	17° 9′ Pisces–0° Aries	غ
	baṭn al-ḥūt	The Belly of the Fish		

STARS AND ASTERISMS

ENGLISH	ARABIC TRANSLITERATION	ARABIC TRANSLATION
Alcor	*al-suhā*	Suha
Aldebaran	*al-dabarān* *al-ʿatīq*	the Follower the Mountain
Algol	*raʾs al-ghūl*	Ghoul's Head
Alioth	*jawn*	Black Horse
Alkaid	*al-qāʾid*	Leader

ENGLISH	ARABIC TRANSLITERATION	ARABIC TRANSLATION
Altair	*al-nasr al-ṭā'ir;*	Flying Vulture
Arcturus	*al-simāk al-rāmiḥ*	the Spear-Bearing Sky-Raiser
Beta Cassiopeiae	*al-kaff al-khaḍīb*	the Dyed Palm
Betelgeuse	*al-jawzā'*	
Canopus	*suhayl*	Suhayl (a proper name)
Capella	*al-'ayyūq*	Capella
Mirzam	*al-mirzam*	Mirzam; moderately bright star
Mizar	*'anāq*	She-Kid
North Star	*najm al-jaddī*	Goat Kid
Pherkad and Kochab	*al-farqadān*	Two Calves
Pleiades	*thurāyā* *al-najm*	the Abundant Little Ones (or the Dewdrops) the Star
Procyon	*al-shi'rā al-ghumayṣā'*	Weeping Star
Sirius	*al-shi'rā al-'abūr*	Sirius who Crossed Over
Spica	*al-simāk al-a'zal*	the Unarmed Sky-Raiser

ENGLISH	ARABIC TRANSLITERATION	ARABIC TRANSLATION
The head of Draco consisting of four stars in a square	*al-ʿawāʾidh*	Camel-Mothers
Vega	*al-nasr al-wāqiʿ*	Alighting Vulture
(A scattered group of stars located beneath the Pleiades. Includes Alpha Menkar and Gamma Kaffaljidhmah)	*al-jazmā*	Amputated Hand

ZODIACAL CONSTELLATIONS

ENGLISH	ARABIC TRANSLITERATION	ARABIC TRANSLATION
Aries	*al-ḥaml*	Ram; Year-Old Lamb
Taurus	*al-thawr*	Bull
Gemini	*al-jawzāʾ, al-tawaʾmān*	Twins
Cancer	*al-saraṭān*	Crab
Leo	*al-asad*	Lion
Virgo	*al-ʿadhrā; al-sunbulah*	Maiden; Grain-Spike
Libra	*al-mīzān*	Scales

ENGLISH	ARABIC TRANSLITERATION	ARABIC TRANSLATION
Scorpio	*al-ʿaqrab*	Scorpion
Sagittarius	*al-qaws; al-rāmī*	Archer
Capricorn	*al-jaddī*	Goat
Aquarius	*al-dalw; sākib al-māʾ*	Water-Bearer
Pisces	*al-ḥūt*	Fish

NON-ZODIACAL CONSTELLATIONS

ENGLISH	ARABIC TRANSLITERATION	ARABIC TRANSLATION
Andromeda	*andrūmīda* *al-marʾah al-musalsalah*	Andromeda Chained Woman
Aquila	*al-ʿuqāb*	Eagle
Argo Navis	*al-safīnah*	Ship
Arrow	*al-sahm*	Eridanus
Big Dipper	*banāt naʿsh* *al-dubb al-akbar*	Daughters of the Bier Great Bear
Canis Major	*al-kalb al-akbar*	Greater Dog
Canis Minor	*al-kalb al-aṣghar*	Canis Minor Little Dog
Cassiopeia	*dhāt al-kursī*	Queen

ENGLISH	ARABIC TRANSLITERATION	ARABIC TRANSLATION
Centaurus	*qayṭūris*	Centaurus
Cetus	*qayṭus*	Cetus
Charioteer	*mamsak al-ʿinān*	Auriga
Corona Australis	*al-iklīl al-junūbī*	Southern Crown
Corvus	*al-ghurāb* *ʿarsh al-simmāk al-aʿzal* *al-ḥibā*	Crow Spica's Throne
Crater	*al-ka'ʾs* *al-bāṭiyyah*	Goblet Dish
Cygnus	*al-dajājah*	Hen
Delphinus	*al-dulfīn*	Dolphin
Draco	*al-tinnīn*	Dragon
Equuleus	*qiṭʿat al-faras*	Piece of the Horse
Eridanus	*al-nahr*	River
Formerly the Little Tortoise; also Lyra	*al-salaḥfāh*	Turtle
Hercules	*al-jāthī*	Kneeler
Hyades	*al-nawq al-ṣighār*	Young Camels
Hydra	*al-shujāʿ*	Hydra Fearless
Lepus	*al-arnab*	Rabbit

ENGLISH	ARABIC TRANSLITERATION	ARABIC TRANSLATION
Little Dipper	*banāt naʿsh ṣughrā* *al-dubb al-aṣghar*	Daughters of the Lesser Bier Little Bear
Lupus	*al-sabuʿ*	Beast
Lyra	*al-salbāq* *al-lūzā* *al-ṣunj al-rūmī*	Lyre Lyra Byzantine Cymbals
Milky Way	*al-majarrah*	Running River
Northern Crown	*qasʿah al-masākīn* *al-fakkah*	Beggar's Bowl
Ophiuchus	*al-ḥayyā*	Snake-Catcher
Orion	*al-jabbār*	Giant
Pegasus	*al-faras al-akbar*	Pegasus; Great Horse
Persus	*barshāwus* *ḥāmil ra'→ al-ghūl*	Perseus Bearer of the Ghoul's head
Piscis Austrinus	*al-ḥūt al-junūbī*	Southern Fish
Serpens	*al-ḥawā*	Serpens
Triangulum	*al-muthallath*	Triangle

Bibliography

Adams, Danielle. *Rain Stars Set, Lunar Stations Rise: Multivalent Textures of Pre-Islamic Arabian Astronomy and the Hegemonic Discourse of Order* [PhD thesis] (University of Arizona, 2018).

"Banāt Naʿsh," in *Encyclopaedia of Islam, Second Edition*, ed. P. Bearman, Th. Bianquis, C. E. Bosworth, E. van Donzel, W. P. Heinrichs (Leiden: Brill, 2012).

Cordero, Jaime Coullaut, *El Kitāb Šams al-Maʿārif al-Kubrà (al-ŷuz' al-awwal)*

de Aḥmad b. ʿAlī al-Būnī: Sufismo y ciencias ocultas [PhD thesis] (University of Salamanca, 2009).

Dietrich, A., "al-Būnī," in *Encyclopaedia of Islam, Second Edition*, ed. P. Bearman, T. Bianquis, C. E. Bosworth, E. van Donzel, W.P. Heinrichs (Leiden: Brill, 2012).

Dykes, Benjamin (ed. and trans.), *The Astrology of Sahl b. Bishr: Volume I: Principles, Elections, Questions, Nativities* (Minneapolis: The Cazimi Press, 2019).

Francis, Edgar Walter. *Islamic Symbols and Sufi Rituals for Protection and Healing: Religion and Magic in the Writings of Ahmad ibn Ali al-Buni* (d. 622/1225) [PhD thesis] (University of California, Los Angeles, 2005).

Gardiner, Noah. *Esotericism in a manuscript culture: Ahmad al-Buni and his readers through the Mamluk period.* [Phd thesis] (University of Michigan, 2014).

Gardiner, Noah. "Forbidden Knowledge? Notes on the Production, Transmission, and Reception of the Major Works of Ahmad al-Buni," in *Journal of Arabic and Islamic Studies*, vol. 12 (2012): 81–143.

Gardiner, Noah. "Stars and Saints: The Esotericist Astrology of the Sufi Occultist Ahmad al-Buni," in *Journal of Magic, Ritual, and Witchcraft*, vol. 12, no. 1 (Spring 2017): 39–65.

Greer, John Michael and Warnock, Christopher (trans.), *The Illustrated Picatrix* (n.l.: Lulu, 2015).

Knight, Michael Muhammad. *Magic in Islam* (New York: TarcherPerigree, 2016).
Lane, Edward William. *Arabic-English Lexicon (Lane's Lexicon)* (London: Wiliams and Norgate, 1863).
Lange, Christian. *Paradise and Hell in Islamic Traditions* (New York: Cambridge University Press, 2015).
Kunitzsch, P. and Knappert, J. "al-Nudjūm," in *Encyclopaedia of Islam, Second Edition*, ed. P. Bearman, T. Bianquis, C. E. Bosworth, E. van Donzel, W. P. Heinrichs (Leiden: Brill, 2012).
Nurbakhsh, Jawad. *Sufi Symbolism*, 6 vols. (London: Khaniqahi-Nimatullahi Publications, 1986–2004).
Pellat, C. "Anwāʾ," in *Encyclopaedia of Islam, Second Edition*, ed. P. Bearman, T. Bianquis, C. E. Bosworth, E. van Donzel, and W. P. Heinrichs (Leiden: Brill, 2012).
Saif, Liana. "From *Ġāyat al-ḥakīm* to *Šams al-maʿārif*: Ways of Knowing and Paths of Power in Medieval Islam," in *Arabica*, vol. 64 (2017): 297–345.
Saif, Liana. *The Arabic Influences on Early Modern Occult Philosophy* (Basingstoke, Hampshire and New York: Palgrave Macmillan, 2015).
Talafha, Mohammed H. and Talafha, Ziad A., "Symbols and Astrological Terms in Ancient Arabic Inscriptions," in *Scientific Culture*, vol. 5, no. 2 (2019): 21–30.
Varisco, Daniel Martin. "The Origin of the *anwāʾ* in Arab Tradition," in *Studia Islamica*, vol. 74 (1991): 5–28.

Index